RED FIGURE VASES
OF SOUTH ITALY AND SICILY

Frontispiece: Calyx-krater with scene from a phlyax play

RED FIGURE VASES
OF SOUTH ITALY
AND SICILY

a handbook

A.D. TRENDALL

596 illustrations

Ellen Machame

THAMES AND HUDSON

738.38209377 TRE

© 1989 Thames and Hudson Ltd, London

Printed and bound in The German Democratic Republic

CONTENTS

Chapter One

GENERAL INTRODUCTION

Historical Background

The term 'South Italian' is generally applied to the red-figured vases made by the Greek colonists (Italiotes) in South Italy and Sicily between *c.* 440 and the end of the fourth century BC. Some of this pottery came to light in the later eighteenth and the nineteenth centuries at various sites in Apulia and Campania and was highly prized because of the interest of its subject-matter. From the later nineteenth century onwards, however, there was a marked change of taste in favour of Athenian vases, especially from the Late Archaic and Early Classical periods, and it is only in the past forty years or so that the increasing quantity of new material from excavations in South Italy and Sicily, together with more detailed studies of the several fabrics, has brought about a certain revival of interest and a reappraisal of their quality. We now have a better appreciation of what South Italian vase-painting has to offer from the standpoints of both style and subject-matter, since it not only illustrates the developments which took place when potters and painters were able to break away from the long-established traditions of mainland Greece but also sheds a great deal of light on the life and customs of the Greek colonists and of the native populations in the fourth century BC, as well as on Greek drama and mythology.

The first classifications of South Italian pottery were largely based upon the find-spots of the vases, and this led to a good deal of confusion; later the local fabrics were broadly consolidated into Lucanian, Apulian and Campanian, and, as the value of a classification based primarily upon stylistic criteria came to be more fully understood, these designations began to assume their true significance. By the end of the last century Paestan had been recognized as an independent fabric and, more recently, it became possible to add Sicilian as a fifth, thanks to the large quantity of red-figured vases brought to light there by excavations since 1950. These five fabrics fall broadly into two main groups, one consisting of Lucanian and Apulian, the other of Campanian, Paestan and Sicilian, and within each group the vases of the component fabrics are fairly closely related in style. There are at present something approaching 20,000 red-figured vases from South Italy and Sicily, of which about 1500 may be classed as Lucanian, over 10,000 as Apulian, some 4000 as Campanian, 2000 as Paestan and over 1000 as Sicilian.

Fig. 1 Map of South Italy and Sicily to show principal find-spots

The fourth century BC saw a decline in the political significance of Athens, and the contraction of Etruscan power in Italy coincides with a marked drop in imports of vases from Greece. In consequence, Athens was forced to seek new markets, which it found in South Russia and the western coast of the Black Sea, in North Africa (Cyrene), and in Spain (Ampurias); this brought about considerable changes in both the style and the subject-matter of the vases, and these do not necessarily find parallels in South Italy, where conditions were rather different and where export markets were not a problem. This may help to explain why subjects connected with the theatre hardly appear on Attic vases of the fourth century, since they were clearly of little interest to the inhabitants of those areas to which these vases were exported, whereas the Greek colonists in South Italy and Sicily seem to have retained a considerable enthusiasm for Greek drama. South Italian pottery, unlike Attic, was not widely exported in the fourth century, and only a very small percentage of the extant vases has been found far from the area in which they were made.

Shapes

The principal shapes used by the first South Italian potters in Lucania and Apulia for their red-figured vases were taken over from those current in Athens in the later fifth century BC. They soon, however, begin to undergo modifications and developments, and it is interesting to note that two shapes in particular, the volute-krater and the pseudo-panathenaic amphora, both of which died out almost completely in Athens after c. 380 BC, continue to be made, in ever-increasing size and quantity, throughout the life of Lucanian and Apulian, although they are not found at all in Campanian and very rarely in Paestan, where red-figure does not come into local production until well into the second quarter of the century. The volute-krater is perhaps the most characteristic of all Apulian shapes – it can reach truly monumental dimensions (many are between 1 and 1.5 metres in height) and its decoration becomes increasingly elaborate. Masks are applied to the volutes on the handles, and swan-heads are sometimes placed at the handle-joins; intricate, and often very beautiful, floral patterns appear on the neck, framing a central figure or a head, and there is an array of superposed palmettes below the handles. Of the other types of krater – bell, calyx and column – the first is in general and frequent use in all fabrics except later Sicilian, the second in general but less common use, but the third is confined to Lucanian and Apulian.

The amphora, of which only the panathenaic form is normally found in Apulian and Lucanian (in contrast to the other fabrics which prefer neck-amphorae), like the volute-krater, becomes increasingly larger and more elaborately decorated, with intricate ornamental pattern-work on the neck and shoulder. The same phenomenon occurs with the loutrophoros, a shape confined to Apulian, which develops spiralling handles on either side of the neck

9

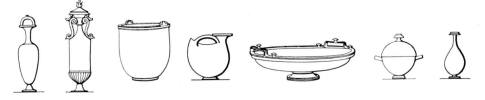

Fig. 2 *Typical South Italian vase-shapes. From left to right: bail-amphora, loutrophoros, situla, askos, dish (knob-handled patera), skyphoid pyxis, bottle*

and may have either an ovoid, or a concave cylindrical, body; the latter, without the handles, is sometimes referred to as a barrel-amphora. In Campania a local variety of amphora, known as a bail-amphora, is widely used; it has a handle, sometimes pierced for suspension, which arches over the mouth [279]. Pelikai, though common in Apulian, are comparatively rare in other fabrics.

Another shape which underwent substantial modification is the *lebes gamikos*; in Campanian and Paestan, in particular, it is often provided with a tall and elaborate lid composed of several sections, one fitting on top of the other, and usually decorated with figured scenes, heads, or animals, giving a somewhat overpowering, and often unbalanced, look to the vase as a whole. The plastic heads or cone-shaped knobs often applied to the shoulders of these vases heighten that effect [308, 403].

Standard shapes like hydriai, lekanides, lekythoi (mostly of the squat variety), oenochoai, skyphoi and cups are in general use in most of the fabrics, but again with a tendency to increase in size, especially in Apulian; kantharoi, rhyta and stamnoi are virtually confined to that fabric. Fish-plates are found in all fabrics except Lucanian; in Apulian they regularly have ornamental decoration within the central depression, elsewhere only very exceptionally, and they may be distinguished from their Attic counterparts by the fact that the bellies of the fish are normally turned towards the central depression and not to the outer rim. Bottles and alabastra make a comparatively late appearance, the former being a particularly popular shape in Sicily, as is the skyphoid pyxis, which is also found at Paestum, though rarely elsewhere. Of the purely local shapes the most remarkable is the so-called nestoris – perhaps better referred to by its Italian name *trozzella* – which appears to derive from a native Messapian shape; it is found in several varieties (*Fig. 3*), of which the most frequent are those with a carinated or ovoid body, side handles, and up-swung handles, decorated with disks, on either side of the neck. The shape is found in early Lucanian and later comes into restricted use in Apulian, but is not found in the other fabrics. An Apulian speciality is the knob-handled patera, a large dish which can reach a diameter of 70 cm, with two flat handles surmounted and flanked by knobs, and decorated normally with a figured scene in the tondo and sometimes with scenes

10

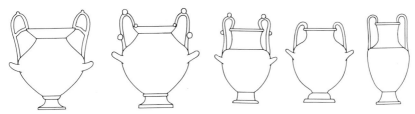

Fig. 3 Types of red-figure nestorides found in Lucanian and Apulian. From left to right: Type I (1 and 2), Type II (3 and 4), Type III (5)

on the exterior. Such vases are frequently depicted in funerary scenes and were presumably used for ritual purposes.

The South Italian artists, in general, and the Apulians, in particular, are fond of decorating large vases with multi-figured compositions on the grand scale. This practice begins at an early stage in Apulian and was probably influenced by the import, at the end of the fifth century BC and in the early years of the fourth, of large volute-kraters from Athens by artists like the Kadmos, Pronomos, Talos and Meleager Painters, several of which have been found at Ruvo. Such vases seem to have had a strong local appeal, and this probably encouraged Apulian artists to imitate them and then to explore to the fullest possible extent the possibilities they offered for even more monumental compositions. This brought about a greater interest in seeking solutions to the problems of perspective and foreshortening, and in making bold experiments to that end, but the vase-painters never quite succeeded in organising a unified picture-space, nor did they give the necessary attention to the requirements of the different vase-shapes, with the result that their compositions tend to lose both a close organic relationship with the surface on which they are painted and a just balance between their individual component parts. It has often been said that the work of some of the great South Italian vase-painters is seen to best advantage in fragments, where one can study the drawing in all its purity, without external distraction; this may be true in some instances where a single figure has survived from a large composition (e.g. *[134]*), but many vases with scenes on a somewhat smaller scale are of very high quality and would more than challenge comparison with any contemporary Athenian products.

Subject-matter

Apart from a host of small vases decorated with the single figure of a youth, satyr, Eros, woman, Nike and, less frequently, of an animal or bird, as well as those depicting a head, most commonly that of a woman, the subjects on vases of medium or large dimensions cover a very wide range and provide us with a good deal of information not only about everyday life and the hereafter, but also

11

about Greek mythology, especially in regard to its connection with the theatre. Scenes associated with Dionysos also play a large part, as is only natural, since he was not only god of wine and of the mysteries, which promise a better after-life to their initiates, but also of drama, which is myth enacted in his honour; hence the relevance of his appearance on many vase-paintings, as well as of scenes inspired by dramatic presentations, since both are highly appropriate on a vase which might be used in the service of the god at a symposium, or else accompany the deceased on their journey to the next world.

Among the most remarkable of all the vase-paintings from South Italy and Sicily are those with theatrical connections, often depicting scenes inspired by Greek tragedies, especially those of Euripides, whose plays seem to have enjoyed great popularity in the fourth century; in these the figures wear elaborately decorated costumes, but not masks, and only very seldom is there any indication of the actual stage. Such scenes may be likened to a modern poster; they normally show us the principal characters in the play, with some indication of the main action (e.g. Andromeda bound to the rock [182]; Niobe mourning at the tomb of her slain children [305]; the meeting of Orestes and Elektra at the tomb of Agamemnon [60]). There is often an assembly of deities in an upper register [210], who may be associated with the plot in some way or else be the speakers of prologue or epilogue. For representations of masks and of the actual stage we must turn to the phlyax vases, e.g. [115, 125, 294, 340–1, 352], which often reproduce scenes from this local type of farce, which may parody well-known myths or give us comic versions of episodes from daily life, in which the characters wear their appropriate masks. The events are often shown as taking place upon a simple stage, supported by posts or columns, and probably set up out of doors for an impromptu type of performance (cf. *Frontispiece*, where the stage has been set up beside a real tree).

Mythology also plays a significant part in the subject-matter; it is not always easy to draw a firm line between myths with theatrical associations and those without, since so many classical legends formed the basis for Greek dramas. The influence of the theatre is, however, probably to be seen in the use of richly-decorated costumes, in the occasional appearance of structures resembling the stage background or of certain types of props (rocks, caves, etc.), and, above all, in the presence of the old retainer (*paidagogos*), who would not have figured in the original myth, but whose presence is appropriate in a drama derived from it, since he often witnesses the denouement, which by reason of its violent nature could not take place upon the stage itself, and then, in his role as messenger, narrates the events to the chorus and the survivors. Also noteworthy is the frequency with which South Italian vase-painters decorate their vases with myths rarely, or never, found elsewhere, and otherwise known to us only from literary evidence (e.g. Callisto, Melanippe, the daughters of Anios); it is perhaps in this field that they make one of their most valuable contributions to our better knowledge of the ancient world. On Athenian vases of the fourth century mythology plays a much smaller role and does not go far beyond certain adventures of Herakles and Theseus, who figure less prominently in South Italian, since they were essentially Attic heroes, or scenes with Europa, Arimaspians and griffins, and Amazonomachies, subjects which might be expected to have a special appeal for purchasers in the Black Sea area.

Another area of great interest and importance is that of the after-life and the cult of the dead. Scenes depicting Pluto and Persephone in their palace in the Underworld, surrounded by some of its more famous denizens, are to be found on Apulian vases, often in association with Orpheus, whose cult is known to have flourished in Taranto (anc. Taras) during the fourth century. Large numbers of other South Italian vases show mourners at grave-monuments of varying types (see pp. 266–7).

Elaborate representations of women at their toilet or preparing for marriage ceremonies appear frequently in Apulian (mostly on pelikai) and Sicilian. Other genre scenes are taken from everyday life – athletes in the palaestra (largely confined to the later fifth and first half of the fourth centuries), banquets, conversation pieces, playing with pets, especially dogs and birds. The reverses of the standard vases usually represent two or three draped youths, in a limited number of stock, and rather monotonous, poses; they are, however, often useful as providing clues to the identity of their painters. The presence in the field above their heads of jumping weights (halteres) or of writing-cases (diptychs) is probably intended to convey a suggestion of the palaestra or the school-room.

One interesting feature of South Italian vases, as distinct from Athenian, is the extensive use made of various types of rocks as seats or foot-rests. These may look like natural outcrops (e.g. [21, 22]), but for the most part they assume a highly stylised form. In Campania, as might be expected in a volcanic area, we find the two main types of rock associated with eruptions – lava flow [282], in which spherulites (vitreous globules) are often embedded, and agglomerate or breccia, made up of fragmented material scattered by the explosive force of the volcano and shown on vases as a mass of small black or black and white dots [280]. On Apulian vases, rocks used as seats look even more artificial; they assume various forms, the most common being 'hollow' rocks and rock-piles, the latter consisting of two or more elliptically shaped pieces, placed one above the other, often outlined in white with a black centre [173, 193]. Such rocks are less common in the other fabrics, notably so in Paestan, where people generally sit upon tendrils or enclosed palmettes [365], or at Cumae where chairs (klismoi) or folding-stools are in frequent use [313].

Inscriptions

By the end of the fifth century, inscriptions had ceased to be a significant element on Greek vases, and in South Italian the part they play – mostly in Apulian and Paestan – is largely confined to the identification of specific figures on the larger and more elaborately decorated vases. They can be of great value, especially when they serve to identify characters in rare myths or when they name the personifications of the locality associated with the story (e.g. Thebes, Crete, Mt Sipylos) or figures like Pothos, Oistros, Poina or Mania. [105] has a couple of metrical inscriptions which might well be quotations from the play represented; [269] gives a short dialogue between Hermes and a man reluctant to obey the summons to go to Hades; pillars and tomb-monuments are occasionally inscribed, the former with a name or the word *termon* (the finishing or turning post), the latter on two occasions with an elegiac couplet celebrating the grave of Oedipus. A few vases by the Darius Painter bear what look like descriptive titles – the Persians, the Tomb of Patroclus. Only two vase-painters sign their works – Asteas and Python, both from Paestum; the signature of a third, a late Apulian, by name Lasimos, is now regarded as a modern addition. *Kalos*-names, as such, do not occur, though the inscription *kalos* appears on a couple of early Lucanian vases, no doubt a lingering echo of the former practice in Athens.

Technique

The technique of making red-figured pottery in South Italy is essentially that of Athens, and it has been fully discussed by J.V. Noble in his *Techniques of painted Attic pottery* and summarized by John Boardman in *Athenian Red Figure Vases: The Archaic Period*, pp. 11–15. It may, however, be noted that the clays of South Italy usually have a somewhat lower iron content than that of Athens, as a result of which they fire to a paler colour. To compensate for this, vase-painters sometimes covered their undecorated vases with a thin wash of yellow ochre and then burnished the surface; in Campania, where the fired clay is often a pale shade of buff, a pink or red wash (made from *miltos* or red ochre) is often added to enhance the colour. Large vases had to be thrown in several sections and the joins smoothed over to produce a continuous curving surface. These joins were susceptible to cracking and fissures are sometimes found on such vases. While many vases were functional, and indeed are frequently shown in use on vase-paintings, others, especially those destined for the tomb, were left with an opening between the body and the foot and thus could not have contained liquids, or else were equipped with fragile, ornamental handles and decorative finials, which would hardly have withstood everyday usage. The inside of volute-kraters is sometimes left unglazed, which would suggest that such vases were not intended to be used as mixing vessels.

On many of the larger Apulian vases (e.g. volute-kraters and amphorae), from about the middle of the fourth century onwards, the subsidiary decoration on the neck or shoulder was often painted in added colours – white, yellow, orange and various shades of red – in the same technique as that used for figures within *naiskoi*. It is probable that it was from this type of decoration that the so-called Gnathia style (named after Egnazia, where many such vases were found) developed, in which the decoration, either ornamental or figural, is painted in colours applied directly to the black-glaze surface of the vase. This technique ran closely parallel to red-figure in the second half of the fourth century, but continues in use for a short period after the latter had to come to an end, at least until the time of the Roman conquest of Taranto in 273.

Chronology

There is rather less external evidence than might be expected on which to base a definitive chronology for South Italian red-figure. The earlier finds are not well documented, and recent excavations in Apulia (especially at Taranto, Gioia del Colle, Rutiglaino, Conversano, Vaste, Canosa and Salapia) and in Campania (S. Maria di Capua Vetere, Caivano and area, Montesarchio, Pontecagnano, Paestum and area), which have yielded a great deal of most valuable comparative material, have failed to produce much (e.g. coins) that would enable precise datings to be made. Nor does the historical evidence greatly assist us, since the history of South Italy in the fourth century is often rather confused as a result of conflicting literary sources.

In Apulia, Taranto reaches the height of its power during the rule of Archytas (*c.* 367–361 BC), and evidence of its prosperity is clearly visible in the extensive production not only of vases, but also of sculptures in both stone and bronze, terracottas and, above all, golden jewellery of various types. After the death of Archytas the native tribes began to rebel against Tarentine hegemony and, unable to cope with the situation, the Tarentines called in the help of Archidamos III of Sparta, who came over in 342 BC with a mercenary force. He was killed at the battle of Manduria in 338 and, if *[226]*, which represents the helmented head of a Greek warrior and bears the inscription *APX*, refers to Archidamos, this would provide valuable external evidence for the dating of that particular vase. In 334 the Tarentines brought in Alexander the Molossian, to help them against the Messapians and the Lucanians; his successful campaigns and his desire for power led to a break with the Tarentines and did much to stir up animosities between the local Greek cities, until his death in 331 put an end to his dreams of empire. He was the uncle of Alexander the Great of Macedon whose exploits in Asia he wished to rival and his presence in South Italy may have inspired the scenes on a few Apulian vases (e.g. *[201]*) which have generally been thought to represent Alexander the Great in battle with the Persian king Darius. Such vases might, therefore, will be dated in the later 30's or early 20's of the fourth century.

In the west, the Lucanians, a people of Samnite origin, had invaded Campania in the fifth century BC and had taken the name of Campani; Capua fell into their hands in 423, Cumae a couple of years later, Poseidonia around the turn of the century, and Laos in 390. As the fourth century progresses, the growing power of Rome leads to conflict between the Romans and the Samnites, with various attempts to stem the Roman advance. During the 330's the Tarentines sent an embassy to the Neopolitans and the closer relations which probably followed may account for the wave of Apulian influence on Campanian and Paestan pottery about that time, Paestum enjoying a brief respite from Lucanian rule between 332 and 326.

One of the more interesting aspects of South Italian pottery is the light which the vases shed upon the contact between the Greek colonists and the native populations, and this is well exemplified in fourth century red-figure, on which we may see many examples of native costumes and armour, which differ considerably from those of mainland Greece. Many of the large Apulian vases may well have been traded for the agricultural produce and wool of the native inhabitants, and it is significant that some at least of the funerary vases show youths in native costume within the naiskos.

In Sicily, during the first half of the fourth century, most of the western part of the island was under Carthaginian domination. Dionysius I was tyrant of Syracuse, consolidating his power in eastern Sicily and South Italy until his death in 367. This was followed by a period of some political upheaval, which might have been a factor behind the apparent migration of potters to Campania and Paestum around this time. The coming of Timoleon in 342 restored order in eastern Sicily; he soon succeeded in driving the Carthaginians out of the principal cities which they had occupied in central and western Sicily, and his resettlements were probably responsible for the notable revival of the pottery industry throughout the island. His rule was succeeded by that of Agathocles, first as *strategos* between 310 and 304, and then as *basileus* (king) from 304 until his death in 289. The finding of datable coins from the reigns of both Timoleon and Agathocles at various sites (in particular, the acropolis at Gela) in conjunction with vases has been of great value in helping to establish fairly reliable dates for the latter; it is significant that there is very little red-figure after 304, when the title *basileus* appears on the coins.

On the overall evidence at present available it seems likely that, except for a few provincial stragglers, the production of red-figure pottery ceased around the end of the fourth century. It is difficult to point to a specific reason for its cessation, but it was probably hastened by political events, not least the growing menace of the advance of Rome, nor can the local vase-painters have been entirely immune to the knowledge that red-figured vases were no longer being produced in mainland Greece. In addition to the late Gnathia vases, a polychrome style flourished briefly at Canosa in Apulia, and at Centuripe in Sicily, during the first half of the third century; the former seems to have drawn its inspiration from some of the vases in the White Sakkos Group, the latter from those of the Lipari Painter and his associates. Thereafter pottery is largely confined to plain black wares, with stamped or relief decoration.

Chapter Two

THE ORIGIN AND DEVELOPMENT OF RED-FIGURE
VASE-PAINTING IN SOUTH ITALY AND SICILY
IN THE LATER 5TH CENTURY BC

Introduction

Until about the beginning of the last third of the fifth century BC the Greek colonists in South Italy and Sicily had been content to import their red-figured pottery from Athens; thereafter they began to supplement these imports with vases of local manufacture. At first, such vases are so closely modelled upon Attic prototypes that it seems likely that the artists responsible for them had either been trained in Athens or were immigrants from that city, seeking other outlets for their skills. This may have been due in part to the effects of the great plague of 430 BC, which must have led to a depletion of the work-force, and that, in turn, may have contributed to a decline in the Attic pottery trade; this becomes increasingly marked as the Peloponnesian War drags on, with a steady decline in the fortune of Athens, culminating in her complete defeat in 404.

To Adolf Furtwängler in 1893 must go the credit for establishing the existence of a local South Italian red-figure fabric in the second half of the fifth century BC. He plausibly connected its origin with the founding of Thurii in 443, but as yet insufficient relevant material has been found in the excavations at that site to provide confirmation of this theory. The discovery at Metaponto in 1973, however, of potters' kilns containing fragments of vases by the Amykos Painter from the end of the fifth century BC and of large quantities of broken vases and wasters by his immediate followers, the Creusa and Dolon Painters, taken in conjunction with the finding of other vases by the Pisticci and Amykos Painters in the immediate neighbourhood, has put beyond doubt that at least for some time in the later fifth and early fourth centuries BC their workshop must have been located in Metaponto. Its products are the forerunners of the developed Lucanian style from the second quarter of the fourth century onwards.

A second school of vase-painters, almost certainly located at Taranto, the largest and most important city in Apulia, seems to have established itself in the last quarter of the fifth century. From the start, its products tended to favour more monumental shapes, like the volute-krater, and to be more elaborately decorated, often with subjects taken from Greek mythology. These vases are the precursors of the developed Apulian style, which, as we shall see, falls into two main groups, one of which has been characterized as 'Plain', the other as 'Ornate', from the difference in the manner in which they are decorated. In the earlier stages of the Metapontine and Tarentine schools of vase-painting, as might be expected, the painters of both seem to have worked in close co-operation and either style reflects the influence of the other. That is why such vases are often referred to as 'Early South Italian', although they might now be better designated 'Early Lucanian' and 'Early Apulian'. It is significant that until *c.* 375 BC vases from the Metapontine school are widely found at sites in Apulia, but thereafter they disappear almost entirely from that area and are rarely found outside the Lucanian hinterland. This suggests that they were probably no longer being made at Metaponto and that the painters had moved to sites further inland, like Roccanova, Anzi, Armento or S. Arcangelo, where what may be termed the 'standard' Lucanian vases of their successors have been found in quantity. Their work is marked by a progressive deterioration in quality, as if the painters were becoming increasingly isolated from the artistic developments taking place in Apulia during the remainder of the fourth century.

Early Lucanian

The earliest South Italian workshop for the production of red-figured vases is that of the Pisticci Painter (named after the small town, some 20 km west of Metaponto, where several of his vases were found) and his two chief colleagues, the Cyclops and Amykos Painters, named from the subjects depicted on two of their major works *[9]* and *[17]*. For the most part they decorate unpretentious vases, especially bell-kraters, with subjects associated with Dionysos and his followers, with daily life (athletes, warriors, etc.), or with scenes of pursuit*[5]*. The last often show Eros *[3]* and may also at times have a mythological connection (e.g. Eos and Kephalos or Zeus and Aigina *[4]*), but, generally speaking, mythology plays a smaller part here than it does in Apulian.

The Pisticci Painter *[1–8]* seems to have begun his career in the thirties of the fifth century, to judge from the parallels between his earliest work and that of Attic artists of this period, like the followers of Polygnotus (notably the Christie Painter) and of the Achilles Painter, or the Barclay Painter and the Painter of the Louvre Centauromachy, from whom shapes, pattern-work and subjects are directly taken over. At first the Pisticci Painter adheres comparatively closely to Attic models, and his earliest work *[1]* is not always easy to distinguish from the originals; soon, however, more individual characteristics begin to develop, especially in the treatment of drapery and the rendering of the draped youths on his reverses, and his later vases draw increasingly further away from those of his Attic counterparts. Noteworthy also is the tendency for the black glaze to lose the lustrous quality it has on Attic vases, and to become duller or more matt-looking.

His favourite shape is the bell-krater, of a type similar to that found at Athens early in the second half of the fifth century, and this he normally decorates with simple two- or three-figure isocephalic compositions, almost invariably with

18

draped youths on the reverses. His pattern-work is very uniform – beneath the rim, above the picture, is a laurel-wreath with rounded rather than pointed leaves, which are sometimes veined; below is a band of meanders with crossed squares, of which two types are in common use, one with an upright cross, and the other with a saltire. On early vases the frame for the cross is generally thick, with a blob in each of the four corners [1]; these tend to break down into strokes of varying thickness [2], with an intermediate phase in which both appear in the same square [5]. Several of his earliest vases, some of which come from the area around Metaponto, are hydriai, usually representing running or standing draped women [1], who hold various objects (tendril, mirror, fillet, etc.) in their hands; others are bell-kraters with satyrs and maenads, or Eros with youths or women [3], and, rather exceptionally on [2] a scene apparently taken from a satyr-play, showing a satyr with a hammer beside a goddess rising from the ground. The lines which mark the folds on the drapery are straight and simple; the outline of the body is often clearly visible through the drapery; the hair is usually shown as a solid mass (in contrast to the contemporary Attic practice); the features are small and not pronounced – the nose tilting up slightly at the tip, the chin rounded, the neck rather thin. The eye is shown as a small black dot for the pupil, between two strokes meeting at an acute angle, with a curving line above for the eyebrow; this perhaps contributes to the rather frozen-looking expression of many of his figures. Hands and feet are not well drawn, and there is a notable tendency to bodily angularity, especially with knees and elbows.

In his more mature period the Pisticci Painter regularly puts three or even four figures [5,8] on the obverse of his kraters and three youths on their reverses [6]. There is little change in their subjects, but in pursuit scenes we often find a bearded figure, holding a sceptre, who looks on impassively [5]. To this period also belong several vases like [7], showing maenads and/or satyrs beside a herm, and a few with mythological scenes of unusual interest, like [8] showing Laocoön at Delphi, where his wife attacks the serpent, entwined round a statue of Apollo, which had devoured one of his sons, or [4] with Zeus, brandishing his thunderbolt, in pursuit of the fleeing Aigina.

It is also perhaps worth noting that a few owl skyphoi have been found at Metaponto in contexts which closely associate them with the work of the Pisticci Painter, and which are therefore almost certainly of local manufacture. Like their mainland Greek prototypes, they are decorated on either side with an owl between olive-branches; they may have two horizontal handles (Type A), or one horizontal and one vertical (Type B), the former being more common in South Italy. They appear also in Apulia during the fourth century and were probably made in Campania and at Paestum as well, but as yet no definitive classification of South Italian owl skyphoi has been published. See, however, F.P. Johnson in *Studies Robinson* ii, 96–105 and *AJA* 59, 1955, 119–124.

A close collaborator of the Pisticci Painter is the Cyclops Painter named after [9], which shows Odysseus about to blind the drunken Cyclops, surrounded by satyrs. Their presence suggests that the subject may have been inspired by a satyr-play like the *Cyclops* of Euripides (c. 406 BC); the artist's emphasis upon the theatrical aspect is a significant expression of that connection between myth and drama which is to play such an important part in later South Italian vase-painting. Of particular interest is the painter's attempt at the rendering of perspective; the Cyclops in the foreground is foreshortened and Odysseus and his companions behind are tiered in receding planes. His style clearly owes much to the work of the Pisticci Painter, but he soon develops his own mannerisms, as may be seen in his treatment of balding satyrs and draped women. The former are often pot-bellied, the latter mostly draped in a chiton with wide sleeves, over which a cloak is wrapped [10]. Their hair is shown as a solid black mass, with a reserved bandeau, often with a spike in front, which encircles it and divides the bunch at the back into two parts; there is a loop of hair over the visible ear, sometimes with a fringe of small curls. His poses often look rather artificial, with something of the effect of a fashion-plate (cf. [10]), and this applies equally to his draped women and his nude youths. He draws hands better than the Pisticci Painter, often with long and tapering fingers, though he pays less attention to the feet, sometimes omitting to indicate the toes. In his attempts to render faces in three-quarter view, as on the Cyclops krater, he goes further than his predecessor, but does not always find his efforts crowned with success.

The most important of the early Lucanian artists is the Amykos Painter [11–19], from whose hand we have well over 200 vases and a considerable number of fragments. Like the Cyclops Painter, with whom he has much in common, he seems to have learnt his art from the Pisticci Painter; his earlier work like [11] strongly reflects the influence of his master's style, especially in the treatment of women, satyrs and youths. As his style develops, it becomes more individual, and we may note an increasing tendency to decorate vases of larger dimensions, perhaps under the influence of the Tarentine school. Among these appears a new shape, the so-called nestoris or *trozzella* (see p. 10). [11] illustrates an example with a carinated body and [12] a slightly later development, with the scenes disposed in panels, either on the upper part of the body, with ornamental pattern-work below as on [12], or on both parts, with a band of palmettes or other patterns between them. This shape becomes fairly popular in later Lucanian, with the body of the vase assuming a more ovoid form [92], but is far less so in Apulian, where it will not be found for nearly half a century; a nestoris in actual use does, however, appear on some early Apulian vases like [37], by the Sisyphus Painter.

[11] and [13–16] illustrate a number of the Amykos Painter's typical stock figures, which are repeated from one vase to another; these include several types of draped women, who may wear a full-sleeved chiton, with a cloak draped over one shoulder [13–15], or stand, with one arm akimbo to produce a bunch of radiating folds at the waist [14]; a fleeing woman with a himation wrapped around her body over the chiton, with collar-like folds at the neck [18], and a

20

woman wearing a peplos with a thick black single or double stripe running down it *[11]*. Often their hair is covered with a sakkos *[13–15]*, instead of having a spiky bandeau or stephane above the brow *[12, 14]*. The youths on the reverses *[16]* show very little change from those on vases by his predecessors, although the himation tends to be drawn more frequently up on to the back of the head.

The tendency to produce vases of rather larger dimensions is very manifest in the painter's mature phase. Here we find large bell- and column-kraters *[18]* or amphorae, with three or four figures on a fairly monumental scale on the obverse; sometimes on the amphorae they are shown on a smaller scale in two separate rows. *[19]* illustrates the only volute-krater attributed to this artist – it represents the Argonauts liberating Phineus from the Harpies – here the figures are disposed at different levels in what is the painter's most ambitious, but not his most successful, work; it may well have been inspired by the monumental vases of his Tarentine contemporaries. Also noteworthy are his large hydriai, like his name vase *[17]*, with mythological scenes represented on the shoulder and, running right round the body of the vase, a frieze of maenads and satyrs or youths and women *[14]*. Such scenes show the painter at his most typical, with a good selection of his stock figures.

Following closely on from the Amykos Painter comes a most important group of vases, several of which were found at Policoro *[24–9]*, the ancient Herakleia, where they may well have been made. Again many of them are of large dimensions, with mythological compositions on the grand scale, which place them among the finest of the early Lucanian vases and comparable to the best Tarentine of the same period. The Group is often referred to by the initials P.K.P., standing for Palermo, Karneia and Policoro, the names of its three chief painters.

The Palermo Painter *[20–2]*, who is the closest of the three in style to the Amykos Painter, owes something also to the Cyclops Painter in his treatment of female figures, especially in regard to drapery, hair-style and the drawing of the face. *[20–2]* well illustrate his characteristic style, in which we should note the rendering of the profile and frontal faces, especially the latter *[22]*, since they now come into wider use; also the emphasis given to the pelvic girdle on his nude male figures, and the rather mannered treatment of the seated draped woman in a somewhat huddled posture *[21]*. The volute-krater *[20]* is his masterpiece – the obverse shows Hermes, Apollo, Artemis and Leto in all their majesty, creating an immediate impression of almost sculptural quality. To the left on this vase is a pillar inscribed with the name of Hermes; another such appears on *[22]*, with the name of the satyr Onnaseuas, and there is a third in New York with that of Marsyas, who leans against it. Vases like these show the Palermo Painter as an artist of great power, fully capable of dealing with major themes in the appropriately monumental manner.

With his work we should compare the famous Karneia krater in Taranto

[23], undoubtedly one of the finest of all South Italian vases, with a majestic Dionysiac scene on the obverse; the reverse is in two registers, the upper showing Perseus terrifying satyrs with the gorgon-head, perhaps inspired by a satyr-play; the lower, *kalathiskos*-dancers beside a pillar inscribed Karneios. They hold, or wear on their heads, the huge basket crowns (*kalathoi*) which were a feature of the dance in honour of Apollo Karneios. A study of the obverse reveals the connection with the Amykos and Palermo Painters in the anatomy of the satyr, the three-quarter face of the ecstatic maenad, and above all in the drawing of the eyes, with the curving upper lid.

Two pelikai [24] and [26] from Policoro stand very close to [23] – one with Poseidon and Athena setting out for the contest to decide which of the two shall be the titular deity of Athens; Poseidon on horseback accompanied by a young warrior [24], Athena in a three-horse chariot driven by a woman [25]. Each side gives a spirited composition, well drawn, with great strength and animation. The second [26] shows on the obverse a scene from the *Herakleidai* – a rare topic in South Italian – with a bearded man (Iolaos), holding a suppliant bough, and standing beside a statue of Apollo on an Ionic column in a sanctuary, with five small children around him; on the left is a bearded man with a herald's staff, probably Copreus come to demand the return of the children, on the right is the goddess Athena, personifying Attica, where Iolaos and the children of Herakles have taken refuge in the sanctuary at Marathon. The richly-patterned dress of .Iolaos suggests the influence of the theatre and the scene would fit in well with lines 48–50 of the *Herakleidai* of Euripides.

This pelike provides a good connecting link with five other vases from Policoro, which may be attributed to a single artist – the Policoro Painter [27–9] – and on which we may note the similarity of the pattern-work, the drapery, and the rendering of the faces in three-quarter or nearly frontal view. Three of the vases are large hydriai (*c.* 45 cm in height), decorated with mythological scenes which run down from the shoulder on to the body of the vase and represent Pelops and Hippodamia, the death of Sarpedon [27] and the vengeance of Medea [28], all themes associated with Euripidean dramas. The other two are pelikai, one with the punishment of Dirce [29], the other with Polynices bribing Eriphyle with the necklace of Harmonia, myths also connected with tragedy; both have draped youths on their reverses. The richly patterned draperies are another indication of theatrical influence. Medea and Dirce appear here for the first time in South Italian vase-painting, and one wonders whether the set from the Policoro tomb might not have been specially commissioned for someone who had a particular fondness for Euripidean drama or had possibly been himself an actor.

The Policoro Painter is fond of three-quarter and frontal faces, and he makes considerable use of flapping drapery; the eyes, however, differ from those of the Palermo and Karneia Painters and, when frontal, have a staring look. Most of his work probably belongs to the early years of the fourth century.

There are several other minor artists associated with the Amykos workshop, of whom perhaps the Arnò Painter [30] is the most interesting, but his drawing is rather heavy-handed, especially in the rendering of the head, which tends to be disproportionately large, and of the drapery which is lifeless. There follows a large group of smaller vases which are contemporary with later Amykan and early Creusa-Dolon, to which brief reference will be made in Chapter Three.

Early Apulian

The second, or Tarentine, school of Early South Italian vase-painters seems to have begun a little later than the first and from the start offers something of a contrast in both style and subject-matter. There are fewer scenes of pursuit or departing warriors, more attention is given to mythology and, in general, the vases are of larger dimensions (e.g. volute-kraters) with figures treated in the monumental manner we have seen in the P.K.P Group; to some measure they reflect the influence of sculpture, apparent also in the choice of such subjects as amazonomachies and centauromachies, which appear in the sculptured metopes or friezes on temples, and indeed at Taranto itself in the form of relief decoration. The artists also seem to remain in closer contact with contemporary Attic vase-painting, some examples of which from the later fifth and earlier fourth centuries, have come to light at Ruvo and other Apulian sites. Its influence is particularly noticeable in the volute-kraters, which reflect the work of Attic artists like the Kadmos and the Pronomos Painters, some of whose vases have been found at Ruvo and therefore might well have been seen by the local vase-painters.

At the head of the Tarentine school stands the Painter of the Berlin Dancing Girl [31–4], so named after his delightful calyx-krater [31] showing a girl dancing to the accompaniment of a flute played by a seated woman beside her. His more mature style may be seen on a bell-krater, the obverse of which [32] shows Orpheus playing his lyre to a black-garbed Thracian, who listens enthralled as he stands before his horse; the reverse design [33] includes two of the artist's favourite figures, the draped woman with long hair and the bearded man, whose cloak is so draped as to leave part of his chest exposed and to go across his waist in a bunch of parallel folds. We see him again on [34], a vase of particular interest for its shape, since this is one of the very few neck-amphorae to be found in Apulia. The shape is taken over from contemporary Attic but obviously proved unpopular in Apulia, where its place from now on is taken by the amphora of panathenaic shape. Precisely the opposite applies to Campania and Paestum where the latter shape is not found. Another characteristic of his work is his very individual meander pattern with thick lines, accompanied by uncrossed squares with a large black dot, almost a blob, placed near the middle of each of its sides [31], and his use of veined laurel leaves below the rims of his kraters and beneath the pictures on [34]. His figures generally have a rather solemn appearance; their features are often angular. Recent finds at Rutigliano, near Bari, included a tomb (T.24) containing seven vases by the Painter of the Berlin Dancing Girl; among them were a volute-krater showing the death of Memnon, an amphora with Adrastos marshalling the forces for the expedition against Thebes, and a pelike with Peleus attacking an Amazon. On all these vases the principal figures have their names inscribed beside them. Several of his other vases show combats with Amazons – perhaps inspired by Attic works of the Polygnotan school – again with identifying inscriptions; Herakles figures in one of them, and also in a centauromachy.

The new vases show him to be a painter of greater significance than had previously been recognized and his work clearly had a considerable influence upon that of both the Sisyphus Painter and the Painter of the Birth of Dionysos; his choice of a wide range of mythological subjects sets a pattern which followed in later Apulian.

His chief colleague and perhaps the most important artist in the Tarentine workshop, is the Sisyphus Painter, so called from the name inscribed on a heart-shaped token held in the hand of one of the youths at the marriage scene depicted on the upper register of a large volute-krater in Munich. Here both sides of the vase are divided into two registers, formally separated by a band of egg-pattern; the lower register on the obverse shows the Argonauts, with Medea, Jason and the Golden Fleece; on the reverse, the Muses are depicted above and a centauromachy, somewhat reminiscent of the Phigalian frieze, below. In the friezes on the neck an Eros crowns Aphrodite between two groups of Erotes at play, on the obverse, and on the reverse there is a horserace.

The division into two separate registers is unusual for a volute-krater, though it may have been inspired by a two-row calyx-krater, common enough in Attic at the time, and indeed found also in the work of the Hearst Painter [42], a contemporary of the Sisyphus Painter, though otherwise rare in South Italian. A better idea of the painter's work is perhaps to be had from his volute-krater in Ruvo [35–6], with the rape of the daughters of Leucippus on the obverse and an Amazonomachy on the reverse. Here there is no formal division of the pictures, although the figures are disposed on two distinct levels.

The quality of the Sisyphus Painter's work shows considerable variation. Beazley referred to the 'peculiar penmanship of his lines' and 'the beauty of the large grave ox-eyed three-quarter heads', and this is well seen on his larger vases like [35], but on the whole his compositions tend to lack internal unity and often consist of a series of detached groups, as in the Amazonomachy on [36]. Characteristic is his treatment of women's drapery, with a particular fondness for long overfalls [37] on their peploi, and for stars or dot-clusters as decorative patterns [35]. [37] is of special interest as one of the first Apulian vases to show youths wearing Oscan or 'native' costume, as well as a woman pouring a libation to one of them from a vase of local shape – the nestoris or *trozzella* – of which we have already seen examples in red-figure by the Amykos Painter [12].

It may be noted that, until about the middle of the fourth century, the column-krater is the only shape in Apulia upon which youths in native costume appear; perhaps it had a special appeal for the native inhabitants of Apulia.

The early work of the Sisyphus Painter includes many bell-kraters, mostly with three-figure compositions depicting Dionysiac or genre scenes, although two depict *kalathiskos*-dancers *[38]* as on the Karneia krater. Two or three draped youths invariably appear on their reverses *[39]*, and this will be the standard decoration for such vases, throughout the life of the fabric. Various stock figures of draped youths will be found – at first they often appear with one arm akimbo and the cloak draped over that arm and shoulder, and across the waist, leaving part of the chest and the other shoulder bare *[39]*, though this fashion becomes less popular as time goes on; for the most part, they are completely draped in their cloaks, with one arm outstretched with a stick in the hand, or else concealed beneath the drapery, to produce the effect either of a 'sling', or a 'sleeve' when akimbo. These fashions were followed, with minor variations, by the later Apulian vase-painters, cf. *[117, 128, 144, 163, 217]*.

In his later phase, of which *[40]* is a good example, the quality of the Sisyphus Painter's work seems to deteriorate; his figures become more stereotyped, and their features more rounded but somewhat coarser; the subjects are less imaginative and largely confined to youths or warriors and women.

Beazley noted the analogy between the earlier style of the Sisyphus Painter and that of the Dwarf and Codrus Painters at Athens, and parallels may also be found with the work of Polion. It seems probable, therefore, that his main activity should be placed in the last two decades of the fifth century, with his latest work running down into the early years of the fourth. The particular significance of the Sisyphus Painter, and to a lesser extent of his slightly earlier colleague, the Painter of the Berlin Dancing Girl, lies in the fact that in their work we may see the origins of the two stylistic trends, which are to characterize later Apulian, and which have been designated 'Plain' and 'Ornate'. The former follows the fashion set by these painters in their smaller vases, especially bell-kraters, with comparatively simple two- or three-figure compositions, little use of added colour, and not much emphasis on ornamental decoration; the latter that of the larger vases like volute-kraters, with mythological and, later, funerary themes, on which we find an increasing use of added colours, and very elaborate pattern-work and floral decoration. For about fifty years the two styles run along parallel lines, the 'Plain' vases perhaps outnumbering the 'Ornate'. From the time of the Iliupersis Painter (*c*. 370–60), however, when Apulian taste turns more to vases of larger dimensions, with monumental compositions illustrating mythological or dramatic themes, with the richly-costumed figures disposed at various levels around various kinds of buildings, there is a substantial increase in the production of 'Ornate', and the 'Plain' style begins to reflect its influence more strongly with a greater use of decorative adjuncts, added colours and more elaborate pattern-work. The range of vases in this style is also extended to include more column-kraters, hydriai and pelikai, but, although in the second half of the century the two styles move more closely together, the essential distinction between them never completely dies out, and 'Plain' vases are still being produced when the fabric comes to an end around 300 B C.

Associated with the Sisyphus Painter are several other artists, who often produced work of very high quality. Among them we may note the Hearst Painter, with his bearded male figures [41] after the manner of the Berlin Dancing Girl Painter, but on the whole drawn with less skill, especially when shown in near-frontal view. What must have been one of his better and more ambitious vases has survived only in fragments; it was a two-row calyx-krater [42] with a vivid representation of Odysseus slaying the suitors; his later and heavier style may be seen on [43] showing Orestes at Athens with a Fury on either side.

Of the other vases associated with the Sisyphus Painter the finest is undoubtedly the large volute-krater [44] showing the binding of Andromeda, while Perseus makes his pact with her father Cepheus. The figures are particularly well-drawn and the composition is nicely balanced, with a sculptural quality like that of Attic vases by the Kleophon Painter and his colleagues. This vase also invites comparison with the volute-krater [21] by the Palermo Painter, with which it has a strong stylistic affinity, providing an excellent illustration of the close connection between the two schools of Early South Italian vase-painting around 400 B C.

The Ariadne Painter, named after [45], which shows on one side the desertion of Ariadne by Theseus, and on the other the departure of Bellerophon, is a late contemporary and follower of the Sisyphus Painter, active in the early years of the fourth century; he is fond of treating mythological subjects in a rather monumental manner, but does so on vases of comparatively small dimensions, with the result that his compositions often look over-crowded and pretentious, as on [46], which shows Bellerophon on Pegasus attacking the Chimaera, flanked by Athena and Poseidon. The Sisyphean influence is clear, perhaps there is also a reflection of the 'Ornate' style of the Painter of the Birth of Dionysos, with whom he must be contemporary. The Ariadne Painter is fond of painting nude male figures with their heads in three-quarter view, and of putting black stripes down his drapery or using them for borders. The appearance of a stamnos is noteworthy – although popular in Athens in the second half of the fifth century, this shape is comparatively rare in Apulian, only about a dozen examples being known, mostly from the middle of the fourth century.

Another artist, whose work is closely connected with that of the Sisyphus Painter, is the Gravina Painter, named after three vases found in very fragmentary state at that site in 1974; they provide a connecting link with the Painter of the Birth of Dionysos. [47] is a volute-krater with an as yet unexplained mythological scene on the obverse – perhaps concerned with the legend of Helen of Troy or with the arrival of the Argonauts at Lemnos – and a boar-hunt on the reverse. The other two were amphorae of panathenaic shape, one *[48]* with Stheneboia plunging into the sea, after being dropped off Pegasus by Bellerophon, the other with youths and women gathered around the statue of a young warrior standing on a plinth. These vases were found with fragmentary Attic vases by the Eretria Painter, who was active in the last third of the fourth century, and are therefore probably to be dated around 400.

If the roots of the 'Ornate' style are to be found in the work of the Sisyphus Painter, it is the Painter of the Birth of Dionysos *[49–55]* who is its chief pioneer, and it is in his vases that the early stage of this style can be seen to best advantage, when the links with Athenian vase-painting of the later fifth century BC, as represented by such artists as the Dinos and Kleophon Painters, the Eretria Painter and the members of the Meidan circle, are at their strongest. Five of his extant vases are volute-kraters, a shape which is to become extremely popular in Apulia, though it dies out in Athens around 380 BC. The greater area which such vases place at the artists' disposal for purposes of decoration allowed them to indulge their taste for large-scale compositions, and led not only to the appearance of more elaborate settings and costumes, appropriate to the great figures of mythology or drama, but also to experiments in the use of perspective and in the rendering of spatial depth. At first these are rather tentative, as may be seen from *[49]*, with the result that the pictures tend to look rather flat, but by the middle of the century a reasonably satisfactory solution to the problem of creating an illusion of depth has been found *[149]*, as well as to that of the foreshortening of buildings *[140, 151]*.

The bodies of most of his volute-kraters are more ovoid and less squat than those of Sisyphus Painter, and they provide the models for the later vases. The volute-handles are still done in open-work, sometimes with added ivy-pattern decoration; masks do not appear until just before the middle of the century, after which the earlier open-work type becomes increasingly rare. On *[49]*, the painter's name vase, representing the birth of Dionysos from the thigh of Zeus, the figures are disposed at different levels over the surface of the vase in a free composition reminiscent of great painting; the compositions on *[53]* and *[54]* are more restricted, but with a substantial amount of overlapping, while on *[50]* and *[51]* they appear in two distinct registers. Here the obverse *[50]* represents the apotheosis of Herakles and the reverse an Amazonomachy, which clearly owes much to those of the earlier vase-painters. The painter is fond of mythological subjects – especially where scenes of combat are involved (Amazonomachy, Centauromachy); *[53–4]* illustrates both of these, set in a rocky landscape indicated by stones and shrubs, with painted or incised ground-lines. The influence of sculpture is again apparent. In his work we may also note the statuesque poses of many of his figures, a reflection of Sisyphean influence, his fondness for frontal or three-quarter faces and his rendering of drapery folds by a number of shorter, broken lines after the manner of the later fifth-century

Athenian painters, but without the preciousness so typical of the Meidias Painter. Noteworthy, too, is his use of elaborate ornamental pattern-work, which is to become one of the most striking elements in late Apulian. On the necks of his volute-kraters we have mythological scenes on a rather smaller scale; female heads, or figures in a floral surround, do not come in until the time of the Iliupersis Painter. A connection with the theatre is to be seen on a volute-krater in Naples showing a sacrifice to Dionysos, with a female mask suspended above. In his later vases like [52], there is an increased use of added white and yellow, as well as a new element of something approaching harshness in his three-quarter faces, which are beginning to assume the tormented look, so characteristic of those on vases by the Iliupersis and Lycurgus Painters, a generation or more later.

[52] shows the god Apollo seated in three-quarter view beside his Doric temple, through the half-open door of which a bronze statue of the god may be seen inside; the attempt at foreshortening of both the columns and the door, as well as the use of high-lights and shading on the statue, painted white, gold and brown to simulate the metal original, well illustrate the new approach towards the problems of perspective, though the painter has failed to relate the recession of the capitals on the temple-columns to the architrave above. Close in style to this vase is [55], showing Alkmene seated in dejection in three-quarter view on the altar, with the pyre of logs in front of it, while a somewhat puzzled Amphitryon comes up, as the thunderbolt of Zeus falls down between them. Here again we may note the refinement of the drawing; also the inscriptions which, on both vases, identify the principal characters, as on [49], a practice which becomes more general with the Darius Painter and his circle in the second half of the century.

It is unfortunate that most of the work of the contemporaries of the Painter of the Birth of Dionysos has come down to us only in very fragmentary condition. [56], with Herakles, Apollo, Artemis and the Dioskouroi, must have come from a krater of considerable artistic merit; better preserved is the volute-krater [57] showing a bearded Herakles about to engage in combat with Kyknos. Beside Herakles, whose normal accoutrements (lion-skin, club, bow and quiver) lie at his feet, is Athena; above is a seated Fury, beside whom stands Apollo, who incited Herakles to fight Kyknos because he had slain pilgrims on their way to Delphi. To right a charioteer, wearing a black cuirass, stands in a two-horse chariot, shown frontally – in an interesting experiment in foreshortening. The eagle, with a snake in its claws, which flies above the head of Kyknos, may be interpreted as an omen of disaster for him.

These vases lead on to the more developed stage of the 'Ornate' style, which is dealt with in Chapter Four.

Early Sicilian

The precise date at which red-figured vases were first made in Sicily is still open to question, but it would not be unreasonable to correlate this event with the Athenian expedition to Syracuse in 415 BC, since that would probably have brought an end to the direct import of Athenian vases. It would perhaps be going too far to suggest that the first Sicilian vases might have been the work of Athenians who took part in that expedition and, like some of their fellows, who saved their lives by being able to recite substantial portions of recent plays by Euripides, gained their freedom through their skill as vase-decorators, but the earliest extant vases which appear to be of local manufacture are so close to certain Athenian vases of the later fifth century that it is not always easy to tell them apart. It is possible that some bell-kraters, mostly from Selinus and Vassallaggi, and therefore to be dated before the Carthaginian conquest in *c.* 410 BC, which have so far been regarded as Attic imports, may, in fact, be of local make, but confirmation of this must await further study; there can, however, be little doubt about the local origin of most of the vases ascribed to the Chequer Painter, who takes his name from the chequer pattern which appears upon some of his vases like *[58]*; they include several of Sicilian provenience, as well as a few from Campania. The earlier work of the Chequer Painter is close in style to that of the Pothos Painter in Athens, especially in his treatment of drapery and the rendering of satyrs; in his later phase, he is nearer to the Jena Painter. His vases, however, may be distinguished from Attic by the appearance of the fired clay, which is generally of a pale pink shade, and by the poor quality of the black glaze, which is dull in appearance, and often flakes off, leaving a rather patchy surface. His favourite shape is the krater; his meanders are regularly accompanied by chequers, though sometimes he uses a saltire square. His manner of rendering the hair is particularly characteristic; it is shown as a mass of curly locks *[58]*, drawn individually, a practice more Attic than South Italian; his drapery has clearly-defined fold-lines, which follow the contour of women's bodies in a swirling manner which recalls the style of the Meidian painters; his noses tend to be small and pointed, with a slight upward tilt. Eros plays a large part in his compositions, which favour genre or Dionysiac scenes rather than mythological themes, though two vases represent different episodes of the death of Pentheus. The draped youths on his reverses *[59]* are very close to Attic prototypes and differ considerably from those on the earliest Lucanian or Apulian vases. His work obviously exercised a considerable influence upon that of the Dirce Painter as may be seen from the latter's choice of shapes and decorative patterns, as well as in his treatment of hair and drapery. The Dirce Painter is an artist of considerable significance not only because he established certain canons of vase-decoration which were followed by his Sicilian successors, but also as the chief 'forerunner' of both early Campanian and Paestan. He decorates a number of vases with mythological themes – the meeting of Orestes and Elektra [*60*], the punishment of Dirce [*61*], the ambush of Dolon, and Philoctetes, as well as one with a phlyax scene, showing Zeus with an attendant and a flute-player. Seven of his vases come from Sicily, including four from the Fusco necropolis at Syracuse, and he is therefore likely to have worked in Sicily, probably at Syracuse; his immediate colleague, the Painter of Naples 2074, who is remarkably close to him in style, may have moved later to Campania, since several of his vases have been found in that area, and one at Paestum.

On the evidence at present available it would seem that there were different schools of vase-painting in Sicily in the earlier fourth century, but that production was on a rather limited scale. From the Syracusan area comes a group of vases associated in style with the work of the Chequer Painter, but of little artistic merit. Recent excavations at Himera in the north-west of the island have brought to light numerous red-figured vases, mostly in a very fragmentary state, several of which would look to be the work of a single artist, who has been called the Himera Painter [*62*], and whose work has some stylistic affinity with that of the Chequer Painter and his followers, as also with that of a group of vases originally attributed to an artist called the Locri Painter [*63*], after the find-spot of several of his vases, and placed in the so-called Intermediate Group. Subsequent discoveries have brought to light more vases by the same painter with Sicilian proveniences (Agrigento, Vassallaggi, Selinunte, etc.), and it seems now probable that this artist was also in origin a Sicilian and that he may subsequently have moved to Locri and established a work-shop there.

In the western provinces of Italy, apart from the so-called Owl-Pillar Group, which includes some sixty vases, mostly Nolan amphorae, decorated in a rather barbarous-looking red-figure style, imitating their Athenian counterparts of the second and third quarters of the fifth century BC and probably of native Campanian manufacture, red-figured pottery does not seem to have been produced before the second quarter of the fourth century. As we shall see in Chapters Five and Six, the earliest vases in that area were strongly influenced by Sicilian, and it seems not unlikely that some of the Sicilian potters may have moved northwards around that time (*c.* 370–60 BC) to establish their own workshops in Campania and at Paestum.

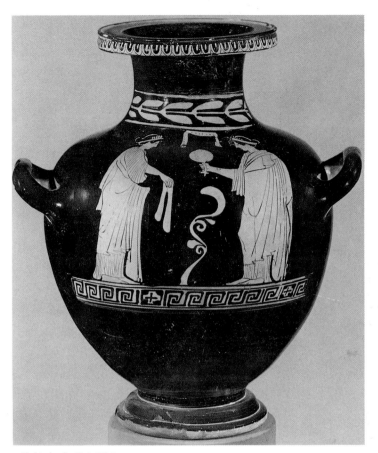

1 Hydria by the Pisticci Painter

2 Krater with lugs by the Pisticci Painter: Anodos of Kore

3 Bell-krater by the Pisticci Painter

4 Hydria by the Pisticci Painter:
Zeus and Aigina

5–6 Bell-krater by the Pisticci Painter:
Pursuit scene/Three draped youths

7 Bell-krater by the Pisticci Painter: Satyrs at herm

8 Bell-krater by the Pisticci Painter: Laocoön

9 *Calyx-krater by the Cyclops Painter*

10 *Bell-krater by the Cyclops Painter: woman and athletes*

11 Nestoris by the Amykos Painter

13 Bell-krater by the Amykos Painter

12 Nestoris by the Amykos
Painter

14 *Hydria by the Amykos Painter: Youths and women*

15–16 *Bell-krater by the Amykos Painter*

*17 Hydria by the Amykos Painter:
Punishment of Amykos*

*18 Column-krater by the Amykos
Painter: Warriors and women*

19 Volute-krater by the Amykos Painter: Phineus and the Harpies

20 Volute-krater by the Palermo Painter: Hermes, Apollo, Artemis, Leto

21 *Bell-krater by the Palermo Painter:*
Youths and women

22 *Skyphos by the Palermo Painter:*
Woman and satyr

23 *Volute-krater by the Karneia Painter: Dionysos; Perseus terrifying satyrs; Karneian dancers*

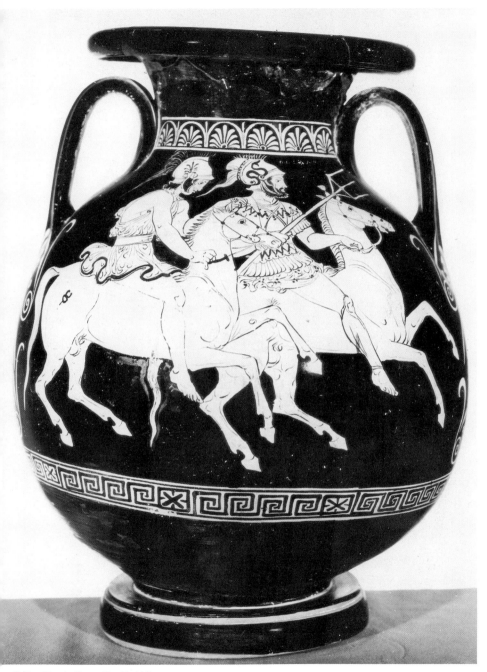

24 Pelike, Karneia Group: Poseidon/Athena

25 Reverse of no. 24

26 Pelike, Karneia Group: The Herakleidai

27 Hydria by the Policoro Painter:
Death of Sarpedon

28 Hydria by the Policoro Painter: Medea

29 Pelike by the Policoro Painter: Punishment of Dirce

30 Amphora by the Arnò Painter

31 *Calyx-krater by the Painter of the Berlin Dancing Girl*

34 *Neck-amphora by the Painter of the Berlin Dancing Girl: Achilles and Briseis*

32–3 *Bell-krater by the Painter of the Berlin Dancing Girl: Orpheus and Thracian*

35 Volute-krater by the Sisyphus Painter: Rape of the Leucippidae

36 Reverse of no. 35: Amazonomachy

37 Column-krater by the Sisyphus Painter: Departure of warriors

38–9 Bell-krater by the Sisyphus Painter: Karneian dancers

40 Bell-krater by the Sisyphus Painter

41 Bell-krater by the Hearst Painter:
Herakles and Nessos

42 Fragmentary calyx-krater by the Hearst
Painter: Odysseus slaying the suitors

43 Bell-krater by the Hearst Painter: Orestes
at Athens

44 *Volute-krater, school of the Sisyphus Painter: Andromeda*

45 *Stamnos by the Ariadne Painter: Theseus deserting Ariadne*

46 *Column-krater by the Ariadne Painter: Bellerophon and the Chimaera*

47 Volute-krater by the Gravina Painter

48 Amphora by the Gravina Painter: Death of Stheneboia

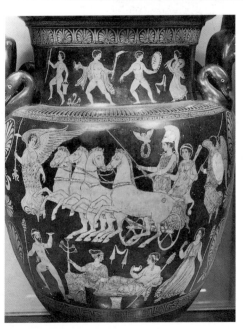

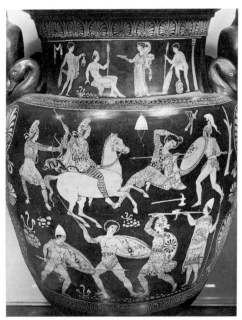

49 Volute-krater by the Painter of the Birth of Dionysos

50 Volute-krater by the Painter of the Birth of Dionysos: Apotheosis of Herakles

51 Reverse of no. 50: Amazonomachy

52 *Fragmentary calyx-krater by the Painter of the Birth of Dionysos: Apollo*

53 *Fragmentary calyx-krater by the Painter of the Birth of Dionysos: Herakles and centaur*

54 *Reverse of no. 53: Amazonomachy*

55 *Calyx-krater by the Painter of the Birth of Dionysos: Alkmene*

56 Fragment of calyx-krater: Herakles, Apollo and youths

57 Volute-krater: Herakles and Kyknos

58–9 *Calyx-krater by the Chequer Painter: Symposium/two draped youths*

60 *Calyx-crater by the Dirce Painter: Orestes, Elektra and Pylades*

61 *Calyx-krater by the Dirce Painter: Punishment of Dirce*   62 *Calyx-krater, Himera Group: Apollo*

63 *Fragmentary volute-krater, Locri Group: Orpheus*

Chapter Three

LUCANIAN

The Metaponto workshop, established by the Pisticci and Amykos Painters in the later fifth century, lasted long enough for a second generation of vase-painters to find employment there for some time. The three principal artists, who must be regarded as the immediate successors of the Amykos Painter, are the Anabates, Creusa and Dolon Painters. Fragments of vases by all three have been found at the kiln-site in Metaponto; comparatively few by the first, but a great many by the other two, which have added considerably to our knowledge of their work. The styles of the three artists show a marked degree of similarity, and this may also be seen in their choice and treatment of the subjects represented in the main scenes, as well as in the rendering of the draped youths on the reverses of their kraters. All three, however, develop certain individual characteristics, and what may be described as the 'standard' style of each of them is fairly easy to distinguish, especially in the more developed stage of their work. We should also note their extremely close connection with some of the contemporary Apulian vase-painters of the 'Plain' style, especially the Tarporley Painter and his school. This is particularly clear in certain vases by the Dolon Painter, and it looks as if for a time he might actually have worked along with the Tarporley Painter, one of whose vases was found near Metaponto. This city is not very far from Taranto, and it would be only reasonable to assume a certain measure of contact between the various potters and painters working in this general area. The same phenomenon may be seen not only in some of the larger vases in the P.K.P. Group (e.g. / 20–3 /), which are closely comparable to those by the Sisyphus Painter, but also in the work of the some of the lesser followers of the Amykos Painter, like the Arnò Painter / 30 /. There is also a large group of smaller vases which have been broadly classified as 'Intermediate'; / 64 / and / 65 / well illustrate their connection with both Amykan work and that of the Creusa and Dolon Painters; / 66 /, with its pleasing picture of Aura (the sea-breeze) seated on a rock by the sea-shore, is related in style both to the Amykos Painter and to Apulian, and in the pattern-work to Attic, since the latter seems to have been inspired by the work of an Athenian artist, the Marlay Painter, one of whose skyphoi was found at Taranto.

/ 67 / gives us the name vase of the Anabates Painter, showing a victorious rider (*anabates*) dismounting from his horse; typical of his earlier work is the wavy black border on Nike's drapery, and the rendering of her mouth, shown as tightly-closed and drawn with a single, slightly downward-curving line. No less characteristic is his treatment of the draped youths on the reverse [68], who wear himatia with thick black borders which, in the case of those facing to left, are wrapped in a sleeve-like fashion over the bent left arm, to fall below it in such a way that the border looks rather like and elongated Greek *pi*. The Painter of Stockholm 12 is a rather inferior imitator of his work, whose drawing, especially of the faces, is much cruder in style.

To the hand of the Creusa Painter, named originally after [77], which was later transferred to the Dolon Painter, over 130 vases may be attributed, enabling us to draw a fairly clear picture of the development of his style from its earliest phase to the final stage of its decline. His connection with the Amykos Painter is established by the discovery in the same tomb at Policoro of a hydria (35303) by that artist together with [69], which is so similar in shape as to suggest it was the work of the same potter; it must belong to the earlier phase of his career and is probably to be dated around 400 BC.

The work of the Creusa Painter is characterized by the frequent repetition of a number of stock-figures, good examples of which may be seen on [69–70] and [72]. They include: *(i)* a draped woman wearing a peplos, often with an overfall, girdled at the waist, with a double black stripe down the lower part of the garment; sometimes a shawl is worn around the shoulders [69–70] or drawn up onto the head to serve as a veil. The fold-lines of the drapery are very clearly marked and on standing figures give an almost columnar effect. The hair is bound up by a narrow bandeau, often with a bunch at the back. The breasts, especially in the later phase, tend to protrude and the folds on the drapery over them to assume a rather scrappy look; *(ii)* a nude male figure (Eros, warrior, youth) standing with the weight on one foot and a corresponding twist of the body [73]; one arm is often akimbo, and a short cloak, fastened at the throat by a brooch, may hang down the back. The draped youths on the reverses [71] generally have a plain black border to their himatia; the one on the left often slightly extends his left hand beneath the himation, to produce a pronounced bulge at the waist.

The bell-krater is again predominant in his choice of shapes, but it is worth noting that he decorates a few volute-kraters, with squatter bodies like those by the Sisyphus Painter in Apulian. Of these [72] is an excellent example and must rank among his better vases, with its unusually elaborate obverse, showing Dionysos and Ariadne amid a number of maenads and satyrs, disposed on different levels, some partly concealed behind rising ground. Both drawing and drapery are thoroughly typical of the painter, and lead on to what may be termed his 'standard' style, which can be seen on fifty or more bell-kraters [70] with a monotonous repetition of stock subjects and figures. On the earlier vases the meanders are accompanied by upright crossed squares, later on by saltires [71, 73]. His range of subjects is limited, and shows little originality; he mostly decorates his vases with two- or three-figure compositions in the Amykan tradition, with Dionysiac themes, or genre scenes, especially with warriors and athletes. He seldom ventures into mythology and, when he does, he mostly invests one of his stock figures with the attributes of Herakles, Hermes, Paris, Iris or whatever hero or divinity he wishes to depict. In his later work, of which [73] is typical, there is a substantial decline in the quality of the drawing, the drapery becomes scrappier, and the heads larger and very heavy-looking; what vitality there was in his earlier work seems almost entirely to have disappeared. His later style finds echoes in the work of a few humble followers, the best of whom is the Painter of the Phlyax Helen, whose name vase [74] shows a singularly ugly Helen of Troy, in Phrygian cap and bridal veil, escorted by two phlyakes with torches. The subject is treated with that rustic humour which so often is found in phlyax scenes; it appears again on a couple of his other vases, showing episodes in the career of Herakles.

The finds at Metaponto have also greatly increased our knowledge of the Dolon Painter, to whose hand some fifty vases may now be attributed, together with large numbers of fragments from the kiln, mostly from his mature phase. At one stage in his career he seems to have worked in very close co-operation with the Tarporley Painter and his followers, and the fact that no fragments of vases from this period were found at Metaponto might indicate that he was at that time actually employed in the Tarporley workshop in Taranto, where he picked up some of the local mannerisms and adapted them to his own use. Of this group [75] is typical; the obverse, which shows three athletes and a woman about to crown one of them with a wreath, is very close indeed to the work of the Tarporley Painter, so are the four youths on the reverse [76], especially the two facing to left with the squiggly fold-lines in the bottom right-hand corner of their himatia, but their heads are heavier, and the straggly hair around their ears, as well as the drawing of their mouths, is more characteristic of the Dolon Painter.

[77] shows another stage in the development of his style. The obverse, which possibly represents Creusa wearing the poisoned crown and drapery sent to her by Medea, shows the fussier treatment of drapery, characteristic of his more mature work; on the reverse [78] the youths, while still close to those on [76] are moving towards the painter's standard treatment of them; the hand-bulge reappears, and two wear a narrow band around their heads. [79], which represents Odysseus consulting the shade of Teiresias, is one of the painter's major works; the figure of Eurylochos to left, wearing pilos and chlamys, with his face in three-quarter view, is characteristic for both pose and drawing.

Of the painter's mature style the fragmentary hydria from the Metaponto kiln [80] affords an excellent example. It is, like the larger hydriai of the Amykos Painter, of kalpis shape, decorated with a figured panel on the shoulder and a frieze running round the body. On the shoulder is a vivid representation of an Amazonomachy, in a series of unusually lively scenes of attack and death, with one particularly striking figure of a Greek warrior, wearing a pilos helmet, his face registering the depths of anguish, as he bears the lifeless and bleeding body of a comrade from the fray. The frieze below consists of figures of Nike, draped youths and draped women which exactly repeat those on some of the earlier vases, and leave us in no doubt they are the work of the same painter. Here too must be placed the painter's name vase *| 81 |*, which shows Odysseus and Diomedes about to ambush Dolon in a somewhat stagey setting of lopped trees. In this vase we see the painter again at his lively best, and we can but agree with Martin Robertson's assessment of it as 'burlesque and wholly successful', in contrast to the more pompous style of *| 79 |*. The reverse shows two youths and two women, in the scrappier and less considered manner of his minor works.

The Dolon Painter also decorated several nestorides, usually with panel scenes on the upper portion and a frieze running right round the lower, though on one the lower part is left undecorated but ribbed instead. *| 82 |* depicts the death of Actaeon, attacked by a number of hounds, against which he vainly tries to defend himself with his sword, while Artemis placidly watches, making a sort of 'there now' gesture. Most of the Dolon Painter's other late vases are bell-kraters with simple compositions, showing Dionysiac or genre scenes; two very fragmentary skyphoi from the Metaponto kiln represent phlyax actors.

The activity of the Creusa-Dolon workshop may reasonably be placed between the end of the fifth century and *c.* 370 BC, since the earlier vases must be contemporary with late Amykan, those of the slightly more advanced phase with the Tarporley Group, and the latest lead up to the work of the Choephoroi Painter. The Metaponto workshop seems to have ceased production early in the second quarter of the fourth century and, when it resumes at a later date, its vases are purely Apulian in style. After the Dolon Painter the manufacture of Lucanian vases seems to have moved to inland centres like Anzi, Armento and Roccanova; their quality begins to decline rapidly, since the vase-painters were clearly out of touch with current artistic developments.

There is, however, one other painter who continues the Amykan tradition, again under a strong Apulian influence. This is the Brooklyn-Budapest Painter, a contemporary of the Creusa and Dolon Painters, and into his work there have now been incorporated the vases once attributed to the 'Painter of the London Pelikai' and the 'Rehearsal Painter', originally thought of as Apulian. The early phase of this painter's work is very strongly influenced by later Amykan (cf. his rocks, shields, striped drapery, the black-figure animals on the rims of the column-kraters) and also finds many parallels in the contemporary vases of the Creusa and Dolon Painters, as well as providing further evidence for the close relations at this period with Apulian.

The column-krater *| 83 |* is a good example of the painter's earlier style, when he is still under Amykan influence. The main scene shows a *komos* with Dionysos, the reverse four draped youths, and very similar scenes appear on several other vases of this shape. The obverse rims are decorated with a frieze of black-figure animals, and all have four-figure compositions on each side. His figures have rather small heads, the noses are pointed, the hair tends to straggle around the ears and the head is often inclined downwards. Women's drapery has a plain black border; sometimes there is a black stripe down it, with hook-folds at the waist, and it may be patterned with dot-clusters; their hair is generally tied up in a bandeau and they often carry a tympanum with a star pattern in the centre. His draped youths [84] are particularly characteristic; those facing right often have the right arm bent in a sort of 'sling' drape, those facing left have one arm akimbo beneath the cloak, often with a stick in the extended right hand, and a slight protrusion of the belly. The lower borders of the cloaks are wavy, and the fold-lines very clearly shown; there is often a series of parallel U-shaped fold-lines over the groin, especially in the later stage. It is the treatment of the draped youths on the reverses of the vases formerly attributed to the 'Painter of the London Pelikai', which show them to belong here.

His subjects are for the most part conventional – Dionysiac or genre scenes with athletes, youths and women – but he occasionally ventures into mythology. [85] gives an unusually lively example of his work, with a very ithyphallic Hermes standing beside a table of offerings, where a woman holds up a wreath before him and a satyr runs up with a thyrsus and a situla; another shows a woman pouring water over a large fish on a chopping block, while a satyr stands by with a big knife.

In his later phase, of which [86] is a good example, the painter makes greater efforts to deal with more elaborate subjects. His drawing also shows certain developments, especially in the rendering of the drapery and the greater use of frontal figures, and the pattern-work becomes more elaborate. The frequent appearance of nestorides, either with [86] or without [87] disks on the high handles, is typical of later Lucanian. [86] gives us a Dionysiac scene, with a reminder of the theatre in the form of a white female comic mask hanging from a vine-branch above the god's head. The drawing, however, lacks the skill and certainty of that on the earlier vases and it looks as if over-ambitious compositions put too great a tax upon his somewhat limited abilities. Other Lucanian artists show the same failing and, when they attempt to rival the monumental vases painted by their Apulian contemporaries, they fall down badly.

Perhaps here we should cast a brief glance at the Sydney Painter, who seems originally to have been of provincial Lucanian origin, to judge from the stylistic affinities between the draped youths on the reverses of his kraters and those by the Brooklyn-Budapest Painter. Later on he may well have moved to Paestum, since several of his vases, both in red-figure and in applied red, have been found at that site. His pattern-work is very characteristic, especially the floral (Fig. 4) which accompanies the palmette-scrolls, and the curving

Fig. 4 Floral pattern by the Sydney Painter

59

leaf with a serrated edge [88]. Also typical is his way of drawing heads and drapery. The former are rather heavy, with staring eyes, open mouths and straggly hair; on the latter the fold-lines are clearly indicated, and there is sometimes a dotted-stripe down the garments of women, in the typical Paestan manner, although it does not appear on the himatia of his draped youths. Women's breasts are clearly defined beneath the covering drapery, with circles to represent the nipples. All these characteristics are clearly visible on [88].

The Choephoroi Painter, named after a series of his vases which show the meeting of Orestes and Elektra at the tomb of Agamemnon in a scene generally associated with the *Choephoroi* by Aeschylus [91], follows on from the Creusa, Dolon and Brooklyn-Budapest Painters, from whom he derives his decorative patterns, his manner of rendering drapery and many of his stock figures. [89–90] clearly indicates his connection with the Creusa Painter, since its reverse might almost be by the hand of that painter, although the obverse with its near-frontal heads, and the bearded figure of Hermes on the left is in the typical Choephoroi style as represented by the vases from which he takes his name [91]. Both his style of drawing and his decorative patterns are very characteristic – especially his treatment of the three-quarter face, framed as it were between straggly locks of hair, of the staring eyes which give many of his figures a look of pained surprise, of the fussy drapery around the waist (a legacy from the Creusa Painter), and of the nude male figures who stand with body in three-quarter view but head in profile, with the weight on one leg, while the other is bent at the knee or crossed over in front.

He also painted several nestorides, of which [92] is a late example. The obverse shows Orestes at Delphi and, in a panel on the neck, Phrixos bringing the ram for sacrifice. The quality of the drawing has greatly deteriorated, especially in the figures on the neck, and the composition is very heavy-handed.

From now onwards, Lucanian vase-painting becomes increasingly provincial; the painters start off with a number of standard themes and stock figures inherited from their predecessors or adapted from contemporary Apulian – both 'Plain' and 'Ornate' – but in the Lucanian hinterland they seem to be cut off from artistic communication and unable to extend their limited repertory or improve the quality of their drawing, which gets progressively worse until it reaches a level that barely falls short of barbarization. This may readily be observed in the work of the last three Lucanian artists – the Roccanova Painter, the Painter of Naples 1959 and the Primato Painter – all active in the second half of the fourth century.

The Roccanova Painter, named from the hypogeum at the site which yielded a large number of his vases, now in the Taranto Museum, together with others of Apulian origin from the workshop of the Darius Painter, thus suggesting a date around 340–30 BC for much of his work, probably began his career a little before that, since the reverses of some of his earlier vases reflect the influence of the Brooklyn-Budapest Painter, although their obverses are often closer to

Fig. 5 Floral patterns by the Roccanova Painter

'Plain' style Apulian of *c.* 360–50 BC. The Roccanova Painter is essentially a provincial artist with a very limited repertory of stock figures which he repeats from one vase to another; there is no originality in his choice of subjects, which are almost entirely confined to genre scenes with youths and women. *[93–4]* show most of his common stock figures; a woman draped in a sleeveless chiton, wearing a thin black girdle with two loops at the waist, ending in dot-clusters, adapted more or less directly from Apulian, and a nude youth, seated or standing, often holding a mirror or a branch in one hand, with a piece of drapery over the other arm. A palmette with scrolls and drop-leaves often separates the figures, when there are only two of them *[93]*.

It may be noted that most of his vases are made from a clay which fires to a pale shade, and the surface is therefore covered with a pink or red wash to improve its appearance; in one group of vases, to which the designation 'Red and White' has been given, the terracotta is left in its natural state for the exposed flesh of female figures, with the result that it looks almost white beside the rest of the surface, creating a sort of bichrome effect. His typical floral patterns (*Fig.* 5) are quite distinctive and very different from those found in Apulian; he is also fond of ornamental patterns in black-figure, especially palmettes. *[96]* is an example of his later work, which is of poor quality; the faces are almost shapeless and entirely devoid of any expression and give the impression that the painter has lost interest in his art.

Like the Roccanova Painter, the Painter of Naples 1959, also active in the second half of the fourth century, draws some of his inspiration from the later work of the Brooklyn-Budapest and Choephoroi Painters, as well as from Apulian of the mid-fourth century. He also frequently repeats stock figures and patterns on his vases, though he gives us a slightly wider range of subjects. From the terracotta of his vases, which is usually of a rich orange shade, it might be deduced that his workshop was located at a different site from that of the Roccanova Painter, perhaps at Anzi or Armento, where a few of his vases are said to have been found, though almost none of them has an established find-spot.

61

[96] shows his typical style and illustrates most of his standard figures. They tend to be rather stocky, with heavy, rounded chins, large eyes, open mouths and a very small upper lip; the mouth often has a slight downward turn, which tends to make his characters look discontented. The most constantly repeated figure is a draped woman, wearing a sleeveless chiton fastened with brooches on the shoulders, or a peplos, with a single thick black stripe running down it and a thick girdle round the waist. Her breasts tend to bulge and over them there are no fold-lines on the drapery; the nipples are sometimes indicated by crosses. She frequently holds a decorated cista, a tambourine, or a mirror with a black centre. Also common is a nude youth, normally carrying a piece of drapery with a wavy black border; his hair has a tendency to straggle over the ears.

The Painter of Naples 1959 painted a number of nestorides, as well as many vases of smaller dimensions, decorated with single figures excerpted from his larger compositions. His followers, like the Acrobat and Dawlish Painters, sink into almost complete barbarism, and it is difficult to think of some of the figures on their vases as human.

The last and most important of the late Lucanian artists is the Primato Painter, to whose school some 250 vases can be assigned. In the early stage of his career his work shows very clearly the influence of the Lycurgus Painter, who flourished in Apulia just before the middle of the century. One might almost think that the Primato Painter, who was named by Beazley after an obscure Italian periodical in which one of his vases was published, had in fact studied under the Lycurgus Painter before moving to Lucania – probably to Anzi or Armento – and establishing a workshop there, since on his vases he continues to repeat subjects and figures from his earlier works, which move steadily further and further away from their prototypes, until they become almost mechanical formulae, with no claims to artistic merit. His work gives one a very clear insight into the fate that can overtake what might have been a decent vase-painter when he finds himself working in isolation and no longer cares about the quality of his products.

His early vases, still very close to Apulian models, show him at his best – the Naples volute-krater with Apollo triumphant on one side, and on the other [97] Herakles running off with the tripod, hotly pursued by Apollo, while a woman looks down from a window above, or [98] showing a balding figure with a cithara (probably a poet), seated in a naiskos, flanked by a woman and a youth, clearly show the strength of the Apulian influence. Even at this comparatively early stage, however, the Primato Painter is beginning to establish those stylistic features which are to mark his more mature work.

Characteristic of the Primato Painter is his fondness for elaborate ornamental patterns, both architectural and floral (egg and dart, cymation, dentils, bead and reel, swastika meanders; vine leaves, lotus and palmettes, etc.), which probably were based on the similar motifs used by the Apulians on the necks of their large volute-kraters, as well as of elaborate palmette designs beneath the handles, often

Fig. 6 Female heads – (a) by the Primato Painter: Copenhagen, Thorvaldsen Museum 132=LCS, p. 175, no. 1020; (b) by a later follower: Vatican U 32=LCS, p. 186, no. 1128

of considerable elegance. His subjects cover a wider range than do those of the other two painters of this period – in his mythological scenes Orestes [99], Apollo, Aphrodite, Achilles and Troilos are represented, as well as his special favourite, Herakles [100], and there are the usual Dionysiac and genre scenes with youths, women and Erotes. Of his stock figures those most frequently found are a flying Nike [100], with swirling drapery, and a flying Eros, a woman with swirling drapery, wearing a high radiate stephane, a youth or woman with a bird perched on one finger, and figures seated on piles of rocks, with black or black and white centres, again of Apulian inspiration. He is fond of ample draperies, which billow out around flying figures, and even his draped youths are often enveloped in a large himation, which projects well out in front of the body, with a mass of collar-like folds at the top.

In his profile faces, figures often have rather sharp chins, beneath a somewhat prominent nose, and staring eyes, which, with the deterioration in the quality of his later drawing, tend to produce a distorted effect. He is fond of frontal faces or in three-quarter view, with a slight tilt of the head, which produces flesh-folds at the neck. Some of his minor works are decorated only with heads; others with animals or birds.

With the work of the followers of the Primato Painter, Lucanian sinks into near barbarism, although his influence persists to the end. A comparison between the two female heads in *Fig. 6*, one by his own hand, the other by a follower, marks the swift decline, and even worse is to follow.

63

64 *Skyphos, Intermediate Group: Satyr*

65 *Lebes gamikos, Intermediate Group*

66 *Skyphos, Intermediate Group: Aura*

67–8 *Bell-krater by the Anabates Painter: Nike and anabates/3 youths*

69 *Hydria by the Creusa Painter*

70–1 *Bell-krater by the Creusa Painter: Warriors and woman/3 youths*

72 *Volute-krater by the Creusa Painter: Dionysos and Ariadne*

73 *Bell-krater by the Creusa Painter*

74 *Bell-krater by the Painter of the Phlyax Helen*

75–6 *Column-krater by the Dolon Painter*

77–8 *Bell-krater by the Dolon Painter*

79 Calyx-krater by the Dolon Painter: Odysseus and the shade of Teiresias

80 Details of fragmentary hydria by the Dolon Painter: Amazonomachy

81 Calyx-krater by the Dolon Painter: Ambush of Dolon

82 Nestoris by the Dolon Painter: Death of Actaeon

83–4 Column-krater by the Brooklyn-Budapest Painter

85 Bell-krater by the Brooklyn-Budapest Painter: Hermes

86 Nestoris by the Brooklyn-Budapest Painter: Dionysiac scene

88 Hydria by the Sydney Painter

87 Nestoris by the Brooklyn-Budapest Painter

89–90 Bell-krater by the Choephoroi Painter

91 *Hydria by the Choephoroi Painter: Orestes and Elektra*

93 *Bell-krater by the Roccanova Painter*

92 *Nestoris by the Choephoroi Painter: Orestes at Delphi*

94 *Lebes gamikos by the Roccanova Painter*

97 Volute-krater by the Primato Painter: Herakles and Apollo

95 Lebes gamikos by the Roccanova
Painter

96 Squat lekythos by the Painter
of Naples 1959

99 *Volute-krater by the Primato Painter: Orestes*

98 *Hydria by the Primato Painter: Lyre-player in naiskos*

100 *Volute-krater by the Primato Painter: Hermes, Herakles, Nike*

Chapter Four

APULIAN

It has already been noted that, almost from the beginning of the fabric, Apulian vases tend to fall into two main groups, one of which may be designated as 'Plain' style, the other as 'Ornate'. The former consists mainly of bell- and column-kraters, hydriai, pelikai and smaller vases; these are decorated with comparatively simple compositions, containing from one to four figures. Their subjects are often associated with Dionysos, as god of both wine and the theatre, with athletics, and with warriors, departing, in combat, or returning home. Many others are decorated only with a head, usually that of a woman; mythological scenes are comparatively rare. In the 'Ornate' group the vases are usually of larger dimensions, especially volute-kraters and amphorae or loutrophoroi, and are decorated in a much more elaborate manner, with tiered compositions including up to twenty or more figures, and with a great deal of subsidiary ornament in added colours (white, yellow, red). Their subject-matter is mostly either mythological or funerary; the myths represented are often connected with the themes of classical tragedies, the funerary scenes, from c. 360 onwards, usually have mourners grouped around a naiskos or a stele. The same painters may decorate their vases in either style, but for the most part, and especially in the first half of the fourth century, they seem to have a preference for one or the other, and thus the distinction between the two groups is more clearly defined. From the middle of the fourth century onwards, the vases of the 'Plain' style, through an increased use of added colours and of subsidiary ornament, tend to approach more closely to the 'Ornate', and artists like the Varrese Painter and his followers (Painters of Bari 12061 and of Louvre MNB 1148) decorate freely in both styles, but the essential distinction in shape, composition and subject-matter remains largely unchanged.

Early 'Plain' Style – the workshop of the Tarporley Painter and his followers

Of the early painters in the 'Plain' style, active during the first quarter of the fourth century, the most important is the Tarporley Painter. He is a pupil and close follower of the Sisyphus Painter, whose influence may be seen in the supple limbs of his youths and the solemn-looking women on his earlier works [101], as well as in the treatment of the draped youths on / *103* /. The drapery, however, looks fussier, and the heads, often almost oval in appearance, tend to be slightly bent forward. Later his drawing becomes more fluid, if less careful, the faces are coarser and drapery-borders become very wavy. Tendrils appear more frequently between the figures; plants, flowers and pebbles are scattered across the ground. The Tarporley Painter favours the bell-krater, which he decorates with Dionysiac or theatrical subjects. / *102* / shows Dionysos holding a mask, / *104* / three actors dressing for a satyr-play, and / *105* / is the first of the long series of Apulian vases decorated with scenes from phlyax plays; it represents the punishment of the thief, with metrical inscriptions which might be quotations from the actual play. Other vases give us genre scenes, especially with athletes; there is little mythology – / *106* / shows one of three vases with Perseus reflecting the gorgoneion for Athena. His reverses invariably depict two or three draped youths; characteristic is the presence of two thick parallel inverted L-shaped lines running down the himation behind the legs / *107* / and of a forked wavy line, rather like a squiggly inverted Y, in the corner / *103* /.

Between his work and that of the Dolon Painter there is for a time a close connection; the two may even have worked together. This is probably also true of some of his associates, like the Klejman Painter or the Painter of Lecce 686.

The immediate successors of the Tarporley Painter, who fall, broadly speaking, into three groups, continue the traditions he had established; their vases mostly have Dionysiac or genre subjects, and, almost invariably, draped youths on the reverses. These, however, are often of value in enabling us to distinguish the hand of one painter from that of another, since they may reflect identifying mannerisms better than do the scenes on the obverse.

In the first group scenes from phlyax plays are popular, often shown as taking place on a simple stage supported by posts; on other vases the theatrical connection is maintained by the presence of masks suspended from above or held in the hand of one of the figures. Warriors in native costume appear more frequently; funerary scenes also become more common, but as yet still of a simple type, with mourners at a stele or grave-column. The most important artist in this group is perhaps the Schiller Painter, whose early work is close to that of the Tarporley Painter, as may be seen from the poses and drapery of his figures / *108* /, and from the youths on his reverses, on whose himatia the Tarporley squiggle is now replaced by something like a lightning-flash. Most of his vases have Dionysiac or genre subjects, but a couple have phlyax scenes, of which / *109* / is of particular interest as giving us an amusing parody of the *Thesmophoriazusae* of Aristophanes. His close associates are the Adolphseck and Prisoner Painters, the latter so named from the battle scenes, with prisoners tied to a tree, which appear on some of his vases, and the Eton-Nika Painter. All are essentially painters of bell-kraters, occasionally with subjects of interest, like the recognition of Theseus on / *110* /, or the semi-comic version of Herakles and the Stymphalian birds on / *111* /. A very productive artist is the Painter of the Long

Overfalls, to whose school over a hundred vases may be ascribed; the women depicted upon them often wear a peplos with a very long overfall *[112]*, and one of the draped youths on the reverses, facing to right, often stands with his body turned to an almost frontal position and his left arm akimbo, enveloped by his cloak *[113]*. Again the scenes are mostly Dionysiac, characterized by the *narthex* (stem of giant fennel) held by Dionysos or one of his followers *[114]*; Artemis Bendis also appears on several vases. A little later come the vases of the York and the Eumenides Groups; one of the more interesting artists in the former is the Rainone Painter, who decorated a couple of phlyax vases, one with a parody of the *Antigone*, in which the two guards have apprehended Antigone, who is carrying a hydria for use in the burial rites of her brother Polynices and who has taken off her tragic mask to reveal the balding head of an old actor beneath it *[115]*. The work of the Eumenides Painter is beginning to close the gap between the 'Plain' and 'Ornate' styles and leads on to that of the Iliupersis Painter, one of the chief exponents of the latter.

The second group, in which the Hoppin, Truro and Lecce Painters are the principal artists, reveals a somewhat different style, with, however, little variation in shape and subject-matter. The Hoppin Painter *[116–7]* is a neat draughtsman, and the influence of the Tarporley Painter is evident in his treatment of both the figures, especially the heads, and the drapery. The latter is very characteristic, with numerous small, broken fold-lines around the waists or over the legs of women. Their hair is usually worn with a bunch sticking out at the back, and is sometimes caught up in a *sphendone*. Youths often wear white head-bands; occasionally their cloaks are decorated with a swastika; this recurs on vases by the Truro Painter and is an indication of the close link between the two. On the latter's vases the fold-lines break up into a multitude of small strokes *[118]*. His drawing of faces tends to be impressionistic, and the hair of his youths can look very straggly. The Lecce Painter's figures are squatter, with rather large heads, often bent forward *[119]*; the anatomy of the bodies of his youths is rendered in greater detail; they look plumper and are often shown in three-quarter view. He prefers to depict figures in motion, rather than in the more static poses favoured by the other painters in this group. In the work of his followers, like the Rohan and the Iris Painters, there is a marked decline in the quality of the drawing, especially of the eyes and the drapery. The latter is, however, responsible for a few entertaining phlyax vases, parodying events in the life of Herakles – gobbling up offerings to Zeus, who brandishes his thunderbolt in impotent fury *[120]*, or resting after his labours. It is from the Hoppin workshop that the first red-figured nestorides come.

The two principal artists of the third group are the Painter of Karlsruhe B9 and the Dijon Painter *[121–8]*. The former's work is closely connected in style with the later vases of the Tarporley Painter, that of the latter provides a connecting link with the Iliupersis Painter. The Painter of Karlsruhe B9 is for the most part conventional in his choice of shapes, but it should be noted that he

76

decorated one of the first Apulian red-figured rhyta [121], a shape destined to become very popular in the second half of the century, and also one of the first knob-handled paterae (usually called dishes). His subjects are mostly uninspired; he prefers two-figure compositions, often with a Dionysiac theme or Eros. His drawing is neat; his figures have soft-looking faces, with small noses. Women's drapery tends to be fussy in the area of the waist (cf. the Hoppin Painter); there is no overfall to the peplos, but down the drapery over the bent leg there often runs a black stripe, following the contour of the leg [122], while over the stiff leg is a series of parallel, vertical fold-lines. The draped youth to left on his reverses often has a long overhang to his himation down the right shoulder, with a black border shaped rather like a capital omega; on the youth to the right it is so draped as to form a sort of 'tail' [123], decorated with two or three U-shaped strokes on their side (cf. the Dijon Painter). The painter is also fond of rocks, both spotted and hollow, on the obverses for people to sit upon; on the reverses a *diptych* or a pair of *halteres* now appears regularly above the youths. Hanging fillets, windows and quartered disks may be used as fillers.

The Dijon Painter, in his early phase, is very close in style to the Painter of Karlsruhe B9 (cf. [124] with [122]); his subjects cover a wider range and include a little mythology, some phlyax plays [125], several scenes with warriors in native costume [126], as well as the usual Dionysiac themes, some of which [127] have theatrical connections. His reverse youths [128] are very characteristic: the one to left generally has a 'sling' drape or the right arm extended, the one to right a 'sleeve' drape. When there are three [128], the central youth often has one arm akimbo beneath his cloak, which is so draped as to leave one shoulder bare, as on many of the reverses in the Long Overfalls Group. In his later phase, drapery tends to have a thick black border, and on moving figures a very wavy lower hem-line (cf. [126]); the youths on his reverses approach those on the early vases of the Snub-Nose Painter, who was probably his pupil. The saltire squares in his meander-bands below the pictures grow larger and more careless as time goes by; tendrils often separate the figures on the obverse; *halteres* and windows appear above on his reverses, but not diptychs.

The Graz Painter is one of his early followers; noteworthy is his preference for nude instead of draped youths on his reverses [129]; they have spindly legs and flat feet, and their faces are often sketchily drawn. He sometimes includes an inscribed pillar in his scenes; several bear the inscription *ΤΕΡΜΩΝ*, probably signifying the boundary-post or finishing line in the palaestra. His obverses mostly show Dionysiac scenes; other vases from this group have mythological or theatrical subjects.

The next generation of 'Plain' style painters is well represented by the Judgement Painter and his associates and followers. [130], showing Zeus wooing Ganymede, looks back to the work of the Schiller Painter; his later work owes more to the artists of the Long Overfalls Group, especially the Bendis Painter, whose draped youths seem to have provided the models for his own, with their pinched faces, straggly hair and thick black borders to their himatia. His subjects draw more on mythology, like his spirited rendering of the death of Callisto, with Hermes rescuing the infant Arcas, or his Orestes at Delphi with the sleeping Furies. Of particular interest is *[131]*, which is closely associated with his work and gives a unique representation of an artist putting the finishing touches to a statue of Herakles, while the hero himself stands by. The Berkeley Painter has a much coarser style, and the Dechter Painter is no better, though *[132]* gives a remarkable version of the Andromeda legend, in which she has been bound to two columns on top of which a pediment has been placed, to produce something of the effect of a temple, probably a distant memory of some stage setting.

The work of the Thyrsus Painter *[133]* is influenced by that of the Lecce Painter in his later stage; his drawing is exceedingly sketchy and looks to have been done in some haste, since on occasions he omits an arm. His faces are angular and his eyes staring; several of his vases come from Paestum and he may have worked there for a time. The Lampas Painter follows on from the Berkeley Painter; his drawing is deplorable and his rendering of anatomy particularly poor, but he is at least innovative in his choice of subjects and his fondness for birds and animals. His favourite shape is the mug, either with neck and knotted handles (Shape 8B), or with offset rim (8N).

The Development of the 'Ornate' Style

It is unfortunate that most of the vases by the immediate successors of the Painter of the Birth of Dionysos, in the first quarter of the fourth century, have come down to us either in a very battered condition or else as comparatively small fragments. Many of them come from Taranto, where the ancient necropolis, deeply buried beneath the modern city, yields from time to time, as a result of building operations, a few scattered remains. The style of the Sarpedon Painter, an artist of considerable originality in both the choice and the treatment of the subjects on his vases, is modelled upon that of the Painter of the Birth of Dionysos and his use of richly-patterned and elaborate drapery for his principal characters, suggests a strong theatrical influence. Fragments, like *[134]* showing the head of Priam, from vases in the Black Fury Group must rank among the finest examples of early Apulian vase-painting, and the anguish on the face of the aged king testifies to the painter's skill in the rendering of emotion. Faces in three-quarter view now become increasingly popular, as better suited to revealing pain, surprise or horror; the tormented look is also very characteristic of the Lycurgus Painter. These vases show the Apulian fondness for the less frequently represented myths, like the death of Sarpedon, the transformation of Callisto into a bear *[135]*, or Erichthonios with the daughters of Cecrops.

The Felton Painter's work provides a connecting link between the early 'Ornate' artists and the school of the Iliupersis Painter. His larger vases, with mythological subjects, are typically 'Ornate' in treatment, with a good deal of added colour, and the figures disposed on different levels, but he also painted a number of smaller vases, which often represent dwarfs or comics [136], with grossly exaggerated bodily features, or heads of youths or satyrs. [137], which is closely associated in style with his work, gives an amusing parody of the legend of Oedipus and the Sphinx.

With the work of the Iliupersis Painter we move into the middle phase of Apulian, in which the larger vases begin to assume those characteristics which become the hall-marks of the developed Apulian style of the second half of the fourth century. We should note, in particular, the increasing use of added colours, with the addition of various shades of red and brown to the standard white and yellow; the elaboration of the subsidiary decoration, especially on the necks of volute-kraters and on the shoulders of amphorae and vases of similar shape; a greater fluidity in the drawing, with more attention to the rendering of perspective and to foreshortening. The Iliupersis Painter is an artist of the highest importance, since it was he who established the canons for the decoration of the monumental vases which appear with increasing frequency, representing mythological, dramatic, bridal or funerary scenes, on which the figures are disposed on two or more different levels. Masks in the form of female heads (sometimes with cow-horns to signify Io), and gorgoneia are now applied to the handles of volute-kraters; the earlier figured or animal frieze on the neck is replaced by a female head or other figures in a floral setting, which is at first comparatively simple, but later highly elaborate and colourful; there is a far greater use of decorative adjuncts in the field – shields, cistae, laurel-trees, flowering plants, etc. – and the 'reflecting pool' [141] makes its appearance.

He also introduced what is to become the almost canonical form of the large Apulian funerary vase [138–9], with mourners around a naiskos on the obverse and a stele on the reverse. For the naiskoi, which can usually be readily distinguished from temples and palaces, see pp. 261–7. He was a highly productive artist to whose hand over a hundred vases can be attributed, covering a wide variety of shapes, and whose style owes much to that of the Dijon Painter, especially in his drawing of human figures and his treatment of drapery. He turns often to mythology for his main subjects; the reverses of his larger vases are usually Dionysiac, a practice which ceases after the next generation. He tends to repeat stock figures, which frequently serve to identify his work. His women generally wear peploi, with a narrow black girdle round the waist; their hair often falls in long curls down their backs or at the side of their faces; they have well-developed breasts, with protruding nipples, and both they and his youths tend to stand on tiptoe. The problems of perspective are boldly tackled, as on his vases showing the temple of Apollo at Delphi [140]. His meander-bands with saltires are modelled on those of the Dijon Painter.

The Iliupersis Painter had numerous followers and their work often reflects his own in both style and subject-matter. Of his closer colleagues the most important is the Painter of Athens 1714, who painted extensively in both the 'Plain' and the 'Ornate' styles and well illustrates the narrowing of the gap between the two just before the middle of the century. */142/* is typical of the 'Ornate' style used on his larger vases and represents a Dionysiac symposium, beneath a hanging female mask, in which a woman is playing a harp, a popular theme in later Apulian. */143/* is a typical minor vase in his 'Plain' style, with a *komos* scene on the obverse and two of his standard type of draped youths on the reverse */144/*. His fondness for 'drop' (small hook-shaped) folds on the drapery should also be noted; the large saltire squares accompanying the meanders look back to those of the Dijon Painter.

/145–6/ illustrate a further stage in the development of the 'Ornate' style, which now begins almost to approach the baroque. The outstanding character-istic of these vases is the richness of their decoration; this finds a counterpart in the architectural decoration of temples and other public buildings in the second quarter of the fourth century, which seems to have provided the models for the ornamental patterns on many of the later Apulian vases. */145/* illustrates this new development; beneath an amorous couple upon a couch is an exuberant floral pattern, rising from a base of acanthus leaf and spreading out laterally with tendrils and bell-shaped flowers. A connection between this type of floral decoration and the flower-paintings of Pausias, who flourished in Sicyon in the second quarter of the fourth century, has been suggested; this may well be the case, as such patterns are also to be found in the early pebble mosaics from Sicyon and Eretria, and a slightly later mosaic, found at Epidamnos in Albania, shows a female head in a floral setting almost identical with those which regularly appear on the necks of Apulian volute-kraters and which are one of the most characteristic features of that fabric. */146/* shows the use of such decoration to provide the setting for a single figure on a vase by the Painter of the Dublin Situlae; a similar treatment will be found on many later Apulian vases, the floral patterns sometimes covering the greater part of the surface of the vase.

/147/ is a vase from this period of special interest, since it shows a seated woman playing a musical instrument, generally referred to as a 'xylophone'. This is at first confined to Apulian vases and has sometimes been identified with the *platage* (rattle) of Archytas; later it appears also on Campanian and Paestan vases but only in their Apulianizing phases, and it must be regarded as essentially Tarentine in origin.

With the work of the Lycurgus Painter (named after the scene on */148/*) and his associates, we reach the culmination of the second phase of the 'Ornate' style. The compositions are now on an ampler scale, involving more figures; greater skill is shown in the handling of perspective and overlapping planes, and in creating the illusion of spatial depth. The Lycurgus school follows the earlier practice of the Iliupersis Painter in decorating the obverses of kraters with a mythological or dramatic subject and the reverses with Dionysiac rather than funerary scenes. The painter himself makes an increasing use of faces in three-quarter view, with the head tilted slightly to one side and with a look of pain or torment on the face [148–9]; his poses are more mannered, even to the extent of looking artificial, as with people leaning against pillars, or women plucking at a piece of drapery above their shoulders or wearing it in the off-the-shoulder style [149]. Drapery is elaborately patterned, sometimes with an inset lozengy stripe down the middle of the garment. Several of his volute-kraters follow the earlier practice of having open-work handles; the decoration on their necks follows the Iliupersic model, with animals or figured scenes, rather than female heads, which, however, tend to appear more frequently on his later works. His mythological subjects cover a wide range – the two here illustrated represent the madness of Lycurgus [148] and the rape of Oreithyia [149]; he is also fond of bridal and erotic scenes, and [150], which depicts mistress and maid in a naiskos with six women grouped around it, is the forerunner of a long series of similar hydriai.

His influence is to be seen in the work of a few associated artists, especially those of the Milan Orpheus Group, and the painters of two volute-kraters, representing Orpheus beside the palace of Pluto and Persephone in the Underworld, both of which seem to look back to a common source, perhaps a fresco or free painting; the elaborate columns with sphinx capitals or the caryatids which support the roof of the palace on [151] are most unusual.

The Development of the 'Plain' Style: Followers of the Dijon Painter

After *c.* 360 there is a rapid increase in vase-production, and workshops must have employed a substantial number of painters. One consequence of this is an extreme uniformity of style, especially in the smaller-sized vases from a given workshop, which sometimes makes it difficult to distinguish between the work of individual painters; nor on the larger vases can collaboration between different artists be excluded. Two distinct schools of painters in the 'Plain' style follow on from the Dijon Painter and, though their products have much in common, each develops its own characteristic style. This period sees the introduction of what is to become the typical Apulian pattern used in conjunction with the meanders below the pictures – the quartered square with a dot in each of the four sections. The 'sling' drape is also modified to produce a 'saucer' effect, by making one arm project much further outward from the body; [155] shows an early stage of this development.

The first school begins with a series of rather dull vases grouped around the Painters of Vatican V14 and Geneva 2754 [152–5], mostly bell- or column-kraters with two-figure compositions and little variety in their subject-matter. The Painter of Athens 1680 [156], who has stylistic connections with the work of the Painter of Athens 1714, is fond of depicting figures in rapid motion, with swirling drapery. He seems also to have Lucanian connections, since his later work is very close to vases like the nestoris New York 52.11.2; one of his late vases was found at Tricarico in Lucania, and it is possible that he moved there at a late stage in his career. His style finds a close parallel in the work of the Schlaepfer Painter, whose reverse youths are very similar, but have a characteristic thick flat-S-shaped line as the upper border to their himatia.

[157], the name vase of the Maplewood Painter, more clearly reflects the influence of the Dijon Painter in the drawing of the faces and the drapery, as well as in the treatment of Oscan warriors in their typical costume. He is a neat draughtsman; his figures have small mouths, the fold-lines on his drapery tend to fall in pairs, and he favours a single or a double stripe down the lower portion of his peploi.

A later artist in this school is the Verona Painter *[158]*, whose vases look like rather crude imitations of those by the Dijon Painter; his drawing is often slovenly, even in his saltire squares. His follower, the Rueff Painter, is even worse.

The second quarter of the fourth century also seen a large increase in the production of minor vases – mostly choes, squat lekythoi, lebetes gamikoi, pelikai and skyphoi, of small dimensions (between 10 and 20 cm in height). They are usually decorated with single figures – a draped woman, Eros, a nude youth or satyr – and reflect the influence of the Dijon and Iliupersis Painters. The individual figures upon them are often adapted from those on the larger compositions of those artists. They look to be the products of what could be termed 'workshop hacks'. *[159–61]* illustrate some typical examples. The Zaandam *[159]* and Choes *[160]* Painters are probably the best; the latter looks to have been influenced by the Hoppin Painter. The Wellcome Group consists mainly of large skyphoi *[161]*, with a single figure on each side; one rim often has a border of wave-pattern, the other of egg. In style they approach the work of the Choes Painter, and the floral patterns follow those on vases of the Hoppin Painter and his associates.

The second school comprises the work of the Snub-Nose Painter and his several associates, from whose hands we have over 500 vases, of which the bell-krater is by far the most common, followed by the column-krater, the pelike and the amphora. The earlier work of the Snub-Nose Painter descends directly from that of the Dijon Painter, though we may note an increase in the decorative adjuncts in the field and a greater use of added white and yellow. The Snub-Nose Painter must have begun his career around 360 B C, and the main period of his activity and that of his associates probably falls between then and c. 340. The artists of this school seldom depart from Dionysiac or genre themes for their subjects. His contemporaries, the Painter of Lecce 660, the Woburn Abbey and Laterza Painters follow his style closely. Others, like the Painter of Ruvo 407–8 or the 'H.A.' Painter (named after a private collection in Milan), decorate amphorae with simple naiskos scenes, which are beginning to draw closer to the 'Ornate' style, although the youths on their reverses still adhere to the standard

'Plain' style tradition. One of the earliest loutrophoroi, with S-shaped handles ending in a lotus-bud, comes from this workshop *[165]*, and is the prototype of what is to become a most popular shape in the second half of the fourth century, when the size of the vase greatly increases and the ornamental decoration on the neck and shoulder becomes much more elaborate *[181]*.

There follows the Schulman Painter, characteristic of whose work and that of his circle is the multiple wavy border on the overhang of the himatia of his reverse youths, and the curious way in which the outer bottom corner tails off into an oblong, down which runs a corkscrew-like curl *[166–7]*. The youths normally wear white head-bands, and the *halteres* above them have a white dot in the centre. His followers tend to paint rather larger bell-kraters, with four-figure compositions on the obverse and a woman with the draped youths on the reverse. *[168]* is typical of their work, though its obverse is more interesting than most, since it shows Dionysos holding a phlyax mask. A less elaborate treatment is to be seen on the vases of the Pittsburgh and Barletta Painters or of the Painter of the Bearded Oscans, whose work leads on to that of the Latiano Painter *[169]*, which must be placed well into the third quarter of the century.

The School of the Varrese Painter

The Varrese Painter, named from the hypogeum at Canosa where some of his vases were found, is a prolific artist and, thanks to a number of large vases (including several hydriai and a tall oenochoe) which have recently come to light, he emerges as one of the more significant painters of the mid-fourth century: his work had a considerable influence not only on his immediate followers, but also on the forerunners of the Darius Painter. Nearly 200 of his vases have survived; of these about a quarter are large and elaborately decorated; the rest, mostly pelikai and bell-kraters, are of smaller dimensions and more akin in treatment to the 'Plain' style. His work is marked by the constant repetition of a number of stock figures and is thus relatively easy to identify. Among these we should note: *(i)* a nude youth, either standing, with one arm covered in a piece of drapery, or seated on a folded drape *[171]*; *(ii)* a standing draped woman, with one leg slightly drawn back and visible beneath the drapery *[171–2]*; *(iii)* a draped woman, bending forward over one raised foot, with one arm resting on the upraised thigh *[172]*; *(iv)* a seated woman, with one leg in front of the other *[173]*.

His figures tend to look rather solemn, even severe, with small, slightly downward-curving mouths; women often have large top-knots, tied with a white ribbon, and wear a small radiate stephane. Characteristic of his drapery are the multiple parallel fold-lines running down it, or across the legs of seated figures *[172]*, and in particular, the rows of parallel, slightly concave, fold-lines on the drapery between women's breasts; his fold-lines often begin or end with a small dot.

On his larger vases there is an extensive use of added colours, especially on the drapery of figures in naiskoi [170], which may well have provided the inspiration for the adoption of the Gnathia technique around this time (c. 360–50), in which the figures are painted in colour directly on to the black-glazed surface of the vase.

The Varrese Painter makes extensive use of mythology for the subjects of his major vases, which include loutrophoroi with elaborate ornamental pattern-work and three large nestorides like [171], with Orpheus heads in relief on the disks, figured scenes on the upper panels between the handles, and ribbing on the lower part of the body; they are comparable with the metal version on [157]. These vases provide a connecting link with the work of the Darius Painter and his forerunners.

His minor vases call for little comment. Apart from a few amphorae with naiskos or stele scenes on the obverse, they are mostly kraters or pelikai with three, or more commonly two, figures on each side [173]. The reverses inevitably represent draped youths, one usually with a 'sling' drape, the other with a 'sleeve', with a squiggly border to the overfall and double wavy lines in the outer corners of the himatia [174]. Many of the figures are seated upon rock-piles; these may have black centres outlined in white, or a row of white dots above a thick white crescent-shaped band on the lower part of each rock in the pile [173]. The pictures are framed between palmette scrolls, often with a single drop-leaf [174].

The style of these vases is continued in the work of a few minor artists, who probably formed part of his workshop; the most important is perhaps the Wolfenbüttel Painter [175–6], on whose vases we may note a similar, if less precise, treatment of the drapery; noteworthy is the way in which the folds of the himation behind the neck and above the shoulder of his draped youths tend to stick up, rather like two small peaks.

The influence of the Varrese Painter may be seen on the vases of the Ginosa and Chiesa Painters; two of the former's amphorae come from the same tomb in Ginosa as a hydria by the Varrese Painter, which suggests at least some connection between them. The Ginosa Painter also puts naiskos scenes on some of his amphorae; on one of them the deceased warrior is represented by his shield and spear [177]; on others the naiskos contains a flowering plant [178], a device common later on.

More significant is the Painter of Bari 12061, to whose hand may now be attributed a volute-krater with a scene showing two suppliant women seated on an altar, menaced by a younger man and a bearded king, each with a drawn sword [179]. The scene, which is repeated on several other Apulian vases, has been referred to the story of the Danaides seeking refuge from Aegyptus and his sons. On the neck in added white is a female head, wearing a crown, in an elaborate floral setting, with spiralling tendrils and palmettes; this becomes the standard decoration in the second half of the century; on the reverse the head is in red-figure in a simpler setting of palmettes. This combination appears with increasing frequency from now onwards. It may also be noted that this volute-krater has open-work handles and a Dionysiac scene on the reverse, thus preserving the earlier tradition, which dies out, with few exceptions, after this vase. *[180]*, the name vase of the painter, shows a metal volute-krater, with a ribbed body, standing in a small naiskos; such metal vases appear on other works by this painter and also on those of the Varrese Painter, thus providing a further link between the two. We may also note the black stripe which runs down one side of women's drapery, following the line of the leg, even when bent; it is a typical mannerism of this painter.

A number of vases which have only recently come to light enable us to recognise as associates of the Varrese Painter several other artists, whose work is also close to that of the Darius Painter. *[181]* is by the Metope Painter, named after the triglyph-metope frieze on the bases of the naiskoi depicted on two of his loutrophoroi; this vase depicts an Amazonomachy, and fragments of an actual limestone frieze with a similar theme have been found in Taranto. His connection with both the Varrese Painter and the Painter of Bari 12061 is clear from the shape and pattern-work of his vases, his rendering of drapery, and his use of added colours; the pilos-helmet worn by the youths on some of his vases also corresponds very closely with that on *[179]*. His volute-kraters have mascaroon handles, and stele scenes on the reverse, in accordance with the standard practice in the second half of the century. *[182]* is his masterpiece; the shape is unusual, being a sort of combination of neck-amphora and loutrophoros, used once before by the Varrese Painter. The obverse shows Andromeda bound on to the rock, with Cepheus beside her and, below, Perseus tackling the sea-monster, on whose back a small Eros is kneeling, to add a touch of sentiment to the scene. The reverse shows four youths and two women at a grave monument in the form of an Ionic column on a high base; the shoulders have red-figure heads, frontal on the obverse, in profile on the reverse, in a floral setting. Parallels for all the supporting figures can be found in the work of the Varrese Painter, and it almost looks as if this vase was painted under his supervision.

The other artist is the Painter of Louvre MNB 1148, who was also originally thought to be one of the minor painters associated with the workshop of the Darius Painter. Numbers of large vases by his hand have, however, recently appeared, and he emerges in consequence as a painter of far greater significance than had previously been thought. He also is a very close follower of the Varrese Painter, as may be seen from his rendering of drapery, but his work shows a high level of individuality, in his drawing of faces, his choice of subjects and his original treatment of them. *[183]* shows his stylistic connection with the Varrese and Metope Painters; it depicts a version of the Niobe legend, in which her brother Pelops and his wife Hippodamia, come to visit her at the tomb of her children. The scene on *[184]* is even more unusual; the upper level of the obverse shows Zeus and Aphrodite in a palace, flanked on the left by Astrape, the personification of lightning, and on the right by Eniautos (the year), a unique figure in vase-painting, and Demeter; below, Zeus, in the guise of a swan, caresses Leda, while Hypnos holds a wand above her head. The Painter of Louvre MNB 1148 decorated a number of smaller vases with stock figures, as well as two stamnoi with youths and Oscan warriors.

Another artist who reflects Varresian influence is the Chamay Painter; his style is more mannered, especially in the posing of his figures and his drawing of drapery. Faces are neatly drawn, if not very skilfully, when seen in three-quarter view; hair is shown as a mass of fine curls, each done separately in diluted glaze; breasts are rounded and set far apart, the covering drapery stretched tightly across them, with parallel fold-lines. His nude male bodies show the growing tendency to effeminacy, from which not even Herakles is exempt [185]. He seems to have had a small following of mannerist painters, who decorate their vases with single figures in a very elaborate setting of floral and scroll-work (cf. the Painter of the Dublin Situlae), a practice copied on some of the smaller alabastra and other vases from the Darius workshop.

Forerunners of the Darius Painter

Following upon the work of the Lycurgus and Varrese Painters is another group of vases, which lead more directly to the Darius Painter and his school. Broadly speaking, it falls into two divisions; the one with funerary subjects, the other mythological. Both are very close in style to the work of the Darius Painter, the latter perhaps nearer to him in spirit, since he is the greatest mythologiser of all South Italian painters.

The two principal artists in the first division are the Gioia del Colle Painter and the Painter of Copenhagen 4223; the *floruit* of the former should be placed around 340 BC in the light of the other material from the tomb which contained his name vase. Both painted a large number of vases, mainly volute-kraters, decorated in what has now become the canonical fashion for funerary vases – mourners at a naiskos on the obverse, at a stele on the reverse. These kraters have mascaroons on the handles, swans' heads (sometimes painted white) at the handle-joins on the shoulders, and on the neck of the obverse either a figured scene or a head in a floral setting, on that of the reverse a palmette composition; beneath the handles are multiple superposed palmette-fans, often of some elegance. The figures within the naiskoi assume increasingly statuesque poses, which may have been influenced by the work of Lysippus, who spent some time in Taranto. More attention is now paid to the architecture of the naiskoi, and there is a more considered attempt at rendering the ceiling-beams in perspective. All the vases of this group are very uniform in style and treatment; [186], the name vase of the Gioia del Colle Painter is typical, and the similarity between his vases and those of the Painter of Copenhagen 4223 [187] is obvious. The latter puts a wider variety of heads (Pan, Orpheus, etc.) on the necks of his volute-kraters, and his floral settings are more elaborate, with a greater use of added red. Youths figure prominently in his naiskoi, sometimes with their squire or their horse; often also with a pet dog [188–9]. Vases with other than funerary subjects are rare; reverses have either four or two figures beside the stele. Their workshop also produced hydriai with naiskos scenes (cf. [170]), but invariably representing women, often wearing attractively-coloured drapery.

The Berlin-Branca Group links the two divisions. On the neck of the obverse of [190] is a female head in added white in a floral setting, as on the vases by the Painter of Copenhagen 4223; on the reverse [191] it is in red-figure, as on those by the Gioia del Colle Painter, and on the body is a typical stele scene. The obverse, however, shows a youthful Herakles, leaning on his club beside a reflecting pool, while Hippolyte holds out her girdle to him. Above are Hermes and Athena, forerunners of the assembly of divinities which from now on will regularly appear in the upper register. The work of this painter includes a powerful Iliupersis in Berlin, and near to it come the vases of the Branca Painter, which include a calyx-krater with another Herakles and Hippolyte scene, and one depicting a remarkable 'Liberation of Prometheus' [192], with a youthful Herakles, who has shot the eagle sent by Zeus to devour the liver of Prometheus and is about to loose the fetters which bind him to a stagey-looking rock (cf. [182]). The reverses figure Dionysiac scenes [193] and perhaps served as models for those on the bell- and calyx-kraters of the Darius Painter. The Branca Painter is a bold draughtsman, fond of putting a halo of curly hair above the faces of figures in three-quarter view, and of treating his themes in a novel way.

Another artist in this group is the Hippolyte Painter, named after a calyx-krater with another version of that story, who is also responsible for one of the finest of Apulian vases of this period [194], which represents Dionysos embracing Ariadne in the presence of a maenad and a satyr, who is pouring wine from a skin into a krater, while a small Eros flies down to crown the couple; beside Dionysos is a satyr-mask, again showing his connection with the theatre, and, suspended above, is a 'xylophone'. The scene has a beauty and elegance seldom equalled in Apulian; Ariadne's filmy drapery revealing the outline of her body beneath it, has a special grace and delicacy. A similar elegance appears on [195] by the Laodamia Painter, with scenes in two registers; below, the fight between the Lapiths and the centaurs at the wedding-feast of Peirithoös, and above perhaps the love-sickness of Phaedra. He, too, is an artist of great ability, especially in his drawing of faces, which he endows with a good deal of expression. His drapery is neat and finely-drawn, and an extensive use of added colour gives a lively look to the vase. A pelike in Kassel by his hand, showing Helen posturing in front of Paris, has a rather more mannered look.

Near to these is the Alkestis loutrophoros [196], which on the upper register of the obverse shows Alkestis bidding farewell to her two children, in the presence of the sorrowing Admetos in whose stead she has offered to die. The lower register and the reverse are less interesting, with five women on the former, and youths, women and Eros on the latter. The body has now assumed the form of a slightly concave cylinder like a barrel, with ribbing at top and bottom; the neck is taller and more slender, the handles more delicate, and the vase itself rests upon a carefully modelled base. The neck is decorated with a variety of ornamental patterns; on the obverse there is also a panel depicting Eros; the shoulders have female heads in red-figure, one in three-quarter view and the other in profile, in floral or palmette settings. It is one of the more impressive vases of this group, and unique in its representation of the death of Alkestis.

The De Schulthess Painter, named after the principal donor of [197], is a newcomer to this group, since his works have only recently become known. This vase shows the arrival of Helen at Troy; in the upper register are Cassandra, seated and looking very apprehensive, Paris, Helen greeted by Aphrodite, and the aged Priam, with a youthful Troilos beside him – all the figures are inscribed. Below is the prow of a ship with the landing ladder, a youth bearing a travel-pack, and a woman running towards a fountain-house (perhaps where Troilos is later to meet his doom). Here again we have a unique subject, treated in a masterly fashion, with drawing of the highest quality. Two other kraters go closely with it; one shows the arms of Achilles [198], the other a gigantomachy [199], with Zeus in his chariot about to hurl his thunderbolt at two giants, who are also attacked by both Apollo and Herakles. At the extreme left, Ge, the mother of the giants, emerges from the earth to entreat mercy; she is painted white and wears orange-yellow drapery with a crimson border. On the neck of the obverse four women, dressed in colourful long robes, join hands in a cyclic dance; it is a scene of unusual beauty, the wavy borders of their garments form an undulating line, which matches the rhythm of the dance. The reverses of all these kraters have stele scenes. Close to these is a calyx-krater [200], also with a unique scene, Oedipus at Colonus, probably to be associated with the Sophoclean drama. The blind king is seated on a large altar in the grove of the Eumenides, personified by a Fury above, with Antigone and Ismene on either side, and Kreon and Polynices standing by.

These vases are all of exceptional interest and importance; they lead directly on to those of the Darius Painter and his school, on which they must have exercised a substantial measure of influence not only in shape and style, but also in their preference for the rarer myths. The Darius Painter and his forerunners all appear to be well versed in Greek literature and mythology and one of the remarkable features of their work is its power to evoke, by means of subtle gestures, poses or expressions, a train of images concerning the past and the future of the various characters they portray.

The Darius Painter and his circle

The Darius Painter exercised a dominating influence on all subsequent Apulian vase-painting. He was the first of the late Apulian vase-painters fully to explore the possibilities which vases of truly monumental dimensions, between 1 and 1.5 metres in height, offer for decoration, and the new canons of composition he introduced made a considerable impact on the work of all his successors. The influence of the early baroque vase-painters and of the Varrese school upon his immediate forerunners has already been noted; the Darius Painter takes the traditions he inherited a great deal further. He handles mythology on a scale not previously attempted, making use of several myths not found elsewhere (e.g. the Daughters of Anios on *[205]*), and he derives many of his subjects from legends which were used by the classical tragedians, especially Euripides, for the source of their plots (Andromeda, Alkmene, Chrysippos, Hecuba, Hippolytus, Hypsipyle, Meleager, Oinomaos), as well as drawing upon the epic poems. Masks, both tragic and comic, also appear on his vases, mostly in a Dionysiac context. The current interest in Alexander the Great's campaigns in Persia in the last third of the century is also possibly reflected on a few of his vases *[201]*, which were obviously inspired by, if they do not actually depict, his battle with the Persian King Darius, and the subject of *[203]*, representing an earlier Darius in council, either at the time of the Ionian revolt in 494 or during the Persian wars of 490–80, was probably chosen for the same reason. He has less interest in funerary scenes, which sometimes appear on his reverses, but very seldom on the obverses. Some vases show bridal preparations or scenes with Eros, especially on pelikai, which seem to be preferred for such themes; they are very popular with his associates and followers *[212]*.

The figures on many of his larger vases are often identified by inscriptions, which on occasions can also be used to give, as it were, a title to the picture like *Persai* on *[203]*, or *Patroklou taphos* on *[204]*. The decorative patterns become increasingly elaborate, probably because of the greater scope offered by the much larger vases; they are again often adapted from architectural motifs (dentils, lesbian cymation, swastika-meanders) and enhanced by the use of contrasting colours. No significant changes occur in the floral patterns on necks or shoulders, but they now are found more frequently on the bands which may be used to separate the upper register on the bodies of vases like amphorae or loutrophoroi from the lower; such bands may also depict friezes of animals, like those on the gilded Tarentine terracotta appliqués, or marine creatures, which enable us to identify a number of fish-plates as products of his workshop.

The Darius Painter is a competent draughtsman; he is fond of faces in three-quarter view, with a triangular forehead in the Praxitelean manner, a slight tilt to the head, and expressive eyes and mouth. The fold-lines of his drapery are clearly defined, but tend to break up across the body; the ripple-like border he gives to overfalls can be highly effective. *[202]* is a good example of his early work, with the comparatively rare subject of Aphrodite and Persephone appealing to Zeus for Adonis. Here most of the figures provide the prototypes for those on his more mature works, in which we note a greater sureness in the drawing and a freer treatment of drapery. His two great vases [203] and [204], showing Darius and the funeral of Patroclus, well illustrate his more developed style, which is perhaps seen to better advantage on a series of calyx-kraters with mythological subjects on the obverses and Dionysiac on the reverses [205–6], since their effect is somewhat less overwhelming than the multi-figured compositions on his monumental vases, and we are in a better position to see the picture as an entity, rather than as a number of contributing elements. [205] and [206] provide excellent examples; the former depicts the three daughters of Anios, who were endowed by Dionysos with the ability to produce olives, corn and grapes respectively, and are here shown with their appropriate emblems, while their father listens to the appeal of Menelaos, who formed part of a deputation sent by the Greeks to enlist the aid of Anios and his daughters in provisioning the Greek host during the siege of Troy. The latter gives an unusual version of the Alkmene story, with the blind seer Teiresias above to left, the eagle of Zeus flying above the altar on which Alkmene, surrounded by a nimbus, is seated, while Amphitryon and a boy hurry up with torches to set fire to the logs of wood in front of the altar, and Kreon stands by on the right.

Many other artists were employed in the workshop of the Darius Painter; his influence is manifest on their vases, but few of these are other than mass products; the same subjects are constantly repeated, and this not only induces a sense of monotony, but often makes the individual hands hard to distinguish. Two of the artists emerge with some measure of individuality, the Perrone and Phrixos Painters, the latter decorating a dish showing Phrixos riding the ram over the sea with a band of fish surrounding it. The fish, which recur as the sole decoration in the tondo of another dish by this painter [207], are of interest since they enable us to attribute to him several fish-plates on which the same fish – especially the black-spotted torpedo, the cuttlefish and the angler-fish, as well as the horn-shell – are also to be found.

The chief of the Darius Painter's successors is the Underworld Painter, named after [209], which represents Pluto and Persephone in their palace, with Orpheus and various denizens of the Underworld around it. Three very large lekythoi (c. 95 cm in height), which are probably early works by this painter, show the close stylistic connection with the Darius Painter. All depict famous scenes of rape – Pluto and Persephone, Eos and Kephalos, the Dioskouroi and the daughters of Leucippus. On the firt two there is a free composition, with the figures arranged on different levels, but on [208] the two scenes are formally separated by a band of scroll-work. The subjects are all treated in considerable detail, and the rape of the Leucippidae presents us also with its aftermath, when the Dioskouroi fought the sons of Aphareus, and Idas, to avenge his slain brother, pulls up the tombstone of his father to hurl against Polydeuces, but is prevented from carrying out his purpose by the intervention of Zeus with his thunderbolt – a scene unique in vase-painting. These lekythoi also show some influence from the Painter of Louvre MNB 1148, especially in the rendering of the faces and the drapery; that of the Darius Painter may be seen in the composition and the handling of the myths. It is even more apparent from a comparison between their larger vases (e.g. *[204]* and *[209]*), both follow the same general principles of decoration, but on those of the Underworld Painter we note a tendency towards over-elaboration. His faces are drawn with less precision; the lines are less clearly defined, often creating a rather petulant expression; the musculature of his nude male bodies is harder and more strongly emphasized, reminding us of some early Hellenistic sculptures. Legs are unduly thin; hair is carefully drawn, often with fine, individual curls in low relief, which may fall down on to the shoulders. Draperies are richly patterned; less important female figures often wear peploi with looped black ribbon girdles; fold-lines are finely drawn, but tend to break up into a series of short strokes. His range of subjects may be less extensive than that of the Darius Painter, but includes some of unique interest, notably *[210]*, which gives the only extant illustration of the story of Melanippe, the subject of two dramas by Euripides. The variety of emotions on the faces of the principals is well expressed, the bewilderment of the herdsman, as he holds out the twin sons of Melanippe by Poseidon, whom he found abandoned and being suckled by a cow, the anger of Hellen, and the anxiety of Melanippe herself, supported by her old nurse. Two kraters represent spirited gigantomachies; others give us a moving scene of the parting of Hector and Andromache, and an unusual version of the Herakles-Atlas legend, in which the youthful hero, with his lion-skin and club, stands beside the enthroned figure of Atlas, next to whom stands Ge, with the serpent-guarded apple-tree of the Hesperides in the distance; above is Selene in a four-horse chariot with gods on either side. *[211]* represents a scene from the *Antiope* of Euripides, on which the upper register shows Amphion and his brother Zethos attacking Lykos, who is protected by the intervention of Hermes, while below is the bull, maddened by Oistros, which has just thrown off the body of Dirce, who lies dead on the ground beside it, the thyrsus nearby reminding us that she was engaged in Dionysiac rites when caught by Amphion and Zethos. To right is the shepherd, who as witness of the scene, will later narrate it as the messenger, and whose presence connects the scene with the drama.

In his latest phase, towards the end of the century, the Underworld Painter's drawing deteriorates rapidly, notably on the face. Many vases, especially pelikai, with genre and bridal scenes *[212]* are products of his workshop; they have little to commend them, except perhaps those by the Siren Citharist Painter, on which the body is divided into two panels, one featuring a head in a very decorative floral setting, the other a typical genre scene with a woman and Eros. On some vases the floral pattern fills almost the whole of the obverse, with a single figure within it.

Most of the vases from the Darius-Underworld workshop so far discussed have been of larger dimensions; in addition to these there are over 2000 of medium or smaller size, mostly decorated with one or two figures adapted from those on the reverses of the major works. They continue the tradition of the 'Plain' style, with modifications to suit the prevailing taste. Their painters are well-drilled, with a consequential uniformity of treatment, giving the impression of mass production. These vases fall into two main groups, one consisting of those of medium size, mostly hydriai, bell- or column-kraters and amphorae, the other of comparatively small vases, with single-figured decoration, including about 1000 depicting female heads.

[213] is typical of the hydriai, which normally represent a youth and a woman, sometimes beside a stele, at others, in converse or following one another. A few have simple naiskos scenes; all have a large fan-palmette below the back handle, with side scrolls. Of the other vases in this group, the work of the Truro Pelike *[214–15]*, Haifa *[216–17]* and Lucera *[218–19]* Painters may be taken as representative – most of their obverses have a youth, satyr or Eros in the company of a woman, and their reverses the usual two or three draped youths, depending upon the size of the vase. The Lucera Painter is of some interest, since it seems to be his vases which influenced the Apulianizing phase in Campania. Later artists include the Flat-head Painter, so named from the flatness of the top of his youths' heads, on which there is a row of upright curls. With the work of the Painter of Vienna 751 and the Forlì Painter, we come to the final stage of the 'Plain' style, when both composition and drawing have deteriorated considerably, and human figures are fast becoming unrecognizable as such. *[220–1]* gives a typical example; an altar or some other object is placed between the two youths on the reverse, whose drapery projects outward to produce a curious sort of pattern around it; their feet have become shapeless lumps, their faces devoid of expression.

Of the smaller vases the most attractive are the alabastra, and a few other shapes, decorated with figures or female heads in floral settings *[222]*, reminiscent of those on the necks of volute-kraters; there is also a series of kantharoi with single figures, usually between berried olive or laurel branches, as well as several plastic vases, which now come into greater use. These may be moulded into various shapes, a crocodile devouring a negro boy, a sphinx or siren, and even the prow of a ship *[223]*; but most are rhyta with animal heads, and on the bowl one, or more rarely, two figures similar to those on the minor vases. The latter cover a wide range of shapes, but are decorated only with commonplace figures and cannot be regarded as much more than workshop pieces.

The practice of decorating a vase with only a profile head goes back at least to the seventh century BC; it continues in Greece throughout the next two centuries, but does not become common until the first half of the fourth, when large numbers of small vases decorated in this manner are found. Heads in

Greece, however, seldom appear as subsidiary decoration, since the vases on which they might have been so used had ceased to be produced soon after *c*. 380. Heads in Apulian appear for the first time as subsidiary decoration on the volute-kraters of the Iliupersis Painter *[141]*; they rapidly increase in popularity and in the second half of the fourth century become an almost standard form of decoration. From *c*. 350 onwards, heads, predominantly female, also appear as the sole decoration on a large range of smaller vases. It is not easy to decide whom the female heads are intended to represent; if they are accompanied by Erotes, it is reasonable to suppose that it would be Aphrodite. In one instance the polos-crowned head on the neck of a volute-krater is inscribed *AΥPA*, but this would not seem to apply generally to such heads, which might well also be thought to represent Persephone, who would be an appropriate choice on a funerary vase. Winged heads are fairly common; they are generally taken to be those of Nike, but some might be those of Eros, who frequently looks very effeminate at this period. Heads in a Phrygian cap are more likely to be Orpheus than Attis, since the cult of the latter had hardly become established in South Italy at this time. Most of the female heads, however, have nothing to distinguish them and had probably lost any particular significance; there is a considerable variety in their treatment, in both hair-style and head-gear.

The Chevron Group comes early in the series (*c*. 350–30) and consists largely of bell-kraters with a figure on one side and a head on the other *[224–5]*; its name comes from the pattern which regularly appears below the rim of most of the kraters. The heads are competently drawn, and the various figures of women, youths or satyrs on the obverses enable us to associate the vases with the later work of the Dijon Painter and the minor products of the Darius workshop. One krater bears on its reverse *[226]* the helmeted head of a Greek warrior with the inscription *APX*; if this were to represent Archidamos III, who was killed at the battle of Manduria in 338, it would provide useful external chronological evidence. *[227]* shows a selection of typical heads by various artists – those by the Painter of Zurich 2660 *[227/3]* are characterized by the looped curls of hair above the brow; in the Winterthur Group by the projecting bow just above the hair over the brow *[227/4]*, in the Monopoli Group by the decoration on the sakkos and the bow on top of it *[227/5]*. Later, the drawing is less careful, the neck more elongated *[227/6]*, and more of the torso tends to be visible. *[227/7]* is typical of one of the latest artists in this group, the Painter of the Kassel Cup, whose characteristic heads, rather poorly drawn, have a long straight nose, a pronounced and rounded chin, and a downward-turned mouth, which gives them a look of discontent or anger.

The Ascoli Satriano Painter is worth a passing mention in this context; he paints vases with both figured scenes and female heads *[227/8]*. Many of his vases come from the north Apulian site which gives him his name, and several reflect a very strong Paestan influence, almost as if he had spent some time at work in that city. His female heads, however, are closer to the standard Apulian style; the hair appears as a large black mass above the brow, the head is covered with a simple *kekryphalos* from which a large bunch emerges at the back. *[228]* is a good example of a mythological scene, representing Herakles, with bow and club, and one of the Hesperides beside the serpent-guarded tree; the heads of the two women are in the painter's characteristic style.

The Patera and Ganymede Painters

The Patera Painter *[229–35]*, named after the long-handled patera which often appears on his vases, is a contemporary of the Darius Painter and is also strongly influenced by the Painter of Copenhagen 4223, especially in his treatment of funerary scenes. He leads on to the Baltimore Painter, whose early work is very close to his in style, and who was almost certainly based in Canosa, to judge from the large number of vases by him or his associates which come from that area. The Patera Painter might well have begun his career in Taranto, then moved to Ruvo where many of the minor vases associated with him have been found, and towards the end of his career worked with the Baltimore Painter in Canosa. He is a prolific artist, who decorated a wide variety of shapes, with a strong preference for funerary scenes on his larger vases. These usually have a naiskos on the obverse and a stele on the reverse *[229–30]*, though the latter is sometimes replaced by two draped youths; one of these often holds up a large cista, with two lines crossing it diagonally, and a large black dot in each of the four quarters *[233]*. The naiskos normally contains only one figure – woman, youth or warrior – with a woman running up on either side, or else a woman on one side and a youth on the other; in the pediment there may be a white disk, but not the more elaborate decoration favoured by the Baltimore Painter. Black and white fillets are tied round the shaft of the stele, which is usually crowned by a pediment or else has a row of offerings, but not a vase, on top. The base often has a thick black fillet looped across it, with three black disks inside each of the two loops. Only on rare occasions does he turn to mythology – mainly on amphorae or loutrophoroi – where we find Pluto and Persephone or Paris and Helen. *[231]*, which comes from Ruvo, is one of his finest works, a dish showing Aphrodite, wearing a long, filmy robe, escorted by Erotes. His column-kraters frequently represent warriors in native costume *[232]*.

Characteristic of the drapery of his reverse youths *[233]* is the wavy black border on the overhang of the himation on the youth to the left, the curlicues in the bottom corners and the way in which the cloak is often so draped as to create the effect of a large open V across the top of the body. Fold-lines on all drapery are boldly drawn, usually in a series of firm, parallel strokes. The Patera Painter likes to depict figures in motion, with a consequential swirling of their drapery. His faces have a rectangular chin; of women's breasts one is usually pear-shaped, the other slightly smaller and pointing upwards. His floral patterns are well drawn, often making use of multiple flowers; added colours, especially different shades of red, heighten their effect. He is also fond of including metal vessels or a piece of armour in his scenes; they are painted in added white and yellow, with shading for the ribbing or for details.

Associated with the Patera Painter are several other artists whose work reflects his influence and provides further connecting links with the Baltimore Painter. The vases in the Groups of the Trieste Owl and Bologna 572 *[234–5]* are particularly close to his lesser works, especially in the treatment of the draped youths on their reverses. His more monumental style is imitated on a vase like *[236]*, or in those of the Seated Women and Stanford-Conversano Groups, but the drawing is somewhat coarser.

There are also several vases with a figured scene on the obverse which may be attributed to the Patera Painter, and, on the reverse, a female head, similar in treatment to those which appear on the necks or shoulders of his volute-kraters or amphorae, and which are repeated as the sole decoration on many vases of the Amphorae Group. It is clear, therefore, that between the Amphorae Group and the Patera Painter there must be a very close connection; indeed some, at least, of the vases in the former might well be by the hand of the latter. We shall see an exactly parallel relationship between the Ganymede and Armidale Painters, and the Baltimore and Stoke-on-Trent Painters; such collaboration is a regular feature of their workshop. The heads on the reverses of some twenty vases of which the obverses are clearly by the Patera Painter *[237/1–4]* give a good idea of the typical Amphorae Group head – the hair is generally enclosed in a sakkos decorated with black and white stripes, which comes to a point at the top, where there is a row of radiating black lines, which presumably indicate open-work. The face has a rather quadrangular look (typical of the Patera Painter); the eyebrow is arched and fairly extended, the upper and lower lines of the upper eyelid may converge to form an acute angle or may run parallel, one being much shorter than the other; the brow-nose line is slightly convex, and there is normally a dot for the nostril and a comparatively small mouth with a downward turn, though later there is a tendency for its size to increase considerably.

That the Ganymede Painter must have worked in close collaboration with the Patera Painter is clear from the correspondence between their styles and subjects. The Ganymede Painter is a rather more ambitious artist, with a taste for more grandiose compositions. His naiskoi usually contain two figures, sometimes with a horse as well, and one, of particular interest, shows Orpheus manifesting himself at the tomb of a poet; on his hydriai, where the flanking figures are always women, the naiskoi contain a flowering plant. He also likes to include pieces of armour, a shield or a cuirass, a pilos-helmet or a petasos, in his naiskoi, thus giving them a somewhat cluttered look. His floral work is very elaborate and painted with some care; on the neck of his name vase *[240]*, Ganymede is carried off by the swan in a floral setting which includes small white birds as well as the usual flowers, spirals and tendrils, but more usually he has a female head in added white, springing from a campanula flower, or a frontal head wearing a radiate diadem (see cover illustration).

His faces are more rounded, especially in the area of the chin, than those of the Patera Painter; women's breasts, however, are treated in a very similar fashion, even greater emphasis being placed on the one that is pear-shaped. His drawing is more fluid and his youths have a softer look. He is fond of figures holding fans, open boxes and cistae, divided by two diagonal lines, but now with white triangles in the four quarters, and sometimes with a round flat cake (*plakous*) on it, topped by a pyramidal one (*pyramis*). The smaller vases repeat figures from the larger compositions and have on their reverses two draped youths who wear white headbands like those of the Patera Painter.

To the hand of the Ganymede Painter may also be attributed a few large vases with mythological scenes – a volute-krater with Amphiaraos before Pluto in the Underworld (a popular theme with the Baltimore Painter), a hydria [241] decorated on the shoulder with Apollo, Artemis and other divinities, and on the body with a frieze showing youths and women beside a small naiskos, and another [242] with a version of the Niobe legend, which shows her, partly petrified, at the tomb of her children, with Hippodamia and Pelops, her brother, on one side of it and her father Tantalos on the other. In front of the tomb is a row of funeral offerings and above to left are the one son and the one daughter, who, according to some versions of the story, escaped the slaughter; the latter sits beside her wool-basket, distaff in hand, since the other daughters were reputedly slain by Artemis, who appears on the right with Apollo, while they were preparing wool.

Some mugs, with figured scenes by the Ganymede Painter on their bodies, have on their lids a very characteristic female head, wearing a striped sakkos, with a white top. The same head appears by itself on a number of other vases [237/5–8]; they have been attributed to the Armidale Painter, who must be the *alter ego* of the Ganymede Painter, since similar heads appear as subsidiary decoration on several of his larger vases. Others, by different painters, are very close to these [237/9]; they must also be products of this workshop, from which some 600 vases of smaller dimensions, decorated with one or two figures associated in style with those of the Patera and Ganymede Painters, have come down to us. The best belong to the Group of the Trieste Askoi, with neat, elegant figures of women, youths and Erotes [243]. A closely related, but less talented, artist is the Menzies Painter [244], whose work is typical of that of a large group (named after him) of minor painters who decorated a host of small vases – oenochoai, epichyseis, skyphoi, kantharoi, lekanides, cups and rhyta – with stereotyped figures, especially Eros, again savouring of mass production [245–7].

The Baltimore Painter and the White Sakkos/Kantharos Group

The Baltimore Painter [248–53] is the most important and significant of the later Apulian vase-painters and, in view of the fact that many of his vases and those of his associates come from the area around Canosa, it is likely that his workshop was located in that city. His vases have much in common with those of his Tarentine contemporary, the Underworld Painter, particularly in regard to their subject-matter, monumental dimensions, multi-figured compositions and ornamental patterns, but they differ greatly in the drawing of the faces and in the rendering of the drapery, in both of which the Baltimore Painter is much bolder and more assertive. He decorates a wide range of shapes, both large and small. His volute-kraters often have scroll-work decoration in white applied to the handles, as well as figures on the blinkers; the neck may be divided into two registers, a narrow one above, with a female head in a floral setting, a deeper one below, with a figured scene, and even the feet may be decorated with figured scenes or with heads amid scrolls and flowers. The feet of large kraters were often made separately and then attached to the body of the vase; they do not always appear to have been painted by the hand which decorated the vase itself. The necks of his amphorae or loutrophoroi are covered with very elaborate ornamental patterns, as well as with the usual heads. The larger vases have either mythological or funerary subjects; genre scenes are confined to the smaller ones. Vases with funerary scenes follow the regular practice of having a naiskos on the obverse and a stele on the reverse; when there is a mythological scene on the obverse, the reverse may have a naiskos, with a youth inside it in red-figure instead of added white. The other naiskoi may hold up to three figures, if female; these will normally wear colourful costumes, with a good deal of orange-yellow and several shades of red. Various objects, and especially pieces of armour, are suspended from the ceiling; in particular, a cuirass (cf. [238]), painted in golden brown to simulate the metal of the original, and shaded to correspond to the musculature of the body (as on [250]); the arm- and neck-holes are painted deep red to show the internal leather lining. Flowering plants, like those of the Ganymede Painter, also appear in the naiskoi, the pediments of which are often decorated with a white disk between two narrow triangles; sometimes there are scrolls flanking a central rosette or a gorgoneion.

His mythological subjects range widely but so far have introduced no new themes. Several depict gigantomachies or amazonomachies, with the figures disposed at different levels, often in very contorted poses or in agony, as reflected in their tortured expressions; others draw their inspiration from epic poetry – Phoinix and Achilles, the arms of Achilles – or from drama – Andromeda, the rape of Chrysippos, Iphigenia in Tauris, Oinomaos; the Underworld is also well represented – the rape of Persephone, Pluto and Persephone, Amphiaraos before Pluto in his palace. Of the less frequently represented themes, the most interesting is perhaps the adjudication of Zeus between Aphrodite and Persephone over Adonis [251], the most dramatic is certainly the slaughter of the Niobids [252]. In most of the scenes there is an upper register of divinities, who look down on the events below. Like the Ganymede Painter, he also paints mythological subjects on the shoulders of large hydriai – chariot scenes are popular in this context, [253] presents a very vivid picture of the rape of Persephone, with the ineffectual intervention of Artemis and Athena. Several very large dishes are decorated in the tondo with genre scenes depicting youths, women and Eros or occasionally a chariot.

His pattern-work is highly complex, but less imaginative and graceful than that of the Ganymede Painter; the spiralling tendrils are thicker, which detracts from their elegance.

His early work is strongly under the influence of the Patera Painter, but as his style develops, it becomes increasingly individual and we may note: (i) his fondness for heads in three-quarter view [253], slightly inclined to one side, with large black pupils in the eyes, a strongly-emphasized lower lip and a heavy nose; on profile heads the mouth tends to become a flat line, above a rectangular chin (cf. the Patera Painter); women's breasts are at first piriform, but later become rounded, the nipples showing up clearly beneath the drapery; (ii) the bold rendering of drapery-folds, often with a transverse line between the breasts running down to the lower part of the garment (cf. the Darius and Underworld Painters); women often wear a small white triangular diadem above the brow; (iii) outlines tend to be thick and look as if they were drawn with a brush that tended to wobble; (iv) horses are stocky, heavy-chested and thick-necked.

Another minor feature, particularly characteristic of the Baltimore Painter and his followers, is the presence of a hydria with a handle shaped like an M, painted in glaze on the visible side [251]. Many of the female heads which appear as subsidiary decoration on the vases of the Baltimore Painter have a very characteristic look; the hair is caught up in a *kekryphalos* with open-work decoration and black and white stripes, and emerges in a bunch at the back, tied with a crinkly white ribbon. Mouth and eye are drawn with fairly thick brush strokes, and at the end of the mouth there is usually a small vertical stroke. Exactly similar heads serve as the sole decoration on a very large number of smaller vases, which have been assigned to the Stoke-on-Trent Painter [254/1–2], who, if he is not the Baltimore Painter himself, must have worked in close collaboration with him; cf. the Armidale and Ganymede Painters. A later development from his heads can be seen on those in the T.C. (Taranto from Canosa) Group, in which the mouth becomes a horizontal gash, with a marked protrusion of the lower lip and a very strong emphasis on the chin [254/3]. Still later are the heads by the Painter of the Macinagrossa Stand [254/4], on which there appears a dot at the base of the nostril, two more, one on each side of the mouth, and a small cluster at the end of it, giving the faces a curiously characteristic look, as if they suffered from some mild form of pimples. The eyes are sometimes highlighted by the addition of a touch of white. The figures on his vases are often seated upon hollow rocks.

The immediate successor and true heir of the Baltimore Painter is the White Sakkos Painter; the close connection between their work may be seen in a large group of the latter's earlier vases, some of which were originally attributed to the Baltimore Painter. In it are included several vases depicting Pluto and Persephone in their Underworld palace, a scene clearly derived from those on some of the Baltimore Painter's volute-kraters; both the pattern-work and the presence of M-handled hydriai testify to the strength of his influence. There is, however, a considerable difference in the actual drawing – faces, especially in three-quarter view, are more impressionistic, with the principal features, like the eyes, mouth and nose, rendered by quickly drawn lines; the treatment of the petasos is remarkable – it rests on the top of the head, as if seen from above / 256 /; the white sakkoi worn by many of the female figures are essentially characteristic of this painter. This group also includes some large loutrophoroi, one with the rape of Chrysippos, another with Pelops and Hippodamia; / 255 / lacks handles, has a head in high relief on the neck, a woman with a cithara emerging from a plant on the shoulder, and a band of fish between the two registers on the body. The fish are the work of the Sansone Painter, noted for his imaginative treatment of cuttlefish, and either point to artistic collaboration between him and the White Sakkos Painter or else to the fact that the two artists are identical. / 256 / is of particular interest for its subject-matter; the main scene represents the stricken Telephos, and on the neck is the same scene as on / 179 /; on the upper register of / 257 / is a group of five women, of whom three have hydriai beside them (Danaides?), below is an elaborate fountain-house.

The White Sakkos Painter also decorated several volute-kraters and amphorae with naiskos scenes, some of which are large and colourful with up to four figures in the naiskos; on others, on which only a single figure appears without supporters, the reverse often is decorated with a female head, painted in a very characteristic manner, which connects it with those on the numerous vases of the Kantharos Group, which must also be products of this workshop. The heads are covered by a sakkos with a double knot on the top and patterned with rays, dots and crosses. A solid mass of black hair, enlivened by a thick white stroke, crosses the forehead; there is a radiate stephane above it, and an elaborate ear-ring. At the upper end of the mass of hair there is a reserved contour with a scalloped edge, not unlike a cockscomb. Heads of this type / 254/6–8 /, with minor variations, are used as the sole decoration on upwards of 600 vases, mostly of smaller dimensions, and including many kantharoi (hence the name of the group), oenochoai of various shapes, dishes, plates, round pyxides and lekanides.

The White Sakkos Painter was also responsible for a large number of smaller vases with figured scenes, mostly showing youths, women and Eros, or frontal heads of either women or Nike in added white; on others, especially kantharoi and tall-necked oenochoai, chariot scenes are depicted. Several of the latter come from the Varrese hypogeum at Canosa and have two registers on the body, the upper with a chariot, the lower with a youth, Eros and a woman. There is often a polychrome female head in relief at the handle-join, and such vases are the forerunners of the polychrome Canosan style of the third century. A slightly later group, which are workshop products rather than the painter's own work, show similar subjects, but more carelessly drawn; the figures are sloppily posed, and males look increasingly effeminate, at times almost hermaphroditic. Women's drapery is marked by bunches of fold-lines at the waist; their breasts are clearly defined, with one often exposed *[259]*. The Stuttgart Group, to which many of these vases may be ascribed, also includes a number of exceptionally large dishes, with chariot scenes in the tondo; this is sometimes divided into two separate zones (cf. the oenochoai), with the chariot above, and a youth, Eros and a woman below. The outer border of the tondo tends to be elaborate, with small figures of Eros or female heads interspersed between the leaves of a vine-wreath. The Varrese hypogeum also yielded a large number of kantharoi decorated with women or Erotes, often badly drawn.

As well as red-figured vases, the White Sakkos Group also includes several volute-kraters, some from the excavations at Ordona, decorated in added colours; they often represent female heads of the Kantharos Group type and must therefore belong here. Their technique anticipates that of the polychrome Canosan style of the early Hellenistic period, but the added colours are very fugitive and often little more than the outline of the figure is left.

Other Late Apulian Vase-Painters

The Patera and Baltimore Painters had several followers, like the Capodimonte and Helmet Painters, who imitated their work without improving upon it, as may be seen in the former's drawing of faces and drapery and in his treatment of the reverses, or in the latter's posing of individual figures, his compositions and his pattern-work. *[260]*, the name vase of the Capodimonte Painter, well illustrates the connection, as do the vases of the Helmet Painter, whose reverses *[261]* regularly show two women running up to a stele (cf. the Patera Painter), which has a black fillet looped around its base. The Helmet Painter is essentially a painter of funerary scenes. On his later vases his drawing shows a decline.

The Painter of Berlin F 3383 *[262]* is closer to the Baltimore Painter. His drapery shows similar bold lines for the folds, often in parallel groups of two; the hem-line is wavy, there is a thick black stripe running down the peplos, and horizontal fold-lines across the space between the breasts, which are rounded, with well-defined nipples. His youths, especially on the reverses, wear white head-bands; they often stand with crossed legs; resting one arm on a pillar, in a Praxitelean type of pose. On *[263]* the two registers are separated by a band of fish; these are close to the work of the Eyebrow Painter, who also decorated a number of fish-plates; the fish are characterized by the well-marked eyebrows above their eyes, and their painter may be identical with the Painter of Berlin F 3383 or else have collaborated with him in the decoration of this vase (cf. the White Sakkos and Sansone Painters).

The Arpi Painter became known only in 1972, when the discovery of a tomb at Arpinova, near Foggia, brought to light a number of late vases by the Baltimore Painter together with several by this hitherto unknown artist, who was named after the site where they were found. His work overlaps that of the Baltimore Painter in its later phase and reflects his influence very strongly. The Arpi Painter is one of the most original and remarkable of all the later Apulian artists, both in his choice and treatment of subjects and in the very individual style of his drawing. [264] shows an almost comic Hephaestus coming to set Hera free from the magic throne; on [265] the slaughter of the Niobids is treated with refreshing novelty, and it was an ingenious device to place Apollo and Artemis on the shoulder of the hydria, from where they are in an advantageous position to shower their arrows from above on to the Niobids below. These appear in a variety of attitudes of supplication, anguish, despair and death, as they vainly try to elude the fatal shafts, though their rather expressionless faces maintain an admirable degree of composure. [266] represents a later stage of his work, with drawing of poorer quality; the obverse, however, has a subject of unusual interest. Above, the thunderbolt of Zeus appears through a colouful nimbus to blast the life out of Semele, while her terrified handmaids look on; below, the infant Dionysos, with a flourishing grape-vine above him, is handed over by Hermes to the nymphs of Nysa. On the reverse a fully-accoutred warrior stands in an unusually elaborate naiskos, which has a triglyph-metope frieze on its plinth; his left leg has a spur attached to it, one of the rare instances of its use at this period.

Later developments from the work of the Arpi Painter may be seen on a few overblown volute-kraters and, in particular, on a series of tall-necked oenochoai, on which a chariot usually occupies a prominent place – Helios, the apotheosis of Herakles, or a gigantomachy [267] in which Zeus, with Hermes as charioteer, attacks the serpent-limbed Typhoeus, while a wind-god produces a furious blast. Others show the death of Aegisthus or genre scenes; in all of them the influence of the Baltimore Painter's later work is clearly to be seen.

Another important artist of this period is the Virginia Exhibition Painter [268], so named because five of his vases, all said to come from the same tomb, made their first public appearance at the exhibition of South Italian vases in the Virginia Museum of Fine Arts in 1982. In style and treatment, and especially in the drawing of the female heads upon some of their reverses, they are comparable to the work of the White Sakkos Painter, although their draped youths, and the use of black fan-palmettes to decorate the bases of stelai are closer to the Painter of Berlin F 3383, of whom this artist would seem to be a follower. [269] is a remarkable vase by the V.E. Painter, the obverse of which shows a youth seated in a naiskos, holding a spear; his hand is grasped by Hermes, above whom is an inscription saying 'off to Hades', to which the youth replies 'I won't'. Such inscriptions are most unusual; the scene may be a distant reminiscence of the legend that, when Sisyphus tricked Persephone into allowing him to return to the world above, Hermes was sent by Zeus to bring him back to Hades, by force if necessary.

Associated with this painter are some smaller vases, less elaborately decorated, but reproducing several of his typical figures, objects and flowers. They consist mainly of tall-necked oenochoai, the mouths and handles of which are painted white, or of kantharoi, with handles terminating in spirals above the rim of the vase and also painted white. Many have female heads on the reverse, close to those in the Kantharos Group, and on the obverse a seated woman or Eros, like those on the later vases in the White Sakkos Group. There are also a few mugs with knobs on the lids in the form of polychrome flowers and, in one instance, the statuette of a woman, again linking this group to the Canosan polychrome style. Such vases must be dated at the very end of the fourth century, or perhaps to the first years of the third.

By the end of the fourth century it has become clear that the red-figure style had worked itself out and that its painters had exhausted their resources. The huge kraters and amphorae of the Underworld and Baltimore Painters and their associates mark the final stage in the attempts of vase-painters to reproduce in their medium multi-figured compositions better suited to the flat surface of a wall; no further developments along these lines were possible. A different approach was necessary and so, in the Hellenistic age, after a short attempt to carry on the old tradition in the polychrome style, plain black or moulded wares take the place of figured pottery. The death throes of Apulian red-figure are to be seen in a few vases which follow on from the work of the painters discussed above, but are now reduced almost entirely to funerary or genre scenes, without any traces of originality and often so badly drawn as to suggest that their painters were not Greeks but natives originally employed for minor tasks in the workshop, and quite incapable of anything beyond hack work. Vases of the Tenri and Foggia-Bassano Groups vainly endeavour to reproduce the later style of the Patera and Baltimore Painters in their feeble naiskos and stele scenes; the Mignot Painter, influenced by the Painter of Berlin F 3383, in his strange vases illustrates the last flowering of the 'Ornate' style, with their colourful obverses, but execrable drawing and pattern-work; a few of them take the form of a Scylla askos [270], a shape more common in Canosan polychrome, of which this vase is a prototype. When we pass to the Painter of B.M. F 339 we can see from his heads that the art of drawing has been almost completely lost [254/9]. They are very clumsy, with emphasis on the frontal sinus, a wavy line for the mouth and a badly-drawn eye, often with the lower lid left out and a very large black pupil. They are the last descendants of the T.C. Group, and on the works of his followers, like the Rennes Painter, complete disintegration has taken place, and the faces are barely recognizable as human; we can go no further.

101 *Skyphos by the Taporley Painter: Eros and woman*

102–3 *Bell-krater by the Tarporley Painter*

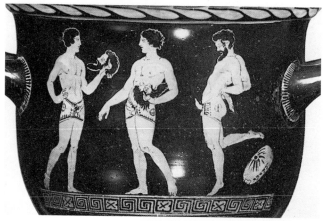

104 Bell-krater by the Tarporley Painter:
Actors preparing for a satyr-play

105 Calyx-krater by the
Tarporley Painter: Scene from
a phlyax comedy

106-7 Calyx-krater by the Tarporley Painter:
Perseus and Athena

109 Bell-krater by the Schiller Painter: Phlyax scene

108 Bell-krater by the Schiller Painter

110 Bell-krater by the
Adolphseck Painter:
Recognition of Theseus

111 Bell-krater, close to the Adolphseck
Painter: Herakles and Stymphalian bird

114 Bell-krater by the Painter of the Long Overfalls

112–13 Pelike by the Painter
of the Long Overfalls

115 Bell-krater by the Rainone
Painter: Phlyax scene

6–17 Bell-krater by the Hoppin Painter

18 Bell-krater by the Truro Painter   119 Bell-krater by the Lecce Painter

120 Bell-krater by the Iris
Painter: Phlyax scene

121 Rhyton by the Painter of Karlsruhe B9

122 Bell-krater by the Painter of Karlsruhe B9

124 Bell-krater by the Dijon Painter

*123 Reverse of bell-krater by the
Painter of Karlsruhe B9*

125 Bell-krater by the Dijon Painter: Phlyax scene

126 Column-krater by the Dijon Painter: Native warrior and two women

129 Reverse of bell-krater by the Graz Painter

127–8 Bell-krater by the Dijon Painter

131 Column-krater, Group of Boston 00.348:
Statue of Herakles

132 Bell-krater, Dechter Group: Andromeda

130 Pelike by the Judgement Painter: Zeus and Ganymede

133 Bell-krater by
the Thyrsus Painter

134 *Fragment of calyx-krater, Black Fury Group:*
Hermes and Priam

135 *Oenochoe, Black Fury Group: Callisto*

136 *Oenochoe, Felton Painter: Apollo and Marsyas*

137 *Oenochoe, near the Felton Painter:*
Phlyax parody of Oedipus

138–9 *Volute-krater by the Iliupersis Painter: Naiskos/stele scene*

140 *Volute-krater by the Iliupersis Painter: Neoptolemos at Delphi*

141 *Volute-krater by the Iliupersis Painter*

142 Calyx-krater by the
Painter of Athens 1714:
Symposium

143–4 Bell-krater by the Painter of Athens 1714

145 Pelike by
the Salting Painter

147 Squat lekythos, Group of Ruvo 423: Woman
playing 'xylophone'

146 Situla by the Painter of
the Dublin Situlae

148 *Calyx-krater by the Lycurgus Painter: Madness of Lycurgus*

149 *Volute-krater by the Lycurgus Painter: Boreas and Oreithyia*

150 *Hydria by the Lycurgus Painter: Naiskos*

151 Volute-krater, follower of the Lycurgus Painter: The Underworld

156 Column-krater by the Painter of Athens 1680: Komos

152–3 Bell-krater by
the Painter of Vatican V14

157 Column-krater by the Maplewood Painter

154–5 Bell-krater by
the Painter of Geneva 2754

158 *Pelike by the Verona Painter*

159 *(below) Cup skyphos by the Zaandam Painter*

160 *(far right) Oenochoe by the Choes Painter*

161 *(above) Skyphos, Wellcome Group*

162–3 *(far left) Bell-krater by the Snub-Nose Painter*

164 *Amphora by the 'H.A.' Painter: Naiskos*

165 Loutrophoros, Group of Lecce 660: Naiskos

166–7 Bell-krater by the Schulman Painter

168 Bell-krater, Grape-vine Group: Dionysos with comic mask

169 Bell-krater by the Latiano Painter

170 Hydria by the Varrese Painter: Naiskos

171 Nestoris by the Varrese Painter

172 Hydria by the Varrese Painter

173–4 *Pelike by the Varrese Painter*

175 *Column-krater by the Wolfenbüttel Painter: Woman and warrior*

176 *Details of reverse of no. 175*

177 *Amphora by the Ginosa Painter: Naiskos with shield and helmet*

178 *Amphora by the Ginosa Group: Naiskos with flowering plant*

179 Volute-krater by the Painter of Bari 12061: Mythological scene (Danaides?)

180 Amphora by the Painter of Bari 12061: Volute-
crater in naiskos

181 Loutrophoros, Metope Group: Naiskos scene

182 Amphora (of special shape), Metope Group: Andromeda

184 Loutrophoros by the Painter of Louvre MNB 1148:
Zeus and Aphrodite; Leda and the swan

183 Loutrophoros by the Painter of Louvre MNB
1148: The Tantalidae

185 Hydria by the Chamay Painter

186 *Volute-krater by the Gioia del Colle Painter: Naiskos with warrior*

187 *Volute-krater by the Painter of Copenhagen 4223: Naiskos with youth and boy*

88 *Volute-krater by the Painter of Copenhagen 4223: Naiskos with youth by horse*

189 *Volute-krater by the Painter of Copenhagen 4223: Naiskos with youth by laver*

190–1 Volute-krater, Berlin-Branca Group: Herakles and Hippolyte/stele scene

192–3 Calyx-krater, Berlin-Branca Group: Prometheus/Dionysiac scene

194 Calyx-krater by the Hippolyte Painter: Dionysos and Ariadne

195 Calyx-krater by the Laodamia Painter: Phaedra (?) Wedding feast of Pirithous

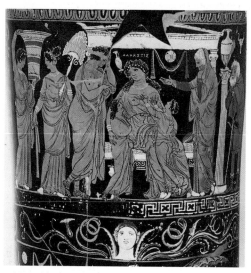

196 *Loutrophoros, near Laodamia Painter: Alkestis*

197 *Volute-krater by the De Schulthess Painter: Arrival of Helen of Troy*

199 *Volute-krater by the De Schulthess Painter: Gigantomachy*

198 *Volute-krater by the De Schulthess Painter: Arms of Achilles*

200 Calyx-krater, pre-Darian:
Oedipus at Colonus

201 Amphora by the Darius Painter:
Alexander and Darius (?)

202 Loutrophoros by the Darius Painter:
Zeus and the judgement of Adonis

203 Volute-krater by the Darius Painter: Darius

204 *Volute-krater by the Darius Painter: Funeral of Patroclus*

205 Calyx-krater by the Darius
Painter: The daughters of Anios

206 Calyx-krater by the Darius
Painter: Alkmene

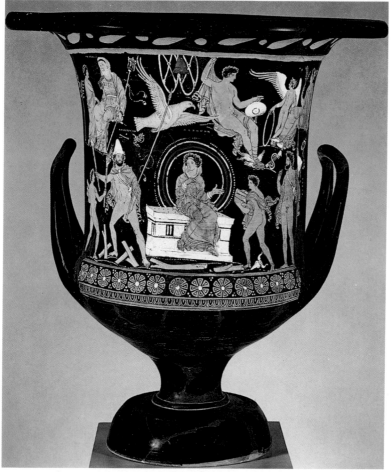

207 Dish, Phrixos Group: Fish

208 Lekythos by the Underworld Painter:
Rape of the Leucippidae

209 *Volute-krater by the Underworld Painter: The Underworld*

210 *Volute-krater by the Underworld Painter: Melanippe*

211 Calyx-krater by the Underworld Painter: Punishment of Dirce

213 Hydria, Darius-Underworld Group: Woman and youth

212 Pelike, Underworld Group: Laver scene

222 (above) Skyphos,
Alabastra Group: Eros

226 Bell-krater, Chevron
Group: Head of warrior
(Archidamos III)

223 Plastic vase in shape of ship's
prow

224-5 (below) Bell-krater,
Chevron Group

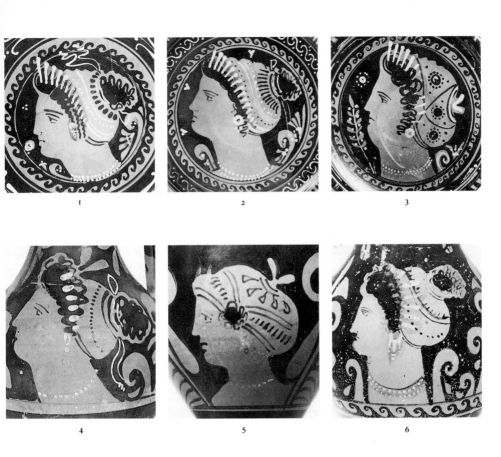

1 2 3

4 5

6

7

8

227 Typical female heads on vases of the Darius-Underworld workshop

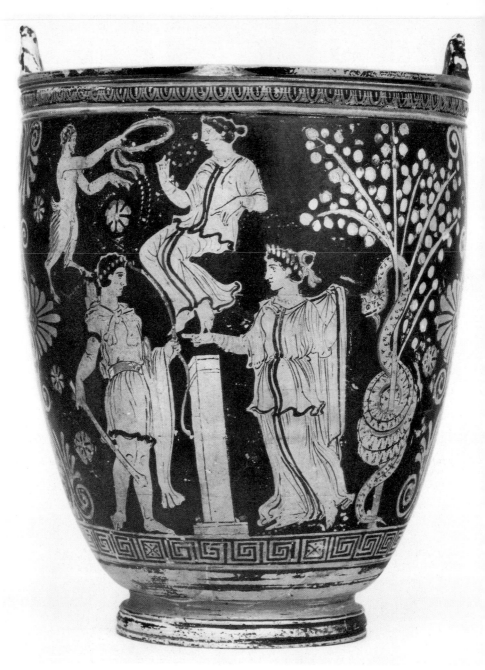

228 *Situla by the Ascoli Satriano Painter: Herakles and Hesperid*

229–30 Volute-krater by the Patera Painter: Naiskos/stele scene

231 *Dish by the Patera Painter: Aphrodite escorted by two Erotes*

232–3 *Column-krater by the Patera Painter: Woman and warrior/2 draped youths*

234–5 Column-krater, Trieste Owl Group   236 Volute-krater by the Painter of New York 17.120.240

1

2

3

4

5

6

7

8

9

237 Female heads by the Amphorae and Armidale Painters

238-9 *Volute-krater by the Ganymede Painter: Naiskos/stele scene*

240 *Neck of volute-krater by the Ganymede Painter: Ganymede and the swan*

241 *Hydria by the Ganymede Painter: Apollo and Artemis*

242 *Hydria by the Ganymede Painter: Niobe*

243 Cup, Group of the Trieste Askoi: Eros

244 Oenochoe (shape 1) by the Menzies Painter

245 Oenochoe, Menzies Group: Eros

246 Rhyton, Menzies Group: Eros

247 Cup, Menzies Group: Eros

248–9 Volute-krater by the Baltimore
Painter: Naiskos scenes

250 Detail of volute-krater by the
Baltimore Painter: Warrior in naiskos

251 (top left) Volute-krater by the
Baltimore Painter: Adonis

252 (top right) Details of volute-krater
by the Baltimore Painter: Slaughter
of the Niobids

253 Details of hydria by the
Baltimore Painter: Rape of
Persephone

1   2   3

4   5   6

7   8   9

254 Female heads on vases by the Stoke-on-Trent Painter and later followers

255 *Loutrophoros without handles by the White Sakkos Painter*

256 *Details of volute-krater by the White Sakkos Painter: Mythological scenes*

257 Volute-krater by the White Sakkos Painter:
Fountain-house

258 Oenochoe, White Sakkos-Chariot Group

259 Dish,
White Sakkos-Stuttgart Group

261 Reverse of amphora by the Helmet Painter: Stele scene

260 Volute-krater by the Capodimonte Painter: Amazonomachy

262 Oenochoe (shape 8) by the Painter of Berlin F 3383

263 Details of barrel-amphora by the Painter of Berlin F 3383

4 Details of amphora by the Arpi Painter: The freeing of Hera

5 Details of hydria by the Arpi Painter: Slaughter of the Niobids

266 Volute-krater by the Arpi Painter: Death of Semele

267 (above) Oenochoe (shape 1), Wind Group:
Gigantomachy

268 Volute-krater by the Virginia
Exhibition Painter

269 Barrel amphora by the Virginia Exhibition
Painter

270 Scylla askos by the Mignot Painter

Chapter Five

CAMPANIAN

Introduction

Of the three main red-figure fabrics in Campania, two seem to have been located in Capua and the near vicinity, and the third at Cumae. Generally speaking, the terracotta is of a comparatively pale shade, a light orange-yellow at Cumae, buff or café-au-lait elsewhere, and a pink or red wash is often applied to the surface to improve its appearance. Added white is used extensively, especially for the visible flesh of women, particularly in the AV and CA Groups. The range of subjects is comparatively limited; mythology plays a smaller part than in Apulian, but very characteristic is the appearance of warriors in Samnite armour (e.g. [314]), with a three-disk breastplate and feathered helmet, or of women dressed in local costume. These find parallels in the tomb-paintings and on a few vases from Paestum, but are quite distinct from those found on Apulian vases. However, in the last third of the century there is a strong wave of Apulian influence on both Campanian and Paestan, probably due to the arrival of migrant artists, and the 'xylophone' and naiskos, hitherto confined to Apulian, appear in the west for the first time, though the typically Apulian volute-krater is not found in Campania, nor are the column-krater, loutrophoros, nestoris and rhyton, and the pelike is extremely rare. [279] illustrates a characteristic local shape, the bail-amphora. Inscriptions of any kind are seldom found.

Red-figure vase-production seems to have begun at Capua shortly before the middle of the century, and at Cumae very slightly later. At the head of the first Capuan school stands the Cassandra Painter, from whom descend, on the one hand, the Laghetto and Caivano Painters, and, on the other, the Parrish Painter and his associates; its later development is seen in the work of the Ixion Painter and it sinks into near barbarism with the Siamese Painter. The second school effectively begins with the Capua Painter, but consists mainly of the AV Group, so called 'because many of the vases in it have been attributed to a fabric of Avella', and comes to an end with the Fillet Group. Both schools have their origin in Sicilian of the early fourth century. The third school was located at Cumae; this is well attested by the extensive finds at that site from excavations there during the last third of the 19th century.

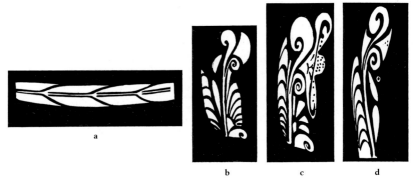

Fig. 7 Laurel and floral patterns on vases of the Cassandra-Parrish workshop – (a) and (b) Cassandra Painter; (c) Parrish Painter; (d) Three-dot Group

The school of the Cassandra Painter and his successors

For the forerunners of the Cassandra Painter we must look to Sicily. It has already been noted that some of the vases by the Dirce Painter and the Painter of Naples 2074 made their way into Campania; early Paestan owes a good deal to them, Campanian rather less. Their followers, however, and in particular, the Prado/Fienga Painter and his school, had a very considerable influence, and many elements in the work of the Cassandra Painter may be traced back to their vases, especially to those of the Revel Painter and the Eros and Hare Painter, who, on the basis of established proveniences, might very well have been active in Campania. The name vase of the Revel Painter [271] comes from the Blacas Tomb at Nola, and it clearly shows the influence of the Prado/Fienga Painter [272] in the treatment of the satyrs and the drapery, and also in its decorative patterns. [273], by the Cassandra Painter, well illustrates his neat figures, with their small heads and finely-drawn faces, as well as his fondness for elaborate pattern-work. To him and his circle may be assigned numerous vases, often of small dimensions, including a few with mythological scenes like Perseus and Andromeda, the birth of Helen, or Alkmene on the pyre. Typical is the presence of a laurel-wreath with leaves shaped like a parallelogram (Fig. 7a), and of a large fan-shaped motif, sometimes with a white border, for the florals in the side scrolls (Fig. 7b). His style is closely followed by the painters in the Spotted Rock Group [274] and by the Laon Painter, whose manner of drawing is sketchier.

The Parrish Painter, named after the former owner of [275], follows closely on from the Cassandra Painter, but lacks the fineness and elegance of his drawing. His figures look coarser, their heads are heavier [276], and their faces are often shown in three-quarter view, but rather carelessly drawn. There is a certain affectation in their poses. On his later vases the quality declines still

158

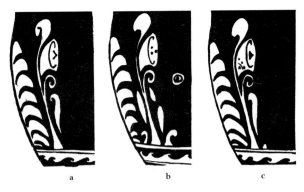

Fig. 8 Floral patterns by – (a) the Laghetto Painter; (b) the Caivano Painter; (c) the Painter of B.M. F 63

further. Characteristic is the presence of a large floral (*Fig. 7c*) with dots on the protruding central stamen and within the curving black line which serves as a border to the petals; also the use of a crossed square with solid black squares on the border of each of the four intersections and in the centre, as on [*277*]. The painter likes to include dogs and horses in his compositions. A few of his vases have mythological subjects – Paris and Helen [*275*], Alkmene, Europa on the bull, Orestes at Delphi – and a couple depict phlyax scenes [*277*]; mostly they depict warriors or youths. A group of lesser artists imitate his work, without improving upon it; their drawing is often sketchy and, at times, slovenly.

The Cassandra-Parrish workshop also included a number of minor artists who decorated numerous vases of comparatively small dimensions, especially neck- and bail-amphorae, with single figures of satyrs, women, or youths, which show little originality. The florals in the side-scrolls are sometimes like those of the Parrish Painter and at others are decorated with a cluster of three dots, which has given rise to its name of the Three-dot Group (*Fig. 7d*); on the necks of the amphorae, there are frequently female heads in profile [*278*], usually with the hair caught up in a sakkos or *kekryphalos*; occasionally the head of a youth or satyr appears instead. Few of the individual artists emerge as real personalities – among these is the Plouton-VPH (= Vienna, Philadelphia, Hamm) Painter [*279*], whose youths look very well-fed or else, like Pooh-Bah, to have been born sneering. The end of this line comes with the Capua Silen Painter, whose drawing is crude and sketchy, but whose dotted flowers look back to those of the Parrish Painter.

The neat and precise style of the Cassandra Painter is best continued in the work of his closest follower, the Laghetto Painter [*280*], who stands at the head of a school which includes the Caivano Painter, the Painter of B.M. F 63, the Errera Painter and several minor associates. The Laghetto Painter starts off in a manner very like that of his master, but soon develops a more individual style, which is copied by his followers. They make a considerable use of added white, yellow and red, which gives their vases a colourful look, and their choice of subjects is of greater interest and variety. The draped youths on the reverses often wear himatia with dotted borders; the cloaks tend to project some distance in front of the body to cover an extended arm; a spray is often held in one hand.

Fig. 8 illustrates the three types of flower which accompany the side-scrolls – (a) with an acute angle in the centre (Laghetto), (b) with three dots and a white stamen (Caivano), (c) a solid black central triangle (B.M. F 63; Errera).

Several vases by the Laghetto and Caivano Painters have been found at Paestum – the latter was originally classed as Paestan – but it now seems better to regard them as Campanians (cf. the use of the bail-amphora), but not to exclude the possibility that either or both might have worked at Paestum for a time; their influence is particularly clear on the work of the Painter of Naples 1778, who is certainly Paestan. Noteworthy is the Caivano Painter's fondness for rocks of the lava flow type (cf. [282]); he also makes considerable use of white dot-clusters, ivy leaves, hanging fillets or bead-chains, phialai, and a half sun's disk with rays as adjuncts in the field above the pictures. Also characteristic is the single palmette leaf, which rises from the ground, sometimes from a small calyx; this is copied in a slightly modified form by the Painter of Naples 1778 (see p. 206). The Caivano Painter has an extensive repertory of stock figures, notably a youth with short hair, blocked-in in black, sometimes with a chlamys hanging down his back and a white pilos, a bearded male figure, a woman in full face, whose hair falls in a series of curly locks on either side of her head and who wears a tunic with a ray-pattern border round the neck [281], and a young satyr with a thyrsus [283]. On a few of his vases we see Samnite warriors with their typical breastplates and crested helmets with an upright feather on either side; others show mythological scenes – the birth of Helen [281], the departure of Bellerophon, the ambush of Dolon [282], the slaying of Troilos, the sacrifice of Polyxena, the death of Myrtilos, the triumph of Apollo over Marsyas, as well as a couple which have not yet been satisfactorily explained.

The Painter of B.M. F 63 [284] is a prolific artist who worked in close collaboration with the two painters just discussed, but whose style of drawing is coarser, as may be seen from the heavier heads of his figures, and their less careful rendering, especially of those below the handles of hydriai or on the necks of amphorae, which tend to assume a rather rectangular look. His hydriai [284], like those of other painters in this school, have broad, flat shoulders, a tapering body and a foot in two degrees with a groove between them; all would appear to be the work of a single potter, and this provides a further connecting link between the various painters who decorated them. The Errera Painter stands close to him in style; he regularly paints the visible flesh of his female figures in white; they normally wear a short peplos with an overfall below a beaded girdle and have long hair which falls down on to their shoulders in rather straggly locks.

160

The Errera Painter likes white wreaths *285* and also makes frequent use of rocks, often with large black dots, but not of the lava flow variety. His subjects are less intriguing and deal mostly with women and warriors. Around these four artists may be grouped a number of minor painters, who imitate their work in both subject-matter and style.

The Ixion Painter, active in the last third of the 4th century, represents the final flowering of the Cassandra school, which after him sinks into near barbarism. He is one of the most important of all the later Campanian vase-painters and his style, while descended from that of the Cassandra and Parrish Painters, also reflects the influence not only of contemporary Apulian but also that of Attic vases of the later Kerch style. He is a monumental painter who decorates large vases, especially amphorae and bell-kraters, with impressive mythological scenes; a bell-krater in Oxford, representing Boreas carrying off Oreithyia *286* is a good example, and, even better, is another, recently acquired by the Louvre, depicting the slaying of the suitors, which crams no fewer than fifteen figures in various attitudes of attack, defence, agony and death on to the obverse. Other vases depict scenes of battle or conflict, a wide range of well-known myths (e.g. Bellerophon and the chimaera, Pelops and Hippodamia), including some which may well be of theatrical inspiration (e.g. Medea slaying one of her children, Orestes at Delphi, the escape of Iphigenia from the Taurians, the murder of Aegisthus, Andromeda); one actually represents an actor, with the satyr mask he has been wearing drawn up on top of his head *287*. He is fond of representing faces in near-frontal or three-quarter view; they often have a flattish look, with a tendency for the mouth to assume a downward turn. Drapery is generally simple, with clearly marked fold-lines, which when drawn transversely, can give it a swirling look. Added colours are widely used, and a few of his vases look almost polychrome, with pink, blue and green as well as the normal white, yellow and red. The draped youths who regularly figure on his reverses *288* often wear large white wreaths around their heads, sometimes with tall white spikes which stick up above the head, giving a somewhat crown-like effect. His pattern-work is elaborate and very distinctive; his palmette-fans often have sprung leaves (i.e. curving inwards instead of outwards); the florals are usually fan-shaped with a white edge and they are sometimes decorated with a line of black dots; on some of the later vases comb-palmettes appear, probably under the influence of the Apulianizing school at Cumae. A constantly recurring and highly individual feature is the single leaf, with a hook at the lower end, which gives it something of the appearance of a jumping-weight or even of a knife (*Fig. 9*).

Fig. 9 *Floral pattern by the Ixion Painter*

From his workshop, perhaps even sometimes from his own hand, come a number of small vases, mostly decorated with single figures, including many, especially skyphoi, depicting a warrior holding a large, round shield and a spear [289]; others have female heads [290], frequently wearing sakkoi, comparable to those which appear below the handles of his hydriai or on the necks of amphorae.

Lastly we may cast a brief glance on the near-barbarized vases which mark the end of this fabric. Some were found with late vases by the Caivano Painter and his followers, which suggests a starting date of c. 320 for the group, in which there are two principal artists, the Atella Painter, who follows on from the later minor artists of the Cassandra workshop, and the Siamese Painter, who lapses into almost complete barbarism. The former has little understanding of human anatomy, his faces are badly drawn, the proportions of the body often awry, with the head too small and the body too long, and exceptionally clumsy feet. The latter rapidly descends into barbarism, and his figures degenerate into something that can hardly be called human [291].

It should be noted that a substantial number of fish-plates are associated with the workshop of the Cassandra Painter and his successors. Like the normal vases, the earliest of these have a Sicilian connection; plates by the Bastis Painter have been found in Palermo, at various sites on the west coast of South Italy, at Agropoli near Paestum, at Paestum itself, and finally at Cumae. Certain plates of the Grassi (*Fig. 10a*) and Lyman Allyn Groups have the typical laurel leaves on the rim, shaped like a parallelogram, and must therefore be associated with the Cassandra workshop. The excavations at Porta S. Prisco in 1970 brought to light one tomb which contained eight vases (including the Andromeda amphora) by the Ixion Painter, together with a fish-plate in a highly individual style (*Fig. 10b*), which, if not by the painter's own hand, must at least be a product of his workshop, and therefore enables us to associate with it some fifty or more other fish-plates. There is also a further group of fish-plates, which are close in style to Paestan, but which look to be Campanian; many of them depict a torpedo (*Fig. 10c*), marked with black and white spots – hence the name Torpedo Group – and they probably come from the workshop of the Laghetto and Caivano Painters, whose connection with Paestan has already been noted.

a   b   c

Fig. 10 Campanian fish-plates – (a) once Los Angeles Market = GRFP IIA/13 (Grassi Painter); (b) Naples 184034 = GRFP 11B/18 (Adelaide-S. Prisco Painter, Ixion workshop); (c) Paestum 31716 (Torpedo Painter)

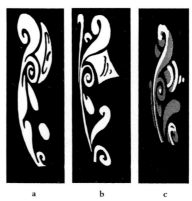

Fig. 11 Florals on vases of the AV Group

a   b   c

The Capua Painter and the AV Group

As with the workshop of the Cassandra Painter, the immediate forerunners of the vases discussed in this section seem also to have been of Sicilian origin. Two artists, in particular, serve to illustrate this connection – the Mad-Man (Madrid-Manchester) and NYN (New York-Naples) Painters. Vases by the former have been found at Lipari and at Paestum, by the latter at Lipari, Laos, Paestum, Pontecagnano and Cumae, which lends support to theory that either or both of them might have moved from Sicily up the western coast to Campania, as may well also have been the case with the Bastis Painter. There are close stylistic connections between their vases and those by the Prado/Fienga and Revel Painters, especially in the drawing of the heads, the rendering of the drapery and decorative patterns, particularly in the florals which appear on the side scrolls beside the fan-palmettes below the handles. Those of the NYN Painter *[292]* lead directly on to the typical florals of the Capua and Whiteface Painters (*Fig. 11*), just as both the latter artists have clearly been influenced by him in their treatment of running draped women. Phlyakes also appear on several of their vases and do so in this group far more frequently than in the preceding one. Otherwise the early vases mostly have banal subjects – women often running in one direction and looking back in other, as on *[292]*, youths, satyrs, Eros.

    The Capua Painter is a prolific but uninspired artist, with a peculiar treatment of female heads, which tend to have long necks, encircled by a necklace of black beads, and to wear a sakkos, patterned with lines and dots and sticking out at the back to cover the chignon. The face has a very linear look, with a pointed nose, a short line for the nostril, thickish lips with a slightly downward-curving line for the mouth, and a vertical stroke for the pupil of the eye *[293/1]*. An oft-repeated figure is a standing or running woman, wearing a long peplos, sometimes with a vertical black stripe, and a sakkos. His draped youths *[293/2]* stand stiffly, wrapped in their cloaks, which often have dot-stripe borders; one hand projects

163

slightly beneath the drapery and often holds a leafy spray. Added white is used extensively for adjuncts and sometimes for the visible flesh of women, a practice very common on vases of the AV Group. There is a limited range of subjects, mostly Dionysiac or funerary; the latter include many stele scenes, but they seem to be generic rather than to deal with any specific legend, even if at times they look to have been inspired by representations of the meeting of Orestes and Elektra. The stele usually consists of a column, on top of which is an anthemion, sometimes flanked by wing-like structures. Other vases show warriors, or women pouring them a libation on their departure or return; large numbers of smaller ones depict single figures or various birds or animals, often of rather inferior quality. *[294]*, by one of his followers, shows a phlyax actor coming upon an infant in swaddling clothes, a scene obviously inspired by Middle Comedy.

The AV Group runs closely parallel to the Capua Painter; it includes three principal artists – the Whiteface/Frignano, Libation and Danaid Painters – and a number of less significant associates. The vases originally attributed to the Whiteface and Frignano Painters have now come together as the work of a single artist in a workshop which produced about 300 extant vases, mostly between *c.* 360 and 330 BC; their subjects are on the whole unimaginative, with only an occasional venture into mythology, like *[295]* with the Hesperides, or *[296]* with a spirited version of Cadmus attacking the dragon by a flowery spring. Very typical are his female figures, often with white flesh, who wear a peplos, with a central black stripe, beneath which their breasts, with small round nipples, are clearly visible. The hair is caught up in a sakkos or *kekryphalos*, and a stephane, either radiate or beaded, is often worn; they commonly hold a box, on top of which is a row of eggs. Youths on the obverses are mostly nude and they often adopt a relaxed pose, in the Praxitelean manner, with one leg flexed at the knee; hands tend to droop in a rather languid fashion; a small white bird may be perched upon them. On the reverses *[297]* the youths are either fully or half draped in their himatia, which normally have plain black borders, and occasionally billow out behind as if caught by the wind; a plain white chaplet is worn round the head or sometimes a beaded or leafy wreath. Small weights in added white regularly appear at the corners of their cloaks. The painter's attempts at rendering faces in frontal or three-quarter view are not very successful.

The typical florals (*Fig. 11b–c*) are either diamond-shaped with black and white strokes across them or fan-shaped with two or more thick white lines. The meander-band below the pictures is not accompanied by crossed squares, but can be replaced by an egg and dot, which is also used at the handle-joins, or by wave-pattern. As with the Capua Painter, there is a large output of smaller vases, either by the painter himself or his workshop associates, of whom perhaps the Andover Painter *[298]* is the most significant; he paints female heads with a rather forbidding look.

Perhaps the most characteristic vases of the AV Group are those by the Libation Painter and his two chief colleagues, the Astarita and Manchester Painters [*299–306*]. They are fond of depicting scenes with Samnite warriors, often in the company of a woman, who wears a cape fastened with a brooch at the throat, and a peculiar local headdress [*300*], of rather medieval aspect. The Astarita Painter's [*299/1*] neat and careful drawing, and his pattern-work and florals, owe much to the Whiteface/Frignano Painter; the draping of the youths on his reverses [*299/2*] is characteristic, on the one facing to left the himation is so draped over the body as to envelop the bent left arm, and then to fall after the manner of a sleeve, the lower portion of which assumes the shape of a parallelogram. Fold-lines are drawn with precision and appear as a series of parallel lines at the top of the cloak, with a collar-like effect. His figures usually have small mouths, with a pouting lower lip and rounded chin; the pupil of the eye is a small black dot, but more correctly placed than on the vases of the Libation Painter, on which, in consequence, figures often have a frozen or staring aspect. He also uses white for the exposed flesh of women and for the chaplets round the heads of his youths. One of the finest of the vases associated with him, a few of which also have mythological subjects, is [*300*], which shows a woman in native costume, with a deep red cape, holding the bridle of the horse her husband is riding; behind her is her maid, with oenochoe and phiale ready for the libation pouring, and below the handles, large female heads.

The vases of the Libation Painter [*301–5*] may be divided into three main groups according to their subjects. On the first are the scenes of libation [*301*] which gave the painter his name; on the second, funerary scenes with women and youths or warriors grouped around some form of grave-monument, in most cases a stele [*302*], rising from a stepped base on which various offerings, like vases, eggs, pomegranates or fillets have been placed, on others an anthemion-like monument or even a statue of the deceased, painted white to simulate the marble or stuccoed stone of the original. On the third are scenes associated with mythology – the ambush of Troilos, Athena equipping Perseus, Iphigenia in Tauris [*303*] – or with Dionysos and the theatre, including several depicting phlyakes, on one of which [*304*] the stage is shown, with the flute-player dressed in the long robe of the musician. [*305*] shows Niobe at the tomb of her slain children; in front of it is a row of offerings. She listens unheedingly to the plea of her aged father Tantalos, and the lower part of her body is painted white to symbolise her forthcoming petrification (cf. [*183, 242*]).

In the work of the Libation Painter and his associates we may note an increasing use of added colours, especially various shades of red, at times almost moving towards polychromy. His florals are fan-shaped with white edges; his meander-bands are accompanied by saltires, but he often uses wave-pattern or strokes beneath his pictures. Windows often appear in the field above, together with various adjuncts like half-shields, phialai, tasselled bead-chains and rosettes. His draped youths usually wear white chaplets; one of them often has his cloak draped over one shoulder to leave the other bare. From his workshop also come numerous small vases decorated with single figures taken from the larger compositions.

One of his later followers is the Manchester Painter *[306]*; his style is very characteristic, and we should note his treatment of the nude male body, with its soft muscles, and of the head, with solid black hair, a tall spiky diadem, staring eye, small depressed mouth and rounded chin. His treatment of the face is distinctive; it is modelled on that of the Libation Painter, but in its mannerism goes a good deal further, until at times it almost becomes a caricature. Typical also are his florals, especially the bell-shaped flower, with a black oval in the centre. In his choice of subjects, he follows closely along the lines of his predecessors – libations to departing warriors, funerary and Dionysiac scenes (one including a phlyax), and an occasional excursion into mythology (Bellerophon).

The work of the Danaid Painter *[307–9]*, while clearly connected with that of the other artists in the AV Group, also reflects a measure of Paestan influence, especially that of the Boston Orestes Painter, in his compositions and pattern-work. His terracotta is of a pale buff shade and a wash, ranging from pink to deep red, is often applied to his vases; much use is made of added white and yellow, but little of red or other colours. In general, his backgrounds are more decorative than those on other AV vases, with an extensive use of plants, saplings and flowers; birds and animals figure extensively in subsidiary roles; ground-lines are in added white. In his larger compositions the figures may be disposed on different levels *[307]*, but he prefers those with only two or three. His drawing of the head and face is very characteristic; the nose is small and often rather pointed; the mouth, also small, is slightly depressed, the chin rounded. The pupil of the eye is a dot, often so placed as to give the figures a rather intent look. Women wear their hair with a large bunch on top of their head; men's hair is short and shown as a solid mass; the usual headdress is a leafy wreath or a string of beads, sometimes doubled. Figures often hold beaded wreaths, on which the beads are attached to the wreath and not placed around it in the usual way. Drapery is simple; women mostly wear a high-girt peplos, without a black stripe or border, and the contours of the body are clearly visible beneath it; their breasts are small and rounded. Many of the Danaid Painter's vases include a female head in the decoration – on the necks of amphorae, beneath the handles of hydriai, or as the main subject. There are two main types – in one the hair is done up in a *sphendone*, decorated with lines and rows of dots *[307]*, in the other it is covered by a sakkos, similarly patterned, with a rosette at the back. White is seldom used for female flesh. *[308]* shows the influence of Paestan, since the elaborate, multiple lid is typical of that fabric; the same is true of the side palmettes. He is less partial to stele or libation scenes, and paints a few vases with interesting mythological subjects, like *[307]*, with Orestes and Elektra, his name vase with the Danaides, or one showing a river-god in the form of a man-headed bull, bearing a woman on his back, while the bust of a veiled woman looks down from a window above *[309]*. A large group of minor vases associated with this painter depict swans, panthers and other animals.

After the painters of the AV Group, there is a swift decline with the Painter of Catania 737 *[310]* and the Fillet Painter *[311]* into near barbarism. The former preserves a closer relationship to the AV Group in his treatment of the hair and of drapery; his side palmettes, with their scrolls and three-petalled florals (*Fig. 12*), are very typical. His drawing is sketchy and is subject to a rapid deterioration; *[310]* is one of his better vases, and shows a draped woman holding a white-bearded mask in her hand; her drapery has his characteristic wave-pattern decoration. His more ambitious vases are less

Fig. 12 *Floral by the Painter of Catania 737*

successful and prepare us for the descent to the Fillet Group *[311]*, where the drawing has almost completely disintegrated and the figures become scarcely human, though the palmettes, florals and chequered squares show the connection with the earlier vases.

The Fabric of Cumae

The fabric of Cumae seems to have come into existence around the middle of the fourth century; it comprises some 1500 vases, so closely interconnected in shape, style, subjects and ornamental decoration that they can hardly be considered as other than products of a single workshop, in which a comparatively large staff of painters and potters was employed. There are three main stages in the development of the fabric, which have been designated Cumae A, B and C. The chief artist of the first stage is the CA (= Cumae A) Painter *[312–16]*, who has two close associates, the Fuscillo *[318]* and LNO Painters. In the later part of his career, the CA Painter comes under the influence of the APZ (= Apulianizing) Painter *[322–5]*, who brought to Campanian many typically Apulian features (e.g. the 'xylophone' and the naiskos), which now appear on the former's vases and on those of his followers like the Painter of New York GR 1000 *[319–20]* or the Boston Ready Painter *[326–8]*. Cumae B consists of the work of the immediate successors of these painters, in which we find a sort of blended style, wherein the Apulian elements have been more fully assimilated, notably the Nicholson and Branicki Painters and their associates *[329–33]*, who must have been active in the last third of the century. Finally, in Cumae C we find a continuation of the tradition of the Rhomboid Group, but with an increasingly impressionistic manner of drawing and a greater tendency towards polychromy *[334–8]*.

The vases of the CA Painter *[312–16]* tend to have a bright and rather pleasing

| a | b | c | d |

Fig. 13 Florals on Cumaean vases

aspect, partly due to the attractive light orange colour of the terracotta and even more to the plentiful use of added white and yellow, with occasional touches of red, for drapery or details, and to the application of a pink to red wash, which is particularly noticeable on the pattern-work. White is also used for women's exposed flesh, and they are often not more than half-draped. The preferred shapes for larger vases are the amphora, hydria and bell-krater, for smaller vases, the skyphos, lebes gamikos and squat lekythos. No calyx-kraters have as yet turned up, but a few new shapes, such as askoi and gutti, appear, perhaps as a result of Apulian influence. The subjects cover a much narrower range than in the other Campanian fabrics. Warriors in Samnite armour play a very prominent part, often in ritual scenes, accompanied by women with offerings, grouped around a stele; sometimes only the women are present. A few hydriai depict naiskos scenes, under the influence of Apulian, further manifest in the 'xylophone' often suspended above the figure in the naiskos, who is invariably female *[314]*. There are also Dionysiac scenes, including symposia with masks hanging above the banqueters *[315]*, but so far this is the only connection with the theatre to be found on this painter's vases. Mythological scenes are very rare; the only certain one at present is the Judgement of Paris on a lekanis lid *[316]*, which well illustrates the work of the CA Painter at its best. We may note, in particular, the delicacy and elegance of his drawing, both in the faces and the drapery, with its fine fold-lines in diluted glaze; it does, however, tend to give his figures, even the warriors, a slightly soft look. The most popular subject for the reverses *[313]* is a draped woman seated on a folding stool, with a tambourine or phiale in her hands, confronting a standing figure, either a youth or a woman, enveloped in a himation; between them there may be a stele, with offerings on top and sometimes with a wreath round the shaft. Saplings play a large part as accessory decoration in the field, with hanging fillets above, or open wreaths, phialai, windows, and tasselled bead-chains suspended from small tablets. The

CA Painter makes frequent use of a fawn-skin as a covering for his seats. The pattern-work is elaborate, especially on the larger vases, where tiers of palmettes, springing from acanthus, with their leaves sometimes outlined in white or, at others, hatched, rise up below the handles; on bell-kraters the pictures are often framed by a tall palmette scroll, with a floral above and a palmette below the central spiral; the latter may take the form of a half-fan, bisected down the middle of the central leaf, the top of which assumes a half-diamond form (*Fig. 13a*), to the shape of which the adjoining leaf is adjusted in a very characteristic manner, or else of a comb (*Fig. 13c–d*), with longer or shorter leaves, especially on the later vases. The florals assume various forms, sometimes decorated with curving black lines (*Fig. 13a*), sometimes with a white stamen (*Fig. 13b*), and later with two petals in profile (*Fig. 13d*), one each side of the raised centre portion. His smaller vases are, as usual, decorated with single figures, usually a woman or a draped youth, but many also depict female heads, similar to those on the necks of his amphorae. These may be of a more elaborate kind with a tall radiate diadem above the brow, and the hair confined in a sakkos, usually decorated with lines and rows of dots, or caught up in a *kekryphalos*, with a large bunch emerging at the back, or else treated in a plainer fashion without the diadem [*317/1–2*].

Two close collaborators of the CA Painter are the Fuscillo [*318*] and LNO (Lausanne-Nostell Priory) Painters, who closely copy his subjects, style and patterns; their drawing is, however, less refined, the faces are heavier and coarser and the reverses usually represent two draped youths, wearing white chaplets or spiky wreaths. Large rosettes with white-tipped petals regularly appear in the upper field. The LNO Painter is unique in Cumaean in that he decorated two vases with phlyax scenes, which do not otherwise appear in this fabric. Probably also to be associated with the CA workshop is a group of about 200 fish-plates, by the Robinson Painter (*Fig. 14a*) and his followers. They are readily identified by his characteristic treatment of the fish, which consist mainly of varieties of

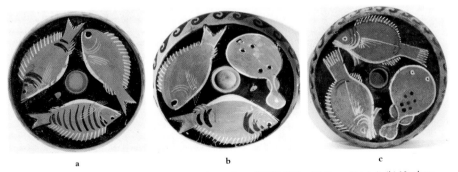

a   b   c

Fig. 14 Cumaean fish-plates – (a) once Los Angeles Market = GRFP IIC/12 (Robinson Painter); (b) Hamburg, Termer coll. = GRFP IIC/20a (Robinson Painter); (c) Naples 205193 = GRFP IIC/76 (Three-stripe Painter)

bream, with a torpedo. Two-banded and striped bream are very popular, their eyes are shown as a large black dot with a white border round the lower part, but not encircling the pupil; torpedoes usually have a round body, outlined in white, and decorated with four black dots, as on *Fig. 14b*. *Fig. 14c* shows a slightly later plate in the 'Three-Stripe' Group, on which the fish have three parallel black lines to indicate the gills and horizontal lines across their bodies; the torpedo has a large cluster of black dots either at the top or at the bottom of its body, with the tail and fins outlined in white.

The Painter of New York GR 1000 *[319]* looks to have been a pupil of the CA Painter, but to have begun at a fairly late stage in the latter's career, since his work is clearly under the influence of the APZ Painter, especially in his treatment of draped youths. Shapes, pattern-work and subjects follow closely after those of the CA Painter, but his figures are treated on an ampler scale and are not normally disposed at different levels on the surface of the vases. The floral patterns accompanying the side palmettes are usually of the two-petal type (*Fig. 13d*), as on the later CA vases. His range of subjects is similarly restricted, but his reverses usually show two or more draped youths *[320]*, wearing thick white head-bands with a row of beads above, although a few copy the standard CA type with a seated draped woman facing a standing draped youth. The female heads on some of his smaller vases show a very characteristic drawing of the mouth *[317/3]*, in which the lips are almost closed, there is a dot at the base of the nostril, a short line for the mouth, and another dot below it; the hair is shown as a round mass over the ear, with a dot-cluster on it to represent an earring.

The contents of two tombs excavated at Cumae in 1878–80 shed some light upon the comparative chronology of these artists and the APZ Painter. Tomb 127 contained three vases by the LNO Painter and three by the Painter of New York GR 1000; Tomb 185, three by the CA Painter, four by the APZ Painter and five by the Painter of New York GR 1000. The general uniformity of shape, style and subject-matter of all these vases suggests that they must have all been painted around the same time, perhaps as a specific commission, probably between 330 and 320. It looks, therefore, as if we should place the Apulian artistic migration around 330 (cf. also with Paestan), perhaps at the time when the Tarentines sent envoys to Naples to try to persuade its inhabitants not to ally themselves with Rome, which in fact they did in 327. The first of the migrant artists is the Ivy-Leaf Painter, whose work is almost purely Apulian, and close in style to that of the Lucera Painter. Several of his vases come from Canosa, where he may have begun his career; others have a Campanian provenience, and his use of white for the flesh of women *[321]* is an indication of assimilation to the local practice. The APZ Painter brings to Campania Apulian devices like the naiskos or 'xylophone', but he decorates Campanian shapes like the bail- or neck-amphora *[322–4]*, he paints the exposed flesh of women in white (not an Apulian practice), and his drapery and reverse youths *[323]* are more in the Campanian fashion than the Apulian, as is his pattern-work. He seems to have become assimilated to Campanian ways very rapidly. He is a prolific artist and over 200 vases may be attributed to his hand, many of them small and trivial pieces. His larger vases often represent groups of white-fleshed women [322, 324–5], sometimes with youths, holding a variety of objects, and as his style develops there is a pronounced elongation of their bodies, leading on to the characteristic style of the Boston Ready Painter [326]. Apart from the naiskoi or related funerary scenes [322], his subjects are dull; the warriors who figured so frequently upon the vases of the CA Group are hardly in evidence, nor does he venture into mythological or theatrical representations. The minor vases often bear female heads [317/4], modelled on those by the Painter of New York GR 1000, sometimes with the face painted white; there is an extensive series of skyphoi decorated with one or two draped youths on either side, which are certainly products of his workshop.

The Boston Ready Painter [326–8], named after his bell-krater in Boston formerly in the collection of Augustus Ready, as Beazley noted, has a style 'very like that of the CA Painter, but strangely exaggerated and stiffened'; this is indeed so, but from the draped youths on his reverses he looks even closer to the LNO Painter and he has certainly been strongly influenced by such a vase as Naples 856 [321] in the Apulianizing Group, as well as by the APZ Painter, especially in his compositions with women, who are very similar to those on the latter's vases. He, too, has a preference for ritual scenes, sometimes with a citharode and often with a laver; warriors appear infrequently and figures are seldom disposed over different levels. He makes extensive use of added white, sometimes of a matt, chalky hue, and at times all the figures on the vase are so painted. His figures are very elongated (cf. with the later work by the APZ Painter), with small heads in proportion to the rest of the body, and he makes extensive use of various adjuncts, notably a white bird perched on the knees of seated figures or on a laver, tall white sprays to serve as fountain-jets in lavers [328], also of incense-burners and cistae. Grave monuments take the form of tall white stelai or of an omphalos-shaped mound. Traces of polychromy in the form of added green or a deep red wash are sometimes to be seen. His scenes are generally static, the combat on Naples 127961 being exceptional, and even there the figures have a somewhat frozen look.

His influence is clearly reflected in the work of the Toulouse Painter, an artist of less ability and little imagination.

With the Nicholson Painter [329–31] we pass to the second generation of Cumaean vase-painters (Cumae B), whose work continues to reflect the tradition established by the CA Painter, but is profoundly affected by the Apulianizing Group, and is therefore best regarded as a development of that blended style we noted in the vases of the Painter of New York GR 1000. The earlier inspiration and skill in draughtsmanship, however, is beginning to fade out; the style is starting to deteriorate, the range of subjects diminishes, and stock themes and figures are repeated from vase to vase with little variation. Added

171

colour is used more sparingly, and the calyx-krater makes a rare appearance in this fabric. Several of the better vases by the Nicholson Painter have been found at Montesarchio (*anc.* Caudium); some depict naiskos scenes *[329]*, and one Nike driving a chariot, which finds an excellent parallel in one of the tomb-paintings at Paestum. Many of his vases are decorated with stock figures – a standing woman wearing a peplos, sometimes with a long overfall, or a seated woman who seems to perch on the edge of a box or similar support *[331]*. His reverses often depict two women at a stele *[330]*, a youth with a seated woman, or two draped youths; the drawing tends to be summary, as if the painter had lost interest in them, and the youths stand stiffly, one arm projecting outwards under the cloak, and a long white ribbon tied round the head and falling down their back. Wave-pattern is preferred below the pictures, which may be framed between bands of chevrons, but more usually by a tall scroll with a white-edged flower and perhaps a narrow comb palmette below it. A few minor artists – the Washington, Rio and Montauban Painters and the Painter of Copenhagen 244 – are closely associated with the Nicholson Painter, whose work they imitate, with a progressive decline in the quality of the drawing, which tends to become scrappy and careless. There are also numerous vases decorated only with female heads, some of which, in a rather stolid style *[317/5]*, seem to be by the Nicholson Painter himself.

The vases of the Rhomboid Group, mainly the work of two artists – the Branicki Painter and the Painter of B.M. F 229 – are contemporary with those of the Nicholson Painter and his followers, but are more individual in style. They show a greater range of subjects, and a persistent use of a filling ornament in the shape of a rhomboid, which gives the group its name. The palmette decoration below the handles and beside the pictures is also highly distinctive *[332]*. In addition to the standard representation of seated and standing women, we find Amazonomachies, symposia, grypomachies, chariots, and scenes seemingly associated with the Judgement of Paris – Athena or Hera preparing for the contest – and, on a later vase by the Painter of B.M. F 229, two Erotes decking Aphrodite. The reverses almost invariably figure two or three draped women *[333]*, standing in a row looking to the left, enveloped in himatia with a thick black U-shaped border at the neck. Otherwise women generally wear a peplos with a long overfall; often with a double black stripe down the centre; the drapery has a peculiarly stiff look, as if it had been starched, with the fold-lines running down in small bunches or radiating outwards with a kind of herring-bone effect. The human figures also tend to look rather stiff and the drawing of prostrate warriors is beyond the capacity of the painter. The work of the Painter of B.M. F 229 follows immediately on from that of the Branicki Painter, but his compositions are a little more ambitious and his vases of larger dimension. His draped women are, however, very similar to those on the Branicki Painter's vases. Both painters also decorated a number of minor vases with female heads *[317/6–7]*, those by the Branicki Painter characterized by a net-work pattern, not unlike a tennis racket, on the sakkos behind the ear *[317/6]*, those of his successors by their extreme heaviness *[317/7]*.

The final stage in Cumaean vase-painting comes with Cumae C, in which considerable modifications and developments take place in shape and decoration. The subjects are mainly concerned with the everyday life of women, and male figures play only a very secondary role. The bottle becomes a popular shape, perhaps under the influence of Sicilian, and is frequently decorated with a female head drawn in a much freer style than previously and enlivened by a touch of pink on the cheeks. The return to colour and even polychromy is noteworthy after the comparative monotony of Cumae B. Most of the vases in C belong to the last years of the fourth or the very beginning of the third century BC, a date which is confirmed by the finding at Teano, Salerno and other sites of such vases together with others decorated with net-pattern or patterns in applied white, as well as plain black wares and vases of the so-called *kemai* type. And it is interesting to note that the red-figure technique appears on some Cumae C vases along with the other techniques referred to, which suggests that they were for a season in active use at the same time, until red-figure gave way to the other varieties.

The vases of the Castelcapuano-White Bird Group are still close in their treatment of human figures to those of the Nicholson and Rhomboid Groups, but *[334]* illustrates the way in which the fold-lines of the drapery are beginning to break up. The process goes a stage further in the work of the Painter of B.M. F 247 *[335]*, where the drawing of the face has become slovenly, though his women look back to those by the Branicki Painter; on a vase like the curious spouted lebes *[336]* the figures have become distorted, though the rhomboid filling ornaments indicate its line of descent. The knob on the lid of this vase takes the form of a bottle decorated in added colour, and the head on the lower portion is rapidly losing any close connection with humanity. Similar heads appear as the sole decoration on some minor vases in this group.

The final phase of the Cumaean red-figure style is to be seen in a small group of vases from Teano. Their connection with the later vases of the CA Group is apparent in the palmette decoration, which is also very like that on the vases of the White Bird Group (cf. the white lines on the palmette stems). Drapery was painted white, though this has now largely disappeared, and a good deal of added colour was used, especially shades of pink. The drawing has become somewhat impressionistic, especially the tiny heads in proportion to much larger bodies, and the remarkable floral setting for the woman and Eros on *[338]* is spectacular, and is again an echo of the contemporary Apulian practice. The head on the reverse of the spouted lebes *[337]* is repeated on many of the smaller vases; the touch of red on the cheek is typical.

Our survey of Campanian may end with three late groups of vases which, however, barely come into the category of red-figure. The first is the so-called *Kemai* Group, a name given to it by Beazley from the inscription, beginning with that word, on a vase in the British Museum. The commonest shape is a small stamnoid or pyxis-like vessel with a lid, sometimes with vestigial handles close to the neck. On [317/8] there is a female head on either side of the shoulder, one in red-figure, the other painted white; they are comparable to those on a number of smaller vases in Cumae C. A *kemai* in Sydney shows five faces in black glaze outline, as on the vases of the Vitulazio Painter. Most other *kemais* are decorated with simple pattern-work, either in black on a reserved ground, or in white on black. The second group is made up of head-cruets; they consist of a concave-sided ring supporting four small lidded vessels of stamnoid form, connected by a central handle-ring for lifting. There is usually a plastic head between the vessels, and the supporting ring is sometimes decorated with female heads in red-figure or with palmettes. Such vases have been found in the Teano necropolis and must be contemporary with the red-figure vases from the same site. The final group consists of the work of the Vitulazio Painter [317/9], who decorates a number of vases, mostly bell-kraters, with female heads drawn in black outline on the pale terracotta of the body of the vase. The heads, drawn in a very impressionistic manner, are often flanked by bands of a stylized leaf-pattern; they are comparable with those on the Sydney *kemai* which, together with the fact that some come from Teano, suggests that they are probably best associated with the latest Cumaean; it is possible they were made at Calvi (*anc.* Cales) since several fragmentary vases have been excavated at that site, and the terracotta is similar to that of the standard Calenian pottery of the late fourth and subsequent centuries.

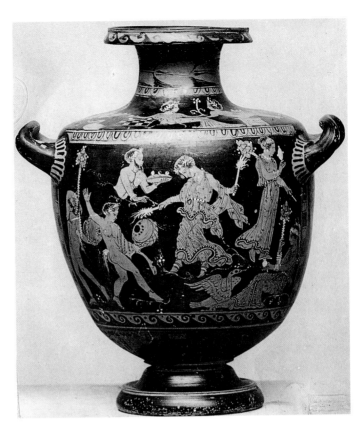

271 Hydria by the Revel
Painter: Komos

272 Calyx-krater by the
Prado/Fienga Painter

273 Neck-amphora by the
Cassandra Painter: Rape of
Cassandra

274 Bell-krater, Cassandra
Group – Painter of Louvre K
491: Centaur/head

277 Bell-krater by the Parrish Painter: Phlyax scene

275–6 Situla by the Parrish Painter: Paris and Helen/youths

278 (above right) Neck-amphora, Three-dot Group: Warrior

279 (right) Bail-amphora by the VPH Painter: Warrior

280 Lebes gamikos by the Laghetto Painter

281 Bell-krater by the Caivano Painter: Birth of Helen

282 Bell-krater by the Caivano Painter:
Ambush of Dolon

284 Detail of hydria by Painter of B.M. F 63

283 Oenochoe (shape 3) by the Caivano Painter: Satyr and woman

285 Skyphos by the Errera Painter

286 Bell-krater by the Ixion Painter:
Boreas and Oreithyia

288 Reverse of bail-amphora by the Ixion Painter

289 Bail-amphora by the Ixion Painter: Warrior

287 Neck-amphora by the Ixion Painter: Satyr-actor

290 Bell-krater by the Ixion Painter: Female head

291 Neck-amphora by the Siamese Painter

293 Skyphos by the Capua Painter

292 Neck-amphora by
the NYN Painter

294 Squat lekythos by the
Foundling Painter: Phlyax

295 Hydria by the Whiteface
Painter: Hesperides

296 Hydria by the Whiteface Painter: Cadmus

297 *Reverse of bell-krater by the Whiteface Painter*

298 *Lebes gamikos by the Andover Painter*

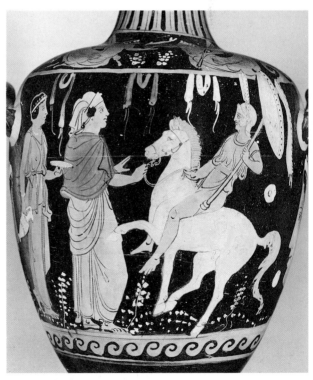

300 *Detail of hydria, Astarita Group: Libation to warrior*

299 *Neck-amphora by the Astarita Painter*

301 Bell-krater by the Libation
Painter: Libation scene

302 Neck-amphora by the
Libation Painter: Stele scene

303 Neck-amphora by the
Libation Painter: Iphigenia in
Tauris

304 Bell-krater by the Libation Painter:
Phlyax scene

305 Hydria by the Libation Painter: Niobe

306 Bell-krater by the Manchester Painter:
Herakles and Hippolyte

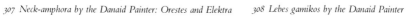

307 *Neck-amphora by the Danaid Painter: Orestes and Elektra*   308 *Lebes gamikos by the Danaid Painter*

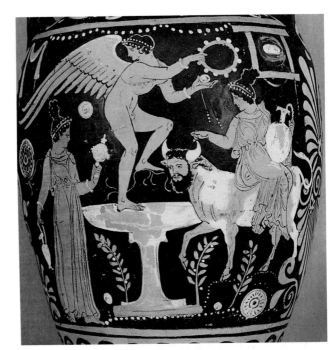

309 Neck-amphora by the Danaid
Painter: Man-headed bull

310 Oenochoe by the Painter of Catania
737: Woman with mask

311 Bell-krater by the Fillet Painter

312-13 Bell-krater by the CA Painter

314 Hydria by the CA Painter: Naiskos

315 Bell-krater by the CA Painter: Symposium

316 Lekanis by the CA Painter: Judgement of Paris

1

2

4

3

5

6

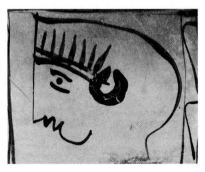

7

9

318 Oenochoe by the
Fuscillo Painter

319–20 Bell-krater by the Painter of New
York GR 1000

321 Skyphoid pyxis, Ivy-Leaf Group

◀ Opposite
317 Female heads on
Cumaean Vases

325 Skyphos by the APZ Painter

*324 Neck-amphora by
the APZ Painter*

326-7 Bell-krater by the Boston Ready Painter

328 Oenochoe by the Boston Ready Painter

329–30 Calyx-krater by the Nicholson Painter

331 Bell-krater by the Nicholson Painter

332 (above right) Bell-krater by the Branicki Painter

333 Reverse of bell-krater by the Branicki Painter

334 *Lekanis lid, White Bird Group*

335 *Lekanis lid by the Painter of B.M. F 247*

336 *Spouted lebes by the Haeberlin Painter*

337 *Spouted lebes, Teano-Tübingen Group*

338 *Lekanis lid, Teano-Tübingen Group*

Chapter Six

PAESTAN

Introduction

The fabric of Paestum is now well attested as a result of the excavations conducted since 1950 in the several cemeteries surrounding the city; these have added about 1000 vases to the previous total and have confirmed Paestum as their place of manufacture. Of all the South Italian fabrics, Paestan is probably the most consistent, and once its stylistic canons had been established by Asteas, they remain virtually unchanged throughout the life of the fabric, modified only to a very limited extent by external influences, except in the later Apulianizing phase.

Paestan clay is characterized by a fairly extensive mica content and it fires to a warm orange-brown colour, which differentiates it from Campanian. Paestan is also the only South Italian fabric in which vase-painters sign their works; we have at present eleven vases signed by Asteas, who in his signature duplicates the first sigma, as he also does in various proper names, and two by Python. Except on the signed vases and on a few others of larger dimensions with more elaborate subjects, identifying inscriptions are rare.

In regard to shapes, Paestan potters were on the whole conservative. Those which appear most frequently are bell-kraters, hydriai, neck-amphorae, lebetes gamikoi, lekanides, squat lekythoi, choes and skyphoi; less common, though not exactly rare, are calyx-kraters, pelikai, stemless cups and other types of oenochoe. So far only four volute-kraters are known, three of which belong to the Apulianizing phase; column-kraters do not appear at all. The bell-krater is the most popular shape; the body assumes an almost cylindrical form, with tall, straight sides, and this, in conjunction with the typical 'framing palmettes', and the wave-pattern below the pictures, serves to identify such vases almost instantly as Paestan. The larger lebetes gamikoi are provided with very tall and elaborate lids *[403]*, which consist of three or four separate elements, usually a lekanis-like base, surmounted by another lekanis and/or a miniature lebes gamikos, and culminating in a knob, which may itself take the form of a vase or even a bird.

The most typical of Paestan decorative patterns is the so-called 'framing palmette', which regularly appears on the larger or medium-sized vases. *Fig. 15* illustrates its development from the earlier stage, at which the side-scroll is still

196

Fig. 15 'Framing palmettes' on Paestan vases

attached to the fan-palmette below the handles, to the standard type with a detached scroll that serves as a frame for the pictures. Towards the end of the fabric the two fans which normally flank the central spiral of the scroll are reduced to one and the spiral is omitted. These 'framing palmettes' are almost completely confined to Paestan, although variations of them are occasionally found in Campanian, or on vases by the Ascoli Satriano Painter, whose work was strongly influenced by Paestan. On large or tall vases, like neck-amphorae or lebetes gamikoi, the pictures are often framed by reserved bands; one or both of their upper corners may be given the form of a triangle by the addition of a reserved band connecting the vertical frame to the stripe below the band of ornamental pattern on the shoulder [*382*]. Meanders with chequered or crossed squares are found below the pictures only on major vases; wave-pattern is in general use otherwise. A laurel-wreath is the standard decoration below the rims of kraters; larger vases may have berried ivy on the obverse, perhaps a legacy from Sicilian. The scroll-work on vases from the workshop os Asteas and Python often terminates in the so-called 'Asteas flower' (*Fig. 16*), since it is characteristic of that painter's work.

Of the patterns used on drapery, by far the most common is the dot-stripe border; it seems to have originated with the 'embattled' border ■ ■ ■ ■ found on vases by the Sicilian forerunners of Paestan, the black squares of which soon break down into dots or strokes. The dot-stripe border becomes, after a short initial phase when only a plain black stripe is used, completely standard on the himatia of draped youths on the reverses, and it is also frequently used for the borders of the piece of drapery across the bodies, or over the arms, of male figures and over the legs of women. It is also extensively used, sometimes doubled, with a white stripe in between, as a decorative pattern down the centre or sides of women's garments, and this is another of the fabric's distinguishing features. Very elaborate ornamental patterns appear on the draperies of divinities or mythological characters; women sometimes wear black garments, often with patterns in added red or white.

Dionysiac scenes predominate on Paestan vases; the god, who usually carries a thyrsus and wears an ivy-wreath, appears either by himself or in the company of

Fig. 16 The 'Asteas flower'

197

one of his followers – a maenad, a satyr or a papposilen – or else in contexts with a theatrical association, provided by a phlyax actor or the presence of a comic mask. Paestan vases with phlyax scenes are perhaps the most successful products of that fabric; those with more elaborate subjects, often of theatrical inspiration [367, 370–1], are usually heavy-handed or overcrowded. Mythology plays a comparatively minor role in Paestan vase-decoration, and funerary scenes, or those showing the departure or return of warriors, are also remarkably rare. The naiskos does not appear at all, and even the simpler form of grave-monument, like the column on a stepped base, is found mostly in mythological contexts, e.g. at the meeting of Orestes and Elektra. Small stelai and altars, however, are of frequent occurence, often flanking the main picture, especially on the smaller vases, but without any very obvious significance. On the more monumental vases, it is typical to have an upper register of busts or half-length figures [349–51], and the head or bust of a woman often appears in a window above the scenes taking place below [364].

Bridal preparations, women grouped around a laver for lustral rites, scenes of courtship with youths bringing gifts to women, are also popular, especially on lebetes gamikoi. The reverses of most Paestan kraters and amphorae normally depict two draped youths, who appear in a very limited number of types; they are either completely enveloped in their himatia, perhaps with one hand exposed, or else the cloak is so draped as to leave a V- or U-shaped opening over the chest or to leave the torso bare. They usually hold some object – a stick, an egg, a strigil or what has been called a 'skewer of fruit'. This consists of a series of round white objects one on top of the other, with no visible means of support; if they were kept in place by some sort of skewer, which is never actually shown, they would probably be cakes rather than fruit. They seldom appear in this particular way outside Paestan; they do not look as if they could be used for juggling and, since they appear frequently in Dionysiac contexts, they may be some form of votive offering. Phialai figure prominently on Paestan vases where they are more often used to carry offerings of various kinds – eggs, cakes, fruit – than for their normal purpose of pouring a libation.

The Workshop of Asteas and Python

Like Campanian, Paestan looks back for its origins to Sicilian red-figure of the early fourth century and, in particular, to the vases of the Dirce [60–61] and Prado/Fienga Groups [272], on which the prototypes of Paestan 'framing palmettes', draped youths and dot-striped drapery will be found. Still closer are the immediate forerunners of true Paestan – the Group of Louvre K 240 – once thought to be the work of Asteas, on whose style they exercised a profound influence. Several of the vases in this group were found on the island of Lipari, and are very close to the work of Asteas in both subject and treatment; so is the name-vase of the group [339], as may be seen by a comparison of the white-haired satyr on it with that on [342]. Several vases with phlyax scenes also belong to this group – a vase from Lipari [340] showing Dionysos watching a female tumbler, while two phlyakes look on in amazement and two figures wearing comic masks look down from windows above, or [341] showing a phlyax with two torches between Dionysos and another satyr who carries a small Eros on his shoulders. Other vases, mostly fragmentary, represent both young and old phlyakes; they wear the usual tights beneath tunic and jerkin, and sometimes a stripe, marking the seam, runs down the legs, a practice typically Paestan. Several of these vases have a Sicilian provenience, and one of them is a rhyton, a shape not found at Paestum; this is perhaps why it now seems safer to regard them as the immediate forerunners of Paestan, rather than as true Paestan.

The early vases by Asteas are very uniform in treatment. The obverses normally depict two figures, one of which will normally be Dionysos [342]; the reverses, two draped youths, with plain black borders to their himatia [343]. [342–5] well illustrate this phase; the former shows Dionysos in the company of an old satyr (cf. [339]), the latter in that of a maenad, who holds in her hand a white-haired phlyax mask (cf. [168]). The ivy-wreath worn by Dionysos on both is very typical of Paestan, as is the treatment of the drapery, on both sides of the two vases. The side-scrolls of the fan-palmettes below the handles are still attached, but on [344] the hooked leaf below the central spiral is replaced by a small fan, and the standard 'framing palmette' follows naturally on from this. Along with the bell-kraters runs a series of hydriai (of kalpis shape) with two- or three-figure compositions, and with large heads, usually of women, beneath the side handles.

That these vases are early works by Asteas seems clear from a comparison between some of the figures depicted upon them and the corresponding ones on his signed vases. Dionysos, the bearded satyr, the papposilen and the young satyr all find counterparts on his signed vases (e.g. [350, 353]), especially on their reverses, as do the female figures with their dot-striped drapery. The 'Asteas flower' (Fig. 16) appears on several of the early vases, as well as on the signed Hesperides lekythos and the Stheneboia hydria. The lekythos [351] and the Berlin phlyax krater [352] are the closest of the signed vases to those referred to above and must therefore rank as the earliest of the signed vases, probably to be dated to the middle of the fourth century.

Before considering the signed vases, we should look briefly at the work of the Painter of the Geneva Orestes [346], who seems to be a close contemporary of Asteas in the earlier stages of his career and whose work also provides a connecting link with the Sicilian forerunners, especially in the treatment of its reverse [347]. The Geneva amphora shows the meeting of Orestes, Pylades and Elektra at the tomb of Agamemnon, with the busts of two Furies above, and with it goes a small fragment in New York [348] showing a woman with a basket on her head, grasping the shaft of an Ionic column (cf. [60] by the Dirce Painter). A hydria in Madrid, with Eros and two draped women, similar in shape and decoration to the early vases of that shape attributed to Asteas, and a small lebes gamikos from the Heraion at Paestum are also by the hand of the Painter of the Geneva Orestes, and the certain provenience of the last suggests that it, and therefore the other three, are true Paestan; this is also supported by the colour and mica content of the terracotta.

Eleven vases bearing the signature of Asteas *[349–55]*, who uses the imperfect tense *egraphe* (painted), have come down to us; they are mostly in rather poor condition, five having been recomposed from fragments with some parts missing, and two, both from Buccino, surviving only in fragmentary form. Most of them are of comparatively large size and decorated with multi-figured compositions, in which the principal characters are identified by inscriptions. Two, the Berlin and Villa Giulia kraters *[352* and *354]*, are specifically associated with the theatre and represent scenes from phlyax plays. Two others, *[355]* and a hydria from Agropoli in Paestum, look to have stage connections, in view of the loggia-like background against which the scenes are set, in the upper portion of which appear busts of various characters (Mania, Iolaos, Alkmene, Aphrodite between two Furies), connected in some way with the stories depicted below, both of which were the subjects of Euripidean dramas. Most of the remaining vases depict mythological scenes – Europa on the bull, Cadmus and the dragon, Phrixos and Helle on the ram, Telephos with the infant Orestes, Orestes at Delphi, Herakles in the garden of the Hesperides; the new fragments from Buccino would seem to have represented a Dionysiac theme.

The mythological compositions normally have the figures arranged in two levels – the main scene taking place below, viewed from above by various divinities and supporting figures. *[349]* shows a slightly more original composition, since the main scene, depicting Europa riding on a white bull over the sea, represented by Scylla and Triton and a number of small fish in added white, with the little figure of Pothos (Desire) flying above, is set in a sort of pentagonal frame, formed by turning the top corners into triangles, in which are placed, on the left, Zeus, Crete and Hermes, and, on the right, Eros, Adonis and Aphrodite.

On the Hesperides lekythos *[351]* the scene is divided into two halves by the apple-tree in the centre, round which the serpent is coiled. On either side below are three figures, Hesperides to left and Herakles with two more to right; above are busts, including those of a satyr and Hermes, with perhaps Hera and another Hesperid.

The two most appealing of the signed vases are *[352]* and the Villa Giulia fragment *[354]*, both with phlyax scenes, rendered with unusual verve and humour. The female masks above, on *[352]*, look back to those on *[339]*; the stage is shown, with the house-door on the left, and as the figures are all named in inscriptions, it is probable that we have here a scene from an actual play. The fragment gives a splendid parody of the rape of Cassandra, in which the roles are reversed, and it is Ajax who clutches the statue of Athena seeking protection from the blow Cassandra is about to deliver; on the right, the wrinkled priestess, raises one hand in a gesture of surprise, while she grasps the temple key in the other.

The reverses of the signed vases normally depict Dionysiac scenes *[350]*; on those of larger dimensions, the figures are in two registers, with a row of busts above and a rather stereotyped group of figures below, normally including Dionysos, a maenad and a satyr. The signed vases are often over-ambitious and it is in his less pretentious works, with their 'agreeable tang of popular provincial art', as Beazley puts it, that we see Asteas at his best; they often have a greater vitality and a better sense of movement, perhaps the result of simpler compositions with only two or three figures. When he makes an effort, Asteas can draw drapery quite well, but too often it is over-elaborate, heavy and lifeless; his faces, too, can be expressionless, looking almost frozen – the Cassandra fragment is a remarkable exception.

A substantial number of unsigned vases may be attributed to the more mature phase of Asteas's work. They fall broadly into two groups, one of which continues the more elaborate style of the signed vases, the other the simpler type of two-figure compositions characteristic of his earlier work. The first includes some vases with Dionysiac scenes of which *[356]* is a good example, showing Dionysos with a bearded satyr and a maenad, and a female mask suspended above; it well marks the transition from his earlier to his more mature style; its reverse *[357]* should be compared with *[353]*. Others have mythological subjects – *[358]* and *[359]* illustrate the legends of Apollo and Marsyas and of Cadmus and the dragon, a rather fuller version than appears on his signed bell-krater. The more elaborate style, in which the figures are very richly garbed, is also to be seen on the purification of Orestes lekythos from Paestum *[360]* and on one in Bochum showing Medea, Jason and the golden fleece. Another group gives us various versions of the Judgement of Paris, once on a volute-krater, a shape rarely found at Paestum; of these *[361]* is perhaps the finest, coming from a tomb in the Contrada Gaudo at Paestum (1972/2), which yielded several other vases in a similar style, as well as a hydria by the Aphrodite Painter, which brings him into a direct association with Asteas. It is interesting to compare *[361]* with *[386]* and see the different approaches of the two painters to the same subject. Some of the vases from the Gaudo tomb depict women wearing black garments with red borders or stripes and patterned with white dot-clusters, like the seated woman on the shoulder of the signed Orestes amphora in San Antonio, and *[363]* has an unusual scene of a youth holding out a grasshopper to a crested hoopoe.

The standard vases are mostly bell-kraters and lebetes gamikoi. The former usually have two figures on the obverse, one of which is normally Dionysos, who appears in the company of his various followers and sometimes with a phlyax actor. The best phlyax vase *[364]* represents Zeus on a love adventure, lighted on his way by Hermes; a splendidly irreverent piece, with the tinsel-crowned head of the god emerging between the rungs of the ladder, as he looks up with an expectant glance to the woman (Alkmene?), whose head is framed in a window above. One at least of the youths on the reverses of these bell-kraters will wear a himation with a dot-stripe border, occasionally both do so.

/ 365 / is typical of the lebetes gamikoi, which mostly represent two women beside a laver, with perhaps a small Eros hovering above, a scene probably to be associated with bridal rituals. A few vases of other shapes belong to this period, including squat lekythoi, oenochoai and, in particular, cups; / 366 / is typical of the last, with a phlyax scene.

Python is known to us from two signed vases, / 367 / the well-known Alkmene krater, and / 368 / a neck-amphora found at Agropoli, representing the birth of Helen. He is a slightly later contemporary of Asteas, with whom he must have worked in very close collaboration, and who had such a profound influence upon his style that it is not always easy to distinguish between their respective works, especially when they are only minor vases. It now seems likely that the group of vases formerly associated with the 'Altavilla Painter' are early works by Python; the youths on their reverses, both of whom wear himatia with dot-stripe borders, lead on to what may be called the standard Python drapery for his reverse youths (*Fig. 17a*), which differs appreciably from that of Asteas, in the greater emphasis given to the dot-stripes and the preference for V- or U-drapings over the chest.

The Alkmene krater / 367 / has a very theatrical, one might almost call it operatic, look, and may have drawn its inspiration from the Euripidean drama, in which the Zeus-sent storm became a 'classic'. / 368 /, which represents the birth of Helen, has a somewhat similar look, heightened by the elaborate costumes worn by most of the characters; of interest is the presence in the upper register of Phoibe, the elder sister of Helen, who is very rarely represented in Greek art. Both vases show the somewhat heavier-handed manner of Python, when dealing with more elaborate mythological subjects. The reverses depict Dionysiac scenes / 369 /, with half-length figures above, as on the vases of Asteas; on the neck of / 368 / there is a siren on the obverse and a female head, wearing a beaded bandeau, on the reverse. Of Python's unsigned vases four also belong to this category; / 370 / may be directly compared with the two Asteas vases dealing with the same subject (e.g. / 359 /); the Orestes krater / 371 / is closest to / 367 / and also illustrates Python's fondness for added colours – the composition is laboured and far too crowded with clumsily-placed figures, e.g. Orestes who looks as if he were pinned to the omphalos. Little wonder that Beazley called it a 'monstrosity'. / 372 / with banqueters at kottabos is rather better; similar symposia appear on several other of Python's vases, including a fragmentary krater rescued from the wreck of the *Colossus*. On a cup from Paestum / 373 / the woman playing the flute for the banqueters is inscribed *EMAYTA*, the interpretation of which remains a puzzle, though it may well be a proper name.

Python's 'standard' vases are mostly bell-kraters, almost all with two-figure

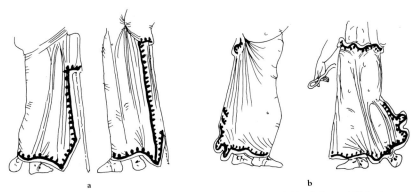

Fig. 17 Dot-stripe borders on the himatia of draped youths on vases (a) by Python and (b) by the Painter of Würzburg H 5739

compositions, showing Dionysos with one of his followers [374], a phlyax actor, a Pan; [376] exceptionally shows Odysseus and the sirens, and is the only krater not to have the pictures framed between the usual side palmettes. The youths on its reverse wear the typical Python himatia [375 and Fig. 17a], and they suggest this vase is better placed here than with the more monumental ones, which do not have draped youths on their reverses. [377] is of special interest as showing a woman in native costume pouring a libation to a warrior, since such scenes are very rare in Paestan, though common enough in Campanian. In this category also may be placed a few neck-amphorae, some with mythological scenes [378], and a number of cups. There is also a large group of rather smaller bell-kraters decorated with a single figure on each side; few have any special interest, since they mainly depict Dionysos, one of his followers or Eros, but [379] is a pleasant exception, showing a phlyax running home after a feast, carrying a tray of goodies on his head and lighting his way with a torch; beside him is a Paestan 'early bird', with a worm in its mouth.

The workshop of Asteas and Python included several other painters, who closely imitated the style of the two masters, and whose personalities are only now beginning to emerge from the 'well-drilled hacks', who painted so many of the minor vases associated with it. Chief of these is the Painter of Würzburg H 5739 [380–1], whose name vase depicts Makaria as a suppliant with two of the sons of Herakles. Among the characteristics of this painter's work, we may note the way in which he tends to break up the dot-stripe border of the himatia on his reverse youths into a series of short parallel stripes (Fig. 17b); how he leaves the area around women's breasts clear, with a series of fine vertical lines running down from beneath them to the girdle round the waist, decorates his garments with one or more horizontal rows of dots or strokes, and puts a dot-stripe border round the top of the peplos at the neck. His heads are comparatively small, and the hair is often shown with a large bunch sticking up at the back, tied round with a white ribbon. The subjects are seldom of much interest, being mostly the normal Dionysiac or genre themes. [382], which shows Orestes about to slay Clytemnestra, is close to this painter in style; the rather later vases of the Kurashiki Painter [383] mark a considerable falling-off in the quality of the drawing.

Two other important painters are associated with the later stages of th Asteas-Python workshop – the Aphrodite Painter and the Boston Orestes Painter. The former is an artist of some significance, and the discovery in 1967 of several vases by him in Tomb 13 of the Contrada Licinella at Paestum opened a new chapter in the history of Paestan pottery, since it showed that Apulian influence made itself felt there earlier than had previously been realised. That the new painter, named after the subject of his large amphora [384] from Tomb 13, must have had an Apulian background and training is clear from his use of elaborate floral and ornamental patterns, which are characteristic of that fabric, as well as from the presence of a 'xylophone' and of hollow rocks, both also typically Apulian devices. It has already been noted that one of his vases was found in the same tomb (Gaudo 1972/2) as a whole series of vases by Asteas in his later period, with which, therefore, the Aphrodite Painter must be contemporary, probably c. 340–330 BC. Once established at Paestum, the Aphrodite Painter soon adapted his style to the current practices of the Asteas-Python workshop, and, although he retains certain Apulian elements in his work, it is not long before he is: (i) framing his pictures, (ii) decorating standard local shapes (e.g. the neck-amphora, the lebes gamikos with a multiple lid), (iii) placing heads below the handles of his hydriai (not commonly done in Apulian), (iv) adopting local ornamental and drapery patterns – berried ivy on the rims of his kraters, 'Asteas flowers', chequer and dot-stripe borders; he even uses the 'skewer of fruit'. In his work we see, therefore, the grafting of one style upon another to produce a sort of composite; there is a close parallel in the work of the APZ Painter in Campania, but not in the later Apulianizing vases at Paestum, where local elements hardly appear.

[384–5] is one of the most remarkable of all the vases found at Paestum. The body on both sides is decorated in applied colour, reminiscent of the Gnathia polychrome style; the scene on the obverse, Aphrodite escorted by two Erotes, is very popular on the necks of Apulian volute-kraters, where added colours would also have been used; the reverse shows youths and women on two levels. On the neck on either side are scenes in red-figure. Hermes standing before a seated woman on the obverse, a woman seated on a pile of hollow rocks on the reverse. The scenes on the body are separated by most elaborate florals with spiralling tendrils of the kind regularly appearing on Apulian vases, especially on the necks of volute-kraters, in the last half of the fourth century. This experiment was perhaps too bold for Paestum, since it was not repeated, although other vases by this painter show a high degree of elaboration in the ornamental pattern-work. *[386]* makes an interesting counterpart to *[361]*, attributed to Asteas; both depict the same characters, but differ considerably in the treatment and posing of the figures. Characteristic of the Aphrodite Painter's work are the drawing of the faces (long, straight nose, fairly thick lips, three lines for the eyebrow and upper lid), the presence of two small lines just beside the knee on male figures, the treatment of the hair (long, in spiralling curls), the presence of a good deal of accessory jewellery and of a loose white band round the lower part of the arm or leg, and the drawing of the fold-lines on the drapery, with clearly defined strokes.

[387] is perhaps the most interesting of the vases not from Tomb 13. It represents Orestes at Delphi, and, most unusually, shows Elektra running off to right, as she is not normally present on this occasion. Above are busts of Poina and Teisiphone looking down from windows – again more in the Paestan manner than the Apulian. All the figures are inscribed. The Aphrodite Painter also decorated several hydriai *[388]* with two- or three-figure compositions in the Paestan tradition, as well as a number of minor pieces.

[389–90], showing the meeting of Orestes and Elektra at the tomb of Agamemnon, gives his name to the Boston Orestes Painter; he is a very close follower of Python, whose influence is apparent in his earlier work, as exemplified in his bell-krater *[391]*. It has a tall, almost cylindrical, body, with a wreath of berried ivy below the obverse rim, and represents a boar-hunt. This seems to have no mythological significance, although its composition, with the figures disposed on different levels, against a rising landscape background, was perhaps inspired by a free painting of the Calydonian boar-hunt. On its reverse are two draped youths, rather in the later manner of Python, to whose work the treatment of the hair and the drapery, as well as the ornamental patterns, owes a great deal. The subject of his name vase *[389]* is repeated on two others, on both of which Elektra wears a black garment with red stripes. On the neck of *[389]*, as on many other Paestan amphorae, is a siren, appropriate for a funerary vase, since it was one of their functions to convey the souls of the dead from this world to the next. *[392]* is one of this painter's typical bell-kraters; they show a high degree of uniformity, mostly depicting Dionysos with one of his followers on the obverse, and the canonical two draped youths on the reverse *[393]*, the latter being particularly monotonous, since the painter uses only two main types, with minor variations. Mythological subjects are comparatively rare, but three of his vases depict warriors, twice in the presence of a woman wearing native costume and offering a libation. The work of the Boston Orestes Painter provides a good connecting link between the standard products of the Asteas-Python workshop and later Paestan, as seen in the vases of the Painters of Naples 1778 and 2585.

Over 500 other vases, mostly of smaller dimensions, come from the Asteas-Python workshop; they are nearly all decorated with single figures, taken from larger compositions, or with female heads, and sometimes with birds or animals. They closely follow the general style of the two principal painters and, indeed, some of them might be minor works of their own hands. Many, however, are drawn hurriedly with indifferent skill and are clearly the works of inferior imitators. Several fish-plates may be assigned to this workshop. Some of the larger ones (*c.* 27–33 cm in diameter) are of particularly high quality and could be by Asteas himself *[394]*. They are characterized by the presence of a large octopus with a dome-shaped body, big eyes and waving tentacles with white suckers; several have berried ivy on the overhanging rim and wave-pattern round the central depression. One such plate was found in the Licinella tomb which contained the group of vases by the Aphrodite Painter, and it is possibly also by his hand, despite its close connection with those assigned to Asteas. With it was found a small 'salt-cellar' in black glaze, which perhaps originally fitted into the central depression.

Later Paestan

The two chief Paestan artists of the last quarter of the fourth century are the Painters of Naples 1778 and 2585 *[395–405]*. At first their styles have a good deal in common, but they diverge considerably as they develop. Both painters approach barbarization in the final stage of their career; this is fully achieved in the work of their followers.

The early work of the Painter of Naples 1778 was very strongly influenced by the Caivano Painter, a Campanian artist who may have worked in Paestum for a time. This is clearly to be seen in the way the hair of his youths falls down on to the shoulders in a series of long locks, composed of a series of thick cross-strokes one above the other *[395]*, or in his treatment of women's drapery, with a fine dot-stripe down the centre or on the borders of cloaks worn across their bodies. It is also to be found in the pattern-work and decorative adjuncts, like the disks or phialai in the field above the pictures, and especially in the individual white-veined palmette-leaf, springing from a white stem (*Fig. 18*). His earlier style is also influenced by the later work of Python and that of the Boston Orestes Painter, as his name vase *[395]* demonstrates. This is one of the last vases to depict a phlyax, and it also shows most of the essential characteristics of the painter's style, of which the alabastron *[396]* gives an even better illustration. The Painter of Naples 1778 decorated several lekanides, lebetes gamikoi and squat lekythoi of fairly large size mostly with youths and women or toilet scenes, and many smaller vases with single figures. In the later phase of his activity his drawing, especially of faces, gets worse, and it is at this stage that he tends to frame the pictures between tall scrolls with only a single downward-pointing fan *[397]*; many of the minor vases are decorated only with female heads, copied from

Fig. 18 Palmette leaf by the Painter of Naples 1778

those on the necks of his amphorae or the lids of the lebetes gamikoi.

[398], an early work of the Painter of Naples 2585, shows a close connection with the later vases by Asteas, especially in the figure of Dionysos; the woman on its reverse and on *[399]*, however, is the forerunner of what will be this painter's most typical figure, repeated from vase to vase. His other stock figures include: *(i)* a seated draped woman, enveloped in a himation, with her right hand projecting outwards *[400]*; sometimes she is only half-draped, with the lower portion of her body covered by a piece of dot-stripe bordered drapery; *(ii)* a standing nude youth, with the weight resting on one leg and a consequent tilt of the body to one side *[401]*; *(iii)* a youth bending forward over one raised foot, holding out some sort of offering to a seated woman *[400]*. This is the painter's most popular theme and it is repeated frequently, with minor variations.

The Painter of Naples 2585 is less inclined to frame his pictures than most of the other Paestan artists; when he does, he uses reserved bands or palmettes similar to those on the vases by the Painter of Naples 1778, but with a much thicker stem and more added white. At first his subjects are mostly of the Dionysiac or genre type, later he branches out into mythology. *[404]*, representing the Judgement of Paris, is perhaps his most remarkable vase of this type, since most of the figures on the obverse are in added colour, and are more expressive of their feelings than usual; *[402]* and *[403]*, both from the same tomb at Paestum, show Danae, receiving the shower of gold, and the birth of Aphrodite. In this later phase the visible flesh of women is usually shown in added white, and this practice is also followed with some of the female heads on his minor vases. Others of his heads are marked by the presence of a large stephane with tall spikes *[405]*.

Both painters also decorated fish-plates; on those by the Painter of Naples 1778 the fish usually have a circle of dots around the eye.

The Floral Painter, named after the floral decoration around the female head on the reverse of a large bottle, is one of the latest of the Paestan vase-painters; he follows on from the Painter of Naples 2585 but also reflects the influence of the Apulianizing Group. *[406]*, found with his name vase, shows the meeting of Orestes and Elektra and well illustrates the decline that has taken place in the quality of the drawing, since the faces are badly drawn and expressionless. His female heads are deplorable, but those on a small group of vases found in 1969 in the Contrada Licinella *[407]* are even worse, and the fabric has become virtually barbarized; with such vases Paestan red-figure comes to its unlamented end.

The Apulianizing Group

Overlapping with the later vases from the workshop of Asteas and Python and those of the Painters of Naples 1778 and 2585 is a comparatively large group of vases decorated in a strongly Apulianizing style; they have been found in a number of tombs at Paestum, especially in the Spinazzo necropolis. In style these vases look almost pure Apulian and might well have been thought of as imports, were it not that they are made from the typically micaceous Paestan clay and have turned up in quantities which would be unexpectedly large for imported wares. We have already noted a similar phenomenon in Campania at the time of the APZ Painter, and it looks as if some of the migrant potters from Apulia, of whom the Aphrodite Painter seems to have been the first, also settled in Paestum. Unlike him, the other artists did not rapidly assimilate to the Paestan style, but continue in their own fashion with comparatively little modification, apart from adopting some Paestan shapes (like the neck-amphora) and ornamental patterns, and in one instance using the typical 'framing palmettes' *[411]*. The general uniformity of subject-matter, style and pattern-work on both the larger and more intact vases from tomb burials, as well as the great mass of fragments from the Heraion and the Agora, suggests that these vases were all the products of a single workshop, more or less confined to the Apulianizing painters, who in this instance seem to have remained apart from the other late Paestan artists. Their work is mostly to be placed in the last third of the fourth century, especially between *c.* 320 and 310 B C, which must mark the *floruit* of the Spinazzo Painter *[413-7]*; the latest vases, which show a marked stylistic deterioration, might go down to the early years of the third century.

The first vases in this group look particularly Apulian, reflecting the style of the Varrese Painter and his immediate followers in the third quarter of the century, and that of the minor artists associated with the workshops of the Darius and Patera Painters. *[408]* and *[409]* are typical examples; it is interesting to note, even at this early stage, the appearance of the bottle and the skyphoid pyxis, which both become very popular later, though they are otherwise rare in Paestan. Neither shape is common in Apulian but both occur frequently in Sicilian at this period. *[409]*, found in the Spinazzo necropolis, illustrates well the Apulian elements – the hollow rock, the open box held by the youth, the hovering Eros; the reverse *[410]* even more so, with an Eros, a fan and a wreath in his hands, walking over plant-strewn ground. Parallels to all these can readily be found in the minor Darian vases or on those of the Menzies Group in Apulian; the drawing, however, is rather different, especially of the drapery and of the palmettes and scroll-work beneath the handles. *[411]* shows a slight degree of Paestan assimilation – the flying Eros is very Apulian, but the 'framing palmettes' and speckled bird are more in the Paestan manner. To this phase also belong a few vases close in treatment to those of the Ivy Leaf Group in Campanian; of these the neck-amphora *[412]* is a good example, with a white-fleshed woman on the obverse, holding a large bunch of grapes, and, on the reverse, a draped youth. The Apulian influence is obvious, but the shape is foreign to that fabric, and both the clay from which it was made and its provenience suggest that it is of Paestan manufacture. These vases lead up to the Spinazzo Group, to which belong the largest and most significant of the Apulianizing vases. Their subjects predominantly represent toilet scenes or bridal preparations, with nude women standing or crouching beside lustral basins, usually in the presence of a small Eros, and often with a neatly folded piece of drapery nearby [413]. The larger vases, lekanides, lebetes gamikoi and skyphoid pyxides, are decorated in a very similar manner and seem to be the work of a single artist, who has been named the Spinazzo Painter. Characteristic of his work is the treatment of women's hair – usually shown as bound up in a *sphendone*, with a large bunch sticking up at the back and divided into three curling locks. The Apulian elements are still evident, but the style has become more individual, and these vases could hardly now be regarded as pure Apulian. With them may be grouped large numbers of smaller vases, including several bottles, dedicated to Hera in her sanctuary at Paestum. They mostly represent women or Eros or both, and the neatly folded piece of drapery regularly appears on them (cf. [413]).

With the large skyphoid pyxis [414–7], also from Spinazzo, we come to a later stage; beneath the handles and between the scenes on the lid there are large frontal female heads, with staring eyes. The obverse shows a typical scene with two women, a youth, Eros and a boy satyr, but the reverse represents two draped youths beside an Ionic column. On the lid are two nude kneeling women with a typical piece of folded drapery on one side, and a flying Eros on the other; they are connected in style with the work of the Painter of Naples 2585. The youths on the reverse, however, recall those on vases by the Painter of Berlin F 3383 and his associates in Apulian. This would suggest a date in the last decade or so of the fourth century, and this is supported by the discovery in the same tomb of another skyphoid pyxis with a female head in applied colour (Gnathia technique), a net-patterned bottle, and some lekanides with simple pattern-work in added colour.

Contemporary with the larger vases, comes a long series of smaller ones decorated solely with female heads, which call for no special comment. [418] illustrates the head on the reverse of a bottle from the Heraion, on the obverse of which is a typical toilet scene; the hair is shown in the so-called 'melon-slice' style, which was popular in the late fourth and third centuries, where it appears in sculpture and on several terracottas and a gold ring from Taranto.

The final stage of the Apulianizing style may be seen on a number of fragments from the Agora at Paestum, on which youths, women, and female heads are depicted in a manner that has become so barbarized that it is not always easy to tell exactly what is represented.

339 Bell-krater by the Painter of Louvre K 240:
Dionysos on panther

340 (above) Calyx-krater, Group of Louvre K 240:
Phlyax scene

341 (above right and right) Calyx-krater, Group of
Louvre K 240: Phlyax scene

342–3 Bell-krater, early Asteas

344–5 Bell-krater, early Asteas

348 Fragment of amphora
by the Painter of the
Geneva Orestes

346–7 Neck-amphora by the
Painter of the Geneva Orestes:
Orestes and Elektra

349 *Calyx-krater signed by Asteas: Europa*

350 Reverse of no. 349

351 Squat lekythos signed by Asteas:
Herakles and the Hesperides

352–3 Calyx-krater signed by Asteas: Phlyax scene

354 Fragment of calyx-krater signed by Asteas:
Phlyax scene

355 Calyx-krater signed by Asteas: Madness of Herakles

356–7 Calyx-krater attributed to Asteas: Dionysiac scenes

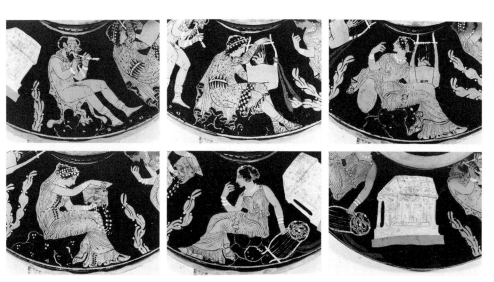

358 Lekanis lid attributed to Asteas: Apollo and Marsyas

359 Lekanis attributed to Asteas: Cadmus and the dragon

360 Squat lekythos attributed to Asteas: Purification of Orestes

361 Oenochoe attributed to Asteas: Judgement of Paris

362 Lekanis lid attributed to Asteas

363 Ring Askos attributed to Asteas: Boy with hoopoe

365 Lebes gamikos attributed to Asteas: Two women at laver

364 (above left) Bell-krater attributed to Asteas: Phlyax scene

366 Cup, attributed to Asteas: Dionysos on griffin and phlyax

367 *Bell-krater signed by Python: Alkmene*

368–9 *Neck-amphora signed by Python: Birth of Helen/Dionysiac scene*

370 *Calyx-krater attributed to Python: Cadmus and the dragon*

71 Bell-krater attributed to Python: Orestes at Delphi

372 *Bell-krater attributed to Python: Symposium*

373 *Cup attributed to Python: Symposium*

377 Bell-krater attributed to Python: Woman and warrior

374-5 Bell-krater attributed to Python: Dionysos and Pan

376 Bell-krater attributed to Python: Odysseus and the Sirens

378 (above right) Neck-amphora attributed to Python: Poseidon and Amymone

379 Bell-krater attributed to Python: Phlyax

380–1 Neck-amphora by the Painter of Würzburg H 5739:
The Herakleidai

382 Neck-amphora: Orestes and Clytemnestra

383 Bell-krater by the Kurashiki Painter

384–5 *Neck-amphora by the Aphrodite Painter: Aphrodite and Erotes*

386 Oenochoe by the Aphrodite Painter: Judgement of Paris

387 Calyx-krater by the Aphrodite Painter: Orestes at Delphi

388 Hydria by the Aphrodite Painter

389-90 Neck-amphora by
the Boston Orestes Painter:
Orestes and Elektra

391 Bell-krater by the Boston Orestes Painter: Boar-hunt

392–3 Bell-krater by the Boston Orestes Painter

394 Fish-plate, Asteas Workshop

395 Bell-krater by the Painter of Naples 1778: Phlyax

396 Alabastron by the Painter of Naples 1778

398 Neck-amphora by the Painter of Naples 2585

397 (above) Bell-krater by the Painter of Naples 1778

399 Reverse of a neck-amphora by the Painter of Naples 2585

400 Cup by the Painter of Naples 2585

402 Hydria by the Painter of Naples 2585: Danae and the shower of gold

401 (above left) Lebes gamikos by the Painter of Naples 2585

403 Lebes gamikos by the Painter of Naples 2585: Birth of Aphrodite

404 *Lebes gamikos by the Painter of Naples 2585:*
Judgement of Paris

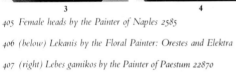

405 *Female heads by the Painter of Naples 2585*

406 *(below) Lekanis by the Floral Painter: Orestes and Elektra*

407 *(right) Lebes gamikos by the Painter of Paestum 22870*

408 Squat lekythos, Apulianising Group

409–10 Skyphoid pyxis, Apulianising Group

411 Bell-krater, Apulianising Group

412 Neck-amphora by the Painter of Paestum 5188

413 Lekanis lid, Spinazzo Group

414–17 Skyphoid pyxis, Spinazzo Group

418 Reverse of bottle:
Female head with
'melon-slice' hair

Chapter Seven

SICILIAN

Introduction

The earlier Sicilian red-figured vases were discussed in Chapter Two, where it was noted that, on the evidence at present available, it looked as if there had been a northward migration of Sicilian potters to Campania and Paestum early in the second quarter of the fourth century BC, since, soon after that date, local red-figure fabrics, which show a strong Sicilian influence in subject-matter, style and ornamental decoration, come into existence in both those areas. In eastern Sicily, especially in the region around Syracuse, production seems to have continued on a comparatively limited scale; the central and western parts of the island, however, were under the domination of the Carthaginians and it was not until Timoleon succeeded in driving them out around 340, that there is a significant increase in the manufacture of red-figured pottery. The fact that many of the sites where such vases have been found have been scientifically excavated, and the finds properly recorded, has enabled a more precise chronology to be established for later Sicilian than for the red-figure fabrics of South Italy. (see p. 16).

The red-figured pottery of mainland Sicily from c. 340 BC onwards shows a remarkable degree of uniformity of shapes, subject-matter and decoration and, in consequence, it is difficult to think of more than a comparatively limited number of centres of production. Stylistically the vases fall into two main groups, although with a certain measure of cross-influence. Many of the vases in the first group come from Syracuse and the surrounding area, or from the territory of Gela, and this gave rise to its being designated the Lentini-Manfria Group, after the find-spots of some of the more significant vases it it; in the light of later discoveries a more comprehensive designation might have been a wiser choice. The second group centres around a number of vases from sites near Mt Etna, like Centuripe, Adrano, or Paternò and has, in consequence, been called the Etna Group. Centuripe has been thought of as a likely centre of production, in view of the large number of vases found in the excavations at that site. Some of the vases in this group are of very high quality and provide a connecting link with those of the Lipari Group, nearly all of which were found on that island; they are of a highly individual and distinctive style, in which added colours play a far larger part than they do elsewhere in Sicilian.

A striking feature of Sicilian vase-painting at this period is the predominance of the feminine element in the subject-matter. Women are represented in conversation together, at their toilet, preparing for marriage ceremonies, in the company of Eros or a winged female figure (usually interpreted as Nike), and, very frequently, by themselves, often seated, gazing expectantly upwards. Female heads also figure extensively, either as the sole design on smaller vases, or on the reverses of larger ones, especially from Lipari. On the vases of the first two groups, Dionysos and the theatre, in which Sicilians seem to have had a particular interest, also figure prominently; it is remarkable that this is not the case in Lipari, in view of the huge number of terracotta figurines from that site, depicting characters from tragedy and Middle or New Comedy. Representations of phlyax plays are fairly common, and the stage on which the action is taking place is often shown *[424]*; most exceptionally, it also appears on two vases with scenes from tragedies, as on *[429]*. Many of the better Sicilian vases, including several from Lipari, seem to reflect the influence of free painting, not only in their composition and the handling of perspective (cf. *[427]*), but also in the drawing of the faces, now commonly shown in three-quarter view, the posing of the figures and in the fluid, flowing fold-lines of the drapery. The nearest parallels will be found on Athenian vases of the third quarter of the fourth century at the height of the Kerch style, in the work of artists like the Marsyas Painter. The draped youths, who appear so regularly on the reverses of vases from South Italy, are hardly found at all in later Sicilian – perhaps because of the virtual absence of kraters or amphorae; when they do appear, it is normally in the company of one or more women.

Also noteworthy, especially at Lipari, is an increasing use of added colours, until some of the vases look almost polychrome, with pastel blue, green, pink and mauve added to the standard white, yellow and red. The Falcone pyxis *[440]* has scenes on it painted entirely in added colours, and, in places where these have now flaked off, various abbreviations of the Greek words for different colours (blue, red, yellow, etc.) are now visible to indicate which one was to be applied (presumably by an assistant) to that particular area.

Decorative patterns show little novelty, though some of those used at Lipari assume characteristic local forms. On smaller vases the scenes are generally framed between palmette scrolls, usually consisting of a single tall leaf, with a half-fan below it. When a floral is used it often takes the form of a Greek E (ε), with solid black centre, sometimes with a touch of white, a form also common in Campanian. The wreath of berried ivy, found on the rims of the earlier calyx-kraters, continues in use; the rims themselves tend to project further outwards, with a more pronounced overhang *[428]*. Sometimes the scene on a vase looks to be taking place on a sort of platform *[431]*; this may be supported by a row of alternating black and reserved squares, which look as if they are intended to represent some sort of architectural feature.

The Lentini-Manfria Group

The Lentini Painter, named from the site, near Syracuse, where several of his vases were found, seems to have been active in the third quarter of the fourth century. *[419]* represents a forerunner of his work; it shows a seated half-draped women and a flying Eros, both popular figures on Sicilian vases; the palmette scrolls between the two figures recall those on some of the earlier Paestan vases by Asteas. *[420]*, from Scordia, is typical of the painter's work, as characteristic of which we may note: *(i)* the seated half-draped woman, who usually wears either a sakkos on her head or a *kekryphalos*, with a small bunch of hair emerging at the back; there is a piece of drapery, with a plain black border over the lower part of her body covering her long and rather thin legs, and swirling out behind them; the breasts are small, protruding slightly with a black dot or circle for the nipple; *(ii)* an Eros, whose wings are outlined in white, with a solid black area (sometimes patterned with white dots) above the wing feathers; he usually wears a bandolier of white beads across the upper part of his body; *(iii)* the white ground-lines, often with dot-clusters, and, as filling ornaments, grapes, phialai, quartered disks and fillets; *(iv)* the presence of a deep pink wash.

We should also note the use of wave-pattern on the rim of the lid of the lekanis and of the band of black vertical strokes on a reserved background between the handles at the top of the bowl; this combination is favoured in Sicilian, later there will be a series of horizontal strokes at each end of the band of verticals *[444]*.

His drawing is neat and precise, especially in the details of the face. There is little variation in the subject-matter. *[421]* is of interest, firstly for its provenience – Spina in the Po delta in north Italy, where one or two other vases of this group have also been found – and secondly for its shape, since the skyphoid pyxis is to become very popular in Sicilian.

The style of the Lentini Painter is continued in a small group of rather larger vases with mythological subjects, decorated in an ampler and more elaborate style of which *[422]* is typical, and in a number of smaller vases, mostly from Gela or Lentini, decorated with single figures. The larger vases lead on to the more monumental work in the Lloyd Group, but, before considering that, a brief glance must be given to the Manfria Group, so named from vases excavated in 1951 at that site, which were found in a deposit which can be dated on numismatic evidence between 338 and 310 BC. The find included several skyphoi, closely connected in style with the work of the Lentini Painter, especially in regard to the treatment of the half-draped woman, and the pattern-work, as may be seen from *[423]*. On this vase the influence of the CA Painter at Cumae is particularly clear, not only in the skin-covered chair upon which Dionysos is seated, but also in the young satyr beside him and in the use of a white spray or a sapling. The drapery is drawn with a lighter hand than on the vases of the Lentini Painter, especially as regards the fold-lines. To this group also belong several phlyax vases, of which [424] shows the typical stage; it looks rather like an open box, outlined in white, with a central support and a flight of steps leading up to it; it is flanked by columns on either side. Here the scene shows a comic Herakles, with Hermes in attendance, and a woman; on another vase Herakles attempts to carry off Auge from a sanctuary, the remainder mostly show scenes from everyday life, rendered with considerable vivacity and expression. Associated in style with these vases are several of smaller dimensions, mostly lekanides and skyphoid pyxides, of which [425] is a typical example.

The larger vases of the Lentini Group lead on to what are amongst the finest examples of Sicilian vase-painting in the period around 330–20 BC. Typical of these is [426], with a laver scene on the obverse and a seated woman with Eros on the reverse; on the one hand, it looks back to the work of the Lentini Painter (cf. [420]), on the other, it looks forward to the work of the Borelli Painter [435–6], especially in the elaborate pattern-work on the lid and below the handles. Also in this area must be placed two remarkable calyx-kraters from Lipari, both with subjects connected with Greek tragedy. One [427] shows Adrastos intervening in the quarrel between Tydeus and Polyneices outside his palace at Argos (cf. Euripides, *Phoenissae* 408 ff.; *Suppliants* 140 ff.), while his two daughters, whom the young men will subsequently marry, stand on the porch of his splendid palace, well drawn in perspective. The other [428] shows the youthful Herakles, with Deianira, her father Oineus and her suitor, the river-god Acheloös, together with Nike, who is about to crown Herakles. This is a splendid illustration of Deianira's opening speech in the *Trachiniae* of Sophocles and would have made an excellent poster for the play. Another instance of Sicilian interest in Greek drama may be seen on [429], which shows, on the actual stage, the scene from the *Oedipus Tyrannus* where the messenger tells Oedipus of the death of his reputed father; Jocasta realises the full implication of his words, while Oedipus does not, thus leading to the tragic conclusion of the play. The different emotions of the principal characters are well brought out, especially the puzzlement of Oedipus; the richly-patterned costumes and the stage setting argue a direct connection with the theatre, even if the two daughters of Oedipus do not appear in this scene in the play itself. Three other calyx-kraters, all from Lipari, are related to the above both in style and in the connection of their subjects with the theatre. [430] represents the Thracian Maron, handing over the skin of wine to Odysseus, with which he will later make the Cyclops drunk; Odysseus is a splendid figure, with shoulder-length hair and wearing the pilos of a traveller. They stand on a low platform, reminiscent of a stage floor, between two women, one inscribed Opora (harvest; autumn), the other, Ampelis (spirit of the grape), characters who might well have had some part, such as speakers of prologue or epilogue, in a play based on the story from the *Odyssey*. Another represents the death of Hippolytus, and the third two maenads with Pan who is playing the flute beneath a grape-vine, from which is suspended a female mask with long hair and white flesh.

Among the best of the monumental vases are those of the Lloyd Group, named after the former owner of [431], with its spirited representation of satyrs pursuing maenads, again on a platform supported by a band of reserved and black squares (as on [427]). Beazley connected it with [419], from the drawing of the hands, in which the two middle fingers are placed close together at some distance from the other two. The drawing is suave, with smooth-flowing lines; the connection with the Lentini vases is clear, so is the influence of Athenian vases of the Kerch style in the third quarter of the century.

[432] is a skyphoid pyxis of exceptional quality; it follows on from [426], but is more monumental in treatment and magnificently drawn, especially in the seated figure of the bride, with the tiny prompting Eros beside her, and the supporting figures of the woman and half-draped youth on the left. The harpist on the lid, and the woman who sits in front of him, deep in contemplation, well illustrate the delicate art of the painter, and look forward to the later Lipari style. The elaborate pattern-work, with its fan-palmettes and sprung leaves and the black-centred flowers, is very close to that on [435]. Numerous smaller vases, decorated with single figures as [433] run parallel to the larger ones, but are drawn in a more summary and less careful manner; many, like [434] are decorated only with a female head.

The later stages of this group are to be seen in the work of the Borelli Painter and his associates, whose activity may be placed in the last two decades of the century. The pattern-work tends to become more elaborate, although the motifs have not changed; the drapery is treated in a still more pictorial manner; the drawing of the face, especially in three-quarter view, becomes sketchier, and the hair looks more straggly. [435-6], the name vase of the painter, illustrates the developments which have taken place, and we note the absence of that suave elegance of some of the figures on the earlier vases. The drawing is scrappier, the fold-lines of the drapery are fussy rather than fluid, the neat profiles are no more. Even the palmettes and scrolls have lost their former precision and the first stages of the coming stylistic break-down are apparent.

Two very fragmentary hydriai in Lentini are contemporary with the Borelli Painter; one [437], shows a woman with Eros, the other probably the rape of Cassandra. The drawing is of rather better quality, recalling that of [432]; fold-lines are finely drawn, usually in diluted glaze, and beneath the handles are female heads, with large and rather staring eyes, which reappear as the sole decoration on a number of vases [438], including some from a tomb-group at Marianopoli in central Sicily, with which were found several black-figured lekythoi of the Pagenstecher class and a pyxis of Lipari type decorated with vine leaves in added colour, which would suggest a date in the late fourth century. [439], from Adrano, which represents a cult scene of some kind, well illustrates the later phase of this style, with its characteristic treatment of the drapery folds. Added colours come into increasing use on these vases and it is here that I should incline to place the famous Falcone pyxis, the obverse of which [440] is entirely in added colour. It has affinities with the polychrome vases from Lipari, but in style seems closer to the vases of Borelli Group, especially in the treatment of the drapery of the Nike and seated woman on the reverse.

The Etna Group

The vases in the Etna Group are the work of several different artists, some of considerable merit; they run parallel to those in the Lloyd and Borelli Groups, but do not include any quite comparable to the large calyx-kraters or skyphoid pyxides, with mythological or dramatic representations. They are mostly of rather smaller dimensions, but often have a more decorative appearance, due to the profusion of plants or flowers in added white, which spring from the ground [441], and to a judicious use also of red and yellow for details, which serves to brighten the pictures, especially in single-figure compositions. The subjects are mainly confined to women, Nike, Eros, female heads and an occasional satyr. Few, if any, would appear to date before *c.* 330 BC.

[441], from Adrano, is typical of the earlier vases in this group. A half-draped Nike kneels beside an altar, to the right of which is seated a draped woman, resting one arm on a tambourine; on the knob is a female head in profile, wearing a sakkos, from which a large bunch of black hair escapes to cover the visible ear. These are all popular themes; the female heads reappear frequently, often with a row of white stripes on the sakkos and a touch of pink on the cheek. The lekanis [442] represents a slightly more developed phase of this style, with a more extensive use of added red and white, and is typical of the work of the Biancavilla Painter, which in turn leads on to the Mormino Painter [443], with his rather more impressionistic style, and very characteristic drawing of the face, with its small, closed mouth and pointed nose, and with a white bandeau round the head.

With the vases of the Cefalù Painter we are coming very close to the work of the Lipari Painter; they have, indeed, recently been placed in the Lipari Group, and at least three of them come from that site, but the drawing of the faces, the rendering of the drapery and the treatment of the pattern-work seem to indicate they are better placed in the Etna Group. The palmette scrolls with the black-centred flowers, the finely-drawn heads of the female figures, the wings of the Erotes, and the half-kneeling satyr-boy all find closer parallels in that group than with the work of the Lipari Painter. Noteworthy also are the two rows of horizontal lines at each end of the row of strokes between the handles of the bowls of lekanides, which are not characteristic of the Lipari Group. [444–5] is a vase of particular interest as representing Apollo, with his cithara, beside the omphalos, and Artemis, with a torch in her left hand, and her right about the neck of a hound. The Cefalù Painter's work has a measure of elegance, resulting from his neat manner of drawing and a good arrangement of the component figures. In spirit it certainly has much in common, not only with the better vases of the Etna Group, but also with the later products of the Lentini-Manfria Group. With the two lekanides in Lipari was found a lekanis decorated with a vine pattern similar to that on the Marianopoli pyxis, and they should therefore be contemporary with the vases from that tomb.

Also to the Etna Group may be assigned about 150 vases decorated only with female heads *[446]*. They fall broadly into two classes, one of which may be described as 'Plain', since there is little subsidiary decoration and only a very limited use of added white; the other as 'Ornate', with a more decorative style and an extensive use of added colour. Of the former *[446/1]* may be taken as typical; *[446/3]* represents a slightly later development, in which the drawing of the face becomes increasingly impressionistic. *[446/6]* is a good example of the earlier phase of the 'Ornate' style, on which we may note the white radiate stephane, the earrings, and the more elaborately patterned sakkos; *[446/4]* is still later, with the hair over the ear breaking up into a series of round curls, which reappear on a number of other heads associated with the one on this vase. The heads on the vases of the Paternò Group *[446/2]* take us a step further; the group consists largely of small round pyxides, with flat lids decorated with ivy-pattern, and a female head on either side of the bowl. The hair is bound up in a *sphendone*, decorated with white stripes, and the part emerging at the back is sprinkled with white dot-clusters. Above the brow is a white stephane, and a large mass of hair beside the ear. The heads are framed between single palmette leaves, with a white inner border, and a small scroll at the base, with a floral in between. In the field there is often a hanging fillet with a tassel at the end, as on many of the larger vases. The drawing of the facial features tends to become sketchier; the cheek may be enlivened by a touch of red. Confronting heads appear on a few vases. *[446/7–8]* mark the final stage, in the so-called White Stripe Group, in which the headdress bears a thick white stripe across it. Here the drawing becomes even more summary and the features are heavy and lifeless.

The Lipari Group

The excavations carried out since 1950 on the island of Lipari, especially in the Contrada Diana, under the direction of Luigi Bernabò Brea and Madeleine Cavalier, have brought to light an enormous amount of material, from the neolithic period onwards. The island was colonized by the Greeks in the sixth century BC and it remained in their hands until the Roman conquest in 252. Over 2000 tombs have so far been excavated and they have yielded a large number of vases, decorated both in red-figure and in applied colour, as well as numerous terracotta masks and figurines, representing characters from Greek tragedy or from Middle and New Comedy. The earlier red-figured vases from Lipari are very different in style from those of the later period and, as we have seen (pp. 29, 158, 198), are closely linked with the origins of Campanian and Paestan. In the later fourth century a local style comes into existence, characterized by the extensive use of a wide range of added colours; these, when applied to a terracotta normally of a comparatively pale shade of buff or brown, sometimes coated with a prepared white slip, produce an effect very different from that of normal red-figure, and perhaps nearer to the fully polychrome style of Centuripe in the third century. The general uniformity of style, subjects and decorative patterns suggests that these later vases are the products of a single workshop, with the Lipari Painter as its principal artist, together with a few associates.

An attempt has recently been made to bring the date of these Lipari vases down to the first half of the third century BC, in the light of the finds of terracottas and a coin-hoard in the necropolis or nearby. The terracottas have been specifically associated with the New Comedies of Menander (c. 343–292 BC) and this is certainly true for some of them, though others could equally well be connected with Middle Comedy and, indeed, several of the masks find parallels in those worn by characters on the phlyax vases or appearing, often suspended above, in various Dionysiac scenes. It is perhaps significant that very few such terracottas have been found in conjunction with Lipari red-figured vases, which from their subject-matter seem to belong to a different world, in which the theatre has no part to play. Shape, style and ornamental patterns all associate these vases closely with others of the end of the fourth century and it would be strange if red-figure vase production continued in Lipari long after it had ceased in Greece and South Italy. The hoard found in 1984 contained some 320 coins of the first half of the third century BC; it was clearly buried for safety, at the time of the Roman invasion of 252, in the wall of the Greek city, but it has no particular relevance for the dating of the vases.

The scenes depicted on the extant vases from the workshop of the Lipari Painter are concerned almost exclusively with women – apart from Eros, no other male figures appear; even the unique lekanis with a mythological subject shows four Nereids bearing the arms of Achilles. The Lipari vases, with their fugitive added colours, like Athenian white lekythoi, were not intended for everyday use, but were expressly designed for the tomb. This perhaps explains the limited range of both their subjects and their shapes. The scenes depicted, which find no close parallels on other South Italian vases, seem to be associated with some special cult, almost certainly connected with the worship of Dionysos, in view of the huge quantities of theatrical terracottas from Lipari; they can hardly depict the preparations for, or rituals of, a wedding on earth, in view of the absence of the groom (contrast the scenes on Apulian pelikai and other vases), and more probably represent the mystical marriage in the hereafter between the dead initiate and the divinity (eschatogamy) or else represent the deceased in the flowery fields of Elysium. The shapes most commonly found – lekanides, sometimes divided internally by clay partitions into separate compartments like a lepaste, lebetes gamikoi, skyphoid pyxides, bottles, usually with a tall, slender neck and a small knob-like stopper, which would have

Fig. 19 Palmettes by the Lipari Painter

contained perfume or unguents – are all associated with wedding ceremonies, and would be particularly appropriate as votive offerings for the after-life.

The Lipari Painter has a highly characteristic style, both in his treatment of female figures and in his decorative patterns [447–51]. His favourite figures, repeated from one vase to another, are: *(i)* a seated half-draped woman, sometimes in three-quarter view, but more often in profile, who rests one arm languidly on a pillar, the arm of a chair, or a tambourine [447]; her rounded breasts tend to sag slightly; the lower part of her body is draped in a white or blue cloak. When the face is seen in three-quarter view, the hair has a central parting in the Praxitelean fashion, and falls down onto her shoulders in straggly locks; *(ii)* a standing woman, wearing a short-sleeved, high-girt tunic, usually holding up some object in one hand; *(iii)* a winged female figure (perhaps Nike), with a touch of blue on the wings, kneeling or bending forward, sometimes to dedicate the girdle of maidenhood upon an altar.

On [448] the seated woman in the centre of the picture holds a sceptre and may well represent Hera, attended by Aphrodite and Eros; on [449] it is likely to be Aphrodite herself, in view of the tiny Eros on her lap; otherwise the women are probably initiates preparing for, or enjoying, the after-life.

The palmette decoration usually consists of a large fan, with a pointed central leaf, springing from an oval core (*Fig. 19a–b*), with a solid black centre; on either side is a tall palmette scroll, with the Greek E type of floral, so common in Sicilian, and below it a small fan-palmette. On later vases the core is more nearly circular (*Fig. 19c*), with a black outer ring, then a reserved one, another black ring, and a small central reserved disk. The lids of skyphoid pyxides are usually patterned with Easter-egg-like objects, sometimes with a blue band around them, with laurel-wreaths linking them [450]. Their reverses are mostly decorated with a large female head, relatively unadorned, and wearing sakkoi patterned only with lines. The knobs of lekanides frequently bear a rosette, with leaves alternately blue and white.

The vases of the White Sphendone Group, on which women's hair is generally shown as bound up in the white *sphendone* [451] which gives the group its name, probably represent a later phase of the work of the Lipari Painter himself; they lead on to the work of the Painter of the Three Nikai [452], several of whose vases were found in the same tomb (298) as those of the White Sphendone Group, with which they must therefore overlap to some extent. He is not such a good draughtsman as the Lipari Painter, as may be seen from his treatment of the face, with its disproportionately small nose and mouth, the small black dot for the pupil of the eye, and a generally heavy-handed approach, which is very apparent on the large female heads on his reverses. Some of the contemporary skyphoid pyxides decorated with female heads have scroll-work or other patterns in added white on their lids, and these provide a connecting link between the red-figured vases and those decorated solely with scroll, vine, geometric or architectural patterns in added colours.

The recent discoveries at many Sicilian sites and, in particular, at Lipari will necessitate certain modifications of the existing classifications of the fabric; they have also enabled us to see the work of several painters, both well-known and new, in a much clearer light. The time is at hand when a complete re-appraisal of Sicilian pottery as a whole will be needed, since it is now becoming easier to trace with greater precision the stylistic connections between vases found at widely separated sites. The present survey should therefore be regarded as still tentative, since it may require a further reassessment when all the material can be studied in greater detail.

420 Lekanis by the Lentini Painter

419 Lekanis lid, forerunner of Lentini Group

421 Skyphoid pyxis, Lentini Group

423 *Skyphos, Manfria Group*

422 *Lebes gamikos, Lentini Group*

425 *Skyphoid pyxis by the Painter of B.M. F 473*

424 *Skyphos, Manfria Group: Phlyax scene*

426 *Skyphoid pyxis by the Painter of the Lugano Pyxis*

427 *Calyx-krater, Adrastos Group: Adrastos*

428 *Calyx-krater, Adrastos Group: Herakles and Deianira*

429 Calyx-krater, Gibil Gabib Group:
Oedipus

430 Calyx-krater, Maron Group:
Maron and Odysseus

431 Calyx-krater, Lloyd Group

432 Skyphoid pyxis: Bridal scene

433 *Squat lekythos: Seated woman*

434 *Skyphoid pyxis, Havana Group:*
Female head

435–6 *Skyphoid pyxis, Borelli Group*

437 *Fragmentary hydria of the Lentini
Hydriai Group*

438 *Oenochoe, Lentini Hydriai Group:
Confronting female heads*

439 *Skyphoid pyxis, Group of Syracuse 51288*

440 *Skyphoid pyxis, polychrome, by the Falcone Painter*

441 Lekanis by the ZA Painter

442 Lekanis by the Biancavilla Painter

443 Lekanis by the Mormino Painter

444–5 Lekanis by the Cefalù Painter: Apollo and Artemis

1

2

3

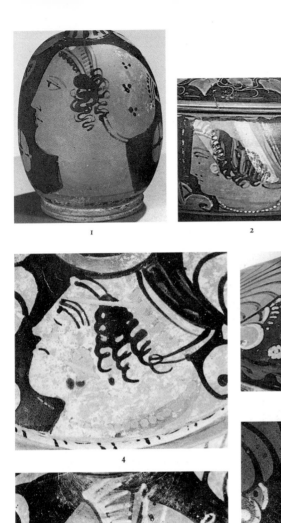

4

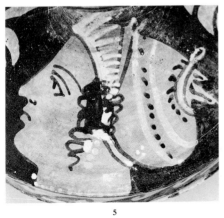

5

6

7

8

446 *Female heads on Sicilian vases*

447 *Skyphoid pyxis by the Lipari Painter*

448 *Skyphoid pyxis by the Lipari Painter: Hera*

449 *Skyphoid pyxis by the Lipari Painter: Aphrodite*

450 Skyphoid pyxis by the Lipari Painter

451 Alabastron, White Sphendone Group

452 Lekanis by the Painter of the Three Nikai

Chapter Eight

MYTH AND REALITY

The vase-paintings of South Italy and Sicily give us an excellent insight into two worlds – one of myth and legend, the other of everyday life. In the former we are concerned with the gods and with their intervention in human affairs, and, since the Greek colonists had no heroic past of their own, with the exploits of legendary heroes like Herakles, Theseus, Perseus or Jason, and of those from the less remote historical past, like Achilles, Agamemnon or Menelaos. In the latter we are dealing with a more real world, in which we see men and women engaged in the varied activities of normal life – for men, athletics, hunting or fighting; for women, weaving and other domestic duties; feasting and revelry for both. The living also must pay their respects to the dead and, since many of the vases we have studied were intended for the tomb rather than for actual use, it is only natural that the hereafter and the cult of the dead should figure largely in their decoration. This at times tends to blur the distinction between the two worlds, and the presence of Aphrodite and Eros, or Dionysos and his followers, in the company of human beings symbolises the union of the two worlds in the hereafter for those initiated into their respective cults and mysteries.

It is perhaps worth noting that on South Italian vases mythological subjects are often treated in a manner very different from that on Athenian vases. The approach might almost be called didactic, as if the vase-painters, and especially those in the schools of the Darius and Baltimore Painters, were anxious to parade their learning, which, at least in some instances (e.g. /256/), looks to have been derived from literary sources now lost to us, but of which echoes remain in later Greek writers like Apollodorus, Athenaeus or Pausanias.

The Gods

One of the most notable features of many of the mythological scenes depicted upon the larger Apulian vases is the presence in the upper register of an assembly of divinities /210/; it will normally include Apollo and Artemis, Athena, Aphrodite and Eros, Hermes or Iris, Pan and, less frequently, Zeus, Poseidon, Ares and Hera, who usually appear only when they have some connection with the events taking place below, which often are connected with the theme of one

255

of the Greek tragedies, or, less frequently, represent an Amazonomachy. The gods also play an important role in the great Gigantomachies which again form the subject of several Apulian vases [199] – Zeus appears in his chariot with Nike, hurling down thunderbolts at the giants, while other gods, even including Aphrodite, take an active part in the fray, and Ge (Earth), the mother of the giants, emerges from the ground with a vain entreaty for mercy. The presence of a number of elements in common between the various representations suggests that these pictures may look back to a single source, probably a lost painting.

The gods appear individually on a very large number of vases, in pursuit of a mortal, to lend a helping hand to a hero, in various mythological contexts. Most frequently found are Aphrodite and Dionysos, both of whom play a very large part in human affairs, as well as in the hereafter.

The birth or *anodos* of Aphrodite [403] appears but rarely; she more often figures in various mythological scenes, especially the Judgement of Paris [316, 404] or with Adonis, and often in the company of a small Eros, who himself plays a very frequent part in bridal scenes, in which he flies towards bride or groom with a wreath in his hands. Aphrodite is often escorted by two or more Erotes [231], either flying beside her, or drawing her chariot; she often holds in her hands a magic wheel or *iynx*, symbolic of the power of love.

Dionysos, in his triple capacity of god of wine, drama and the mysteries, appears more often than any of the other divinities. We see his birth after the thunderbolt of Zeus had blasted Semele [266], his concealment in the thigh of Zeus [49], his handing over by Hermes to the nymphs of Nysa; he is often present at symposia, in the company of maenads or satyrs, or in scenes connected with the stage; he appears also with his consort Ariadne [194]. His power is well illustrated by such scenes as the madness of Lycurgus [148] or the death of Pentheus. He is also probably to be identified with the youthful male figure, holding thyrsus, phiale or bunch of grapes, who is to be found on so many South Italian vases; here we should see him in his role as god of the mysteries, offering his initiates a better life in the hereafter, where he will be in mystic communion with them.

Apollo and his sister Artemis, who usually wears huntress costume, are also very popular. They appear with their mother Leto and Hermes on [20]; Apollo alone may be seen on several vases beside his statue in the temple at Delphi [52], and as the triumphant musician in the contest with Marsyas [358], in which the Muses acted as judges. Artemis appears as the vengeful goddess with him at the slaughter of the Niobids [252], by herself at the transformation of Callisto and Actaeon, and as intervening with Athena in their vain attempt to prevent Pluto from carrying off Persephone [253]. She may also be found on several Apulian vases in her guise as Bendis, a Thracian goddess whose worship was introduced into Athens in the time of Pericles and with whom she became assimilated.

Athena is represented as playing the flute, and, on seeing her reflection in a mirror, casting it away for the imprudent Marsyas to pick up; reflecting the gorgoneion in a pool [106], before attaching it to her aegis, taking part in the Judgement of Paris [316]; lending a helping hand to Herakles or Perseus, or with the daughters of Cecrops on the Athenian acropolis. She appears frequently as the representative of Athens or Attica [26], after her victory over Poseidon, and she is normally to be seen in full panoply.

Zeus – apart from assemblies or scenes on Olympus, like the judgement over Adonis – is usually shown in hot pursuit of some mortal woman, Leda [184], Thalia, Europa [349], Aigina [4], or of the youthful Ganymede [130], who on South Italian vases is usually carried off by a swan instead of an eagle [240]. Signs of his intervention are apparent from the presence of thunderbolts in scenes with Alkmene, the Dioskouroi, or the rape of Persephone, to ensure that his will is carried out.

Of Hera, his consort, we see comparatively little; she appears at the Judgement of Paris [361], in a preferential position in Paestan, since she had a special sanctuary in that city; she appears as a bride in Sicilian; on one occasion she suckles the infant Herakles, on another she is freed from the magic chair by a rather comic Hephaestus [264], who himself appears again to set in motion the fiery wheel to which Ixion was bound at her request. Ares also is seldom seen, except in gigantomachies.

Hermes, as messenger of the gods, or his female counterpart Iris [251], who may be distinguished from Nike by the herald's staff she carries, appears with comparative frequency, but usually in a secondary role. Demeter [184] and her daughter Persephone appear mainly in scenes connected with the Underworld; they are characterized by the cross-bar torches or ears of corn which they hold. Demeter goes in quest of her ravaged daughter, with the help of the Corybantes; Persephone is carried off by Pluto in his chariot, and then is present by his throne in his palace in Hades [209], from which Hermes comes to summon her back to earth in due season, whence she must again return when the time comes. The two goddesses also appear in the departure of Triptolemos from Eleusis to bring corn to mankind.

We see Poseidon, usually identifiable from the trident he carries, with his consort Amphitrite, or with Amymone, as she goes to draw water from the spring, and once he carries off Amphithea, who is not otherwise known in this context. Pan is a popular deity [374], either in substantially human form, with small goat-horns, or as part human part goat; he often indicates a rustic setting and usually holds his pipes (*syrinx*) or a hunting-stick (*lagobolon*), or both. Helios [268], Selene, and Eos (Sun, Moon, Dawn) figure on many vases, especially on the necks of volute-kraters, where their heads are often surrounded by a halo-like nimbus and where they may be used to indicate the time of the action. Eos is often shown in pursuit of either Tithonos or Kephalos, the former normally holding a lyre, the latter as a huntsman; such scenes are popular in early Lucanian, but thereafter are infrequent.

Personifications, often inscribed, are also a regular feature on South Italian vases. They may indicate the place of the action (Athens, Sikyon, Thebes), the country concerned (Asia, Hellas, Crete), a river or a mountain (Neilos, Dirke, Sipylos), or a season (Opora; cf. also Ampelis); they may stand for various natural phenomena – the wind (Boreas), the breeze (Aura), the clouds, or lightning (Astrape); they can also stand for various abstractions or emotions, like Dike (justice), Phthonos (envy), Pothos (desire), Poina (punishment), Mania (madness), and in this category we may also place the Furies and other demons.

The Trojan War

The 'tale of Troy' is well represented on South Italian vases, and the story begins well before the expedition of the Greeks to bring Helen back. The stage for this was set by the judgement of Paris, who awarded the prize to Aphrodite, who had bribed him with the promise of the hand of Helen, the most beautiful of all Greek women, born from the egg *|368|* resulting from the union of Leda and Zeus in the guise of a swan *|184|*, and at the time the wife of Menelaos, King of Sparta. Her departure from Sparta and her arrival with Paris in Troy *|197|* are depicted; these events are followed by the marshalling of the Greek fleet under Agamemnon and Menelaos. In the course of the journey to Troy, Achilles, son of Peleus and Thetis, whose tempestuous wooing appears on several vases, by mistake attacked Telephos, King of Mysia, and wounded him in the thigh. Telephos later sought out the Greeks in order to have his wound cured by the man who gave it to him, and, to further his purpose, he seized the infant Orestes in order to persuade Agamemnon, the child's father, to bring him to Achilles to be healed, after which he agreed to guide the Greeks to Troy. En route they stopped at Delos, where they encountered Anios, whose three daughters, endowed with the power to produce corn, oil and wine, are later to help victual the Greek fleet *|205|*.

Achilles is also to be seen either lying in wait for Troilos, as he waters his horse at the fountain-house, or else pursuing him on the Trojan plain and dragging him from his horse by the hair, a motif also popular in Amazonomachies.

Several of the more notable episodes in the Trojan War itself, as recounted in Homer's *Iliad*, are also illustrated, especially those in which Achilles plays a prominent part – his converse with Phoinix and the embassy to him (Book ix), the bringing by his mother Thetis and the supporting Nereids of the armour *|198|* made for him by Hephaestus (xix), his dragging of Hector's body round the wall of Troy (xxii), the funeral of Patroclus (xxiii), and the ransom of Hector's body by Priam (xxiv). Other scenes include the parting of Hector and Andromache (vi), the capture of the horses of Rhesos (x), the ambush of Dolon (x), and the death of Sarpedon (xvi), whose body is borne back to Lycia by Sleep and Death. The sack of Troy is also vividly depicted – the rape by Ajax of Cassandra in the temple of Athena *|273|*, later to be the cause of his suicide as a result of the wrath of the goddess; Menelaos coming to exact vengeance upon

Helen but, overcome by her beauty, allowing the sword to drop from his nerveless hands; Aeneas supporting the aged Anchises, all shown against a general background of upheaval and destruction.

Events after the *Iliad* are also well represented – the late arrival of the Amazons to aid the Trojans, the death of Penthesilea at the hands of Achilles, the rescue of Philoctetes, the theft of the Palladion, the death of Priam and the homecoming of the various Greek rulers. Agamemnon returns, with Cassandra as one of the spoils of victory, to his palace at Mycenae, where he is murdered by his wife Clytemnestra and her lover Aegisthus; his death is later avenged by his son Orestes and his daughter Elektra, whose meeting at their father's tomb is a very favourite theme *[60]*. The adventures of Odysseus on his homeward journey are also illustrated – his meeting with the Thracian Maron *[430]*, who gives him the skin of wine with which he is later to make the Cyclops Polyphemus drunk *[9]*, his passing by the Sirens' rock *[376]* and through the straits between Scylla and Charybdis, his calling up of the shade of Teiresias and finally his slaying *[42]*, with the assistance of his son Telemachus, of the suitors who had for so long plagued his faithful wife Penelope.

Herakles and other Heroes

The deeds of Herakles figure less prominently on South Italian vases than upon Attic, although the main episodes in his life are fairly well represented. Scenes connected with his twelve labours are now less popular, except perhaps for the apples of the Hesperides *[351]* and the girdle of Hippolyte *[190]*, the latter now taking place in a peaceful outdoor setting in which the Amazon queen hands over the girdle to him without a struggle. More unusual is the almost comic version of the Stymphalian birds on *[111]*. His various adventures with centaurs are well shown – with Pholos, with Eurytion *[54]*, and with Nessos, whom he slays with an arrow for attempting to carry off his wife Deianira. We see him also in bondage to Omphale, in his fight with Kyknos *[57]*, in his drunken visit to the palace of Admetus and his subsequent rescue of Alkestis, and, in particular, with Busiris, the Egyptian king who foolishly tried to slay him. His madnesss is also shown, and his final apotheosis *[50]* when he rises triumphant from his funeral pyre and is taken to Olympus in a chariot driven by Athena or Nike. He also figures in a number of comic scenes, inspired by satyr or phlyax plays, in which we see him feasting, robbed by satyrs while he supports the world in place of Atlas, mocking both Apollo at Delphi and his master Eurystheus during his time of bondage to him. His many triumphs are often marked by the supporting presence of Athena or by Nike offering him a crown.

Theseus appears infrequently – we see his recognition by Aigeus *[110/1]*, his dealing with the Marathonian bull, his setting out for Crete and his abandonment of Ariadne *[45]*; also his participation in the battles with the Amazons, and with the centaurs at the wedding feast of Peirithoös *[195]*, with whom he is punished in the Underworld for their defiance of the gods.

The adventures of Jason and the Argonauts provide the subject-matter for a few vases – the fight with Amykos [17] and the freeing of the blind King Phineus from the Harpies [19] take place on the route to Colchis, where Jason falls in love with Medea, the daughter of King Aetes and with her aid succeeds in securing the golden fleece from its serpent-guarded tree. Medea, brought back to Corinth as Jason's bride, is about to lose him to Kreon's daughter, when she takes a frightful revenge upon the pair, by slaying her two sons by Jason and encompassing the death of his bride-to-be by means of a poisoned robe and crown [77]; she then escapes to asylum in Athens in the dragon-chariot sent by the Sun, where she becomes the wife of King Aigeus, bearing him a son, with whom she returns to her native land.

Many other of the great heroes of mythology are also celebrated. Perseus, son of Danae and Zeus, who appeared to her as a shower of gold [402], is shown as a child put to sea in a chest with his mother; later we see him equipped by Athena with a sickle and the cap of invisibility for his attack on the gorgon Medusa, whom he beheads, using her severed head to petrify the sea-monster sent to devour Andromeda and, in a somewhat different context, to terrify satyrs in a comic play. Pelops is seen with Oinomaos taking the requisite oaths before their chariot race, in which he bribed the latter's charioteer, Myrtilos, to remove the lynch-pins from the wheels of his master's chariot, thus bringing victory to Pelops, who claims Hippodamia as his bride and carries her off triumphant; we see them later visiting his sister Niobe, when she is mourning at the tomb of her slain children [183]. Meleager appears in the famous boar-hunt together with Atalanta; Bellerophon takes leave of Proitos and Stheneboia, with the fatal letter, which he delivers to Iobates in Lycia and, after slaying the fearsome chimaera, returns to Greece, where he takes Stheneboia for a ride on Pegasus and dumps her in the sea [48]. Cadmus attacks the serpent guarding the well-spring at Thebes [370]; Phrixos escapes with Helle on the golden-fleeced ram to Colchis, escaping death at the hands of his father Athamas, but losing his sister Helle on the way to Colchis, where the ram was duly sacrificed and its fleece hung up on a tree in the grove of Ares.

The story of Oedipus is one of the best-known of Greek legends. The background to it appears on several vases showing the rape by Laios, his father, of Chrysippos, son of Pelops, who, after his son's death, called down a curse upon Laios and his descendants. Oedipus unwittingly slays his father and goes on to Thebes to solve the riddle of the sphinx (shown in both serious and comic versions), marry Jocasta (his true mother) and have two sons and two daughters by her. We see him with the seer Teiresias, with the messenger from Corinth who comes to tell him his reputed father is dead [429], and finally as a blind old man in the grove of the Eumenides at Colonus [200], the last two scenes certainly connected with dramatic representations of the story; one of them [429] actually depicts the stage on which the principal characters are standing.

The subsequent histories of their two daughters, Antigone and Ismene, and their two sons, Polynices and Eteocles, are also shown on a number of vases.

Various episodes from the expedition of the Seven against Thebes, the subject of a lost epic poem and of dramas by Aeschylus and by Astydamas, are also illustrated. *[427]* shows an early stage in the story when Adrastos, King of Argos, intervenes in the fight between Tydeus and Polynices which broke out one stormy night outside his palace. He composed their quarrel, married them to his two daughters, and undertook to restore Polynices to his throne in Thebes, usurped by his brother Eteocles. He marshals the expedition which included Amphiaraos, the seer, albeit against his will, since he knew he would not return, but was bound by an oath to his wife Eriphyle, who had been bribed by Polynices with the necklace of Harmonia, to ensure the participation of Amphiaraos. A couple of vases show his departure, enjoining his two sons to avenge him, and others depict him, after the earth had gaped open and swallowed up his chariot, standing before Pluto in his palace in the Underworld.

Two other heroes worthy of mention are Amphion and his twin brother Zethos, especially as the former was the husband of Niobe and brother-in-law of Pelops, both of whom also figure prominently as the subjects of South Italian vase-paintings. Amphion and Zethos were the twin sons of Antiope by Poseidon; she fled to Sicyon, but was captured by Lykos and brought back to Thebes to serve his wife Dirce as a slave. The two children were exposed, but found and reared by a herdsman. Amphion became a great musician, having been presented by Hermes with a cithara; Zethos preferred the martial arts. Later, Antiope's bonds were magically loosed, she joins her two sons, who take revenge on Dirce and Lykos by binding the one to a wild bull and attacking the other, who is saved only by the intervention of Hermes. This is the scene on *[211]*, which seems also to be connected with the lost *Antiope* of Euripides, not only by the presence of the 'herdsman', but also by Dirce's thyrsus, since in the play she was performing Dionysiac rites when caught. The twins then become rulers at Thebes, and in the building of the walls the stones went into place of their own accord at the music of Amphion.

Amphion married Niobe, whose children were slain by Apollo and Artemis when their mother boasted about them to Leto; several vases *[305]* show Niobe mourning at the tomb of her slain children, where she is entreated by her aged father Tantalos to desist and return to normal life, and also by her brother Pelops. She is turned to stone, signs of which are apparent on several of the representations, and placed on Mt Sipylos in Lydia.

Many of the myths and legends referred to here formed the basis for the plots of Greek tragedies, and the vases which serve to illustrate them merit consideration in their own right.

Dramatic themes

A noteworthy feature of vase-painting in South Italy and Sicily is the frequency with which the scenes depicted upon the vases appear to have direct connection with the stage, and this probably reflects the desire of the Greek colonists there to see either new plays or revivals of classical Greek tragedies. Here South Italian differs from Athenian vase-painting of the fourth century, since the latter has no comparable representations, its products being intended for export to areas where Greek drama would not have been in such demand.

Comic actors, locally known as *phlyakes*, take part in the performances of a wide range of farces, which parody the deeds of gods and heroes, or give a humorous twist to the events of everyday life. They wear the appropriate costumes and masks, and the scene is often shown taking place upon a stage, usually of a simple or impromptu type, consisting of a floor supported by posts or columns, to which access may be had by a flight of steps, and from which the actors may depart through a door on one side or the other. Satyr-plays are less frequently represented and it may well be that they had gone out of favour in the fourth century, since most of them are of comparatively early date, like / 1 / or / 9 /, perhaps connected with the *Hammerers* (*Sphyrokopoi*) of Sophocles and the *Cyclops* of Euripides. / 104 / shows actors dressing for such a play, and other vases show Perseus terrifying satyrs with the gorgoneion or satyrs stealing the weapons of Herakles, while he is supporting the globe in place of Atlas, who has gone to get him the golden apples of the Hesperides.

With tragedy we are on rather less sure ground, since only two vases, both of Sicilian origin (*e.g.* / 429 /), show the stage on which the action is taking place, although other vases (e.g. / 427 /) give at least a suggestion of a stage setting. The characters are never masked, but they do wear elaborate costumes, which are probably of theatrical inspiration. The presence of a paidagogos or old retainer, who will later serve as the messenger to narrate the tragic events which could not be performed on the stage, is another indication of a theatrical connection, since he would have no part in the actual myth. It has already been suggested that the scenes shown on many of the vases would make admirable posters for the plays concerned; the vase-painters probably drew their inspiration from an actual performance which remained in their memory and influenced the representation on the vases. It seems likely also that at least some of the figures within the funerary naiskoi were actors or poets, who would have been held in high esteem, and we know also that there were revivals of classical Greek tragedies, especially those by Euripides, and these may have served as a stimulus to the vase-painters. We know very little of the contemporary tragedians like Astydamas and Chaeremon, whose works have almost completely perished, but it would seem that they handled the old myths in a very different way from the earlier tragedies, and this might explain the somewhat unusual treatment of them on several vases (e.g. / 206 /). The illustrations of numerous lost plays, like the

Prometheus Unbound, Melanippe, Chrysippos, Alkmene, etc. are of considerable value for the help they may give towards their reconstruction.

The various episodes in the story of Orestes and Elektra referred to by Aeschylus in his *Oresteia* find frequent representation on South Italian and Sicilian vases, especially the meeting of Orestes and Elektra */307/*, often also with Pylades, at the tomb of Agamemnon, as described in the opening lines of the *Choephoroi*; the murder of Aegisthus and Clytemnestra is followed by scenes showing Orestes at Delphi, seeking refuge at the omphalos from the tormenting furies, being purified by Apollo, and finally winning his freedom after the trial in Athens. */192/* shows Prometheus bound to his rock, about to be freed by Herakles who has just shot the eagle sent by Zeus to devour the liver of Prometheus, probably inspired by the lost Aeschylean drama; the Danaides and their punishment in Hades is perhaps connected with his *Suppliants*, and reference has already been made to scenes associated with the *Seven against Thebes* and his lost *Niobe*.

Sophoclean drama is less frequently illustrated; */429/* and */200/* show scenes from his two Oedipus plays and */428/* the principal characters in the *Trachiniae*; others show Philoctetes in his cave, the suicide of Ajax, Antigone before Kreon, and, possibly, Creusa with Ion and Xuthus and the Pythia at the temple of Apollo in Delphi. When, however, a vase shows just a simple scene like Ajax committing suicide with nothing to connect it with the stage, it is more likely to depict the pure myth rather than any dramatised version of it.

It is, however, Euripides, whose plays seem to have provided continual inspiration for the vase-painters during the fourth century, from the early years of which comes the tomb found at Herakleia, with several vases depicting Euripidean themes (*Antiope, Medea, Herakleidai*). Thereafter we have many illustrations of extant plays (*Bacchae, Andromache, Hippolytus, Alcestis, Iphigenia in Aulis* and *in Tauris, Hecuba, Medea*) as well as many of those which have not survived. *Andromeda* is particularly well represented, from the pact made between Cepheus and Perseus that he should have Andromeda if he slew the monster, to the freeing of Andromeda, and Cassiopeia's entreaty for her forgiveness. On some vases Andromeda is bound to poles or tree-trunks */414/*, perhaps an echo of the Sophoclean version, on others to the rock or cliff-face */185/* as in the Euripidean play. Also well-represented is the rape of Chrysippos, the theme of one of Euripides' best-known plays, and the first occasion on which homosexual love had been treated as a dramatic theme, and Alkmene, who is shown seated on the altar beside the pyre against a background of a rainbow or nimbus, representing the effect of the water Zeus ordered the Clouds to pour down to quench the flames, when his thunderbolts failed to achieve this purpose. But for the lost plays, perhaps the most remarkable is the Melanippe krater */210/*, by the Underworld Painter, which has only recently come to light and would appear to illustrate one of his most famous plays, *Melanippe the Wise*. The scene is both touching and dramatic. Aiolos, the husband of Melanippe, looks on while the herdsman shows the exposed twin sons Melanippe has borne to Poseidon to Hellen, the father of Aiolos, who orders them to be put to death. Melanippe stands by, with the old nurse, in an attitude of resignation and dejection; to left is her brother Kretheus, who holds a crown above a horse, which may well be an allusion to their mother Hippe, who was transformed into a mare, and whose appearance and intercession at the end of the play brought it to a satisfactory conclusion. It is a vase of unique interest and, like so many others from South Italy, it provides an important link between art and literature.

Everyday life

Representations of different aspects of the everyday life of men and women are extremely numerous, though children play only a very small part in them. We see youths engaged in various sporting activities – running, wrestling, jumping, riding, etc. – in the palaestra, sometimes in the presence of their trainer or of Nike; the frequent appearance of jumping weights (*halteres*) as a decorative ornament above the draped youths on the reverses of many vases is certainly an allusion to the palaestra, just as the diptych is of the schoolroom. As the fourth century progresses, sporting scenes greatly diminish in frequency and youths tend to look more effeminate, with softer bodies and, at times, overdeveloped breasts, though not quite to the stage of hermaphroditism found in Hellenistic sculptures. Revel scenes with youths and women hurrying off to a party, or at a symposium, are also popular; courting or the offering of gifts is frequently depicted and a small Eros hovering above one or other of the principal characters suggests that marriage is in the air. However, couples seldom go beyond an amorous embrace; the gay abandon of archaic and early classical Greece finds little place in the fourth century. By themselves women may indulge in domestic pursuits like spinning or winding wool; more often they are shown making their toilet or performing ritual lustrations, in which case they may appear naked. Otherwise they mostly wear normal Greek costume – a chiton or a peplos, the latter often with a long overfall, with a girdle at the waist. Sometimes the main garment is made of a very light, filmy material which clearly shows the contours of the body beneath it; this was a Tarentine speciality woven from the filaments of certain types of mussels, which produced a fabric of a silky, golden hue. Cloaks (*himatia*) are often draped across, or completely over, the body, and sometimes drawn up on top of the head at the back with the effect of a veil. A variety of jewellery is worn – earrings, necklaces, bracelets, anklets, etc.; the hair may be completely covered by a *sakkos*, caught up in a *kekryphalos* or tied in a *sphendone*; a radiate *stephane* is commonly worn above the brow; sometimes there is a tiara-like crown, or a *polos*. On Apulian, Campanian and Paestan vases, women are often dressed in native (Oscan) costume, or a blend of native and Greek. Characteristic of the former is a cape, fastened at the throat, a turban-like headdress of curiously medieval aspect, and a long overfall below the girdle at the back. This costume is worn especially in ritual scenes, where the woman is offering a libation to a departing or returning warrior. Men also wear a local costume, in scenes both of everyday life and of battle, where it is accompanied by the appropriate armour. The basic costume consists of a short tunic reaching down to the top of the thighs, decorated with various combinations of black stripes, sometimes ornamented also with swastikas. Their armour normally consists of helmet, cuirass and greaves, with a shield and two spears. The helmets are often of Attic type with a crest and are further adorned by two upstanding feathers stuck into tubes attached one to each side; occasionally Celtic helmets appear on Apulian vases, a reminder of the presence of Celtic mercenaries in that province in the fourth century. Also common is a conical type of helmet (*pilos*), which can be made of metal and have a crest attached to the top, but is more usually of felt or fur, on which small tufts of hair are often visible. Breastplates or cuirasses in Apulia are of the 'muscled' variety, matching on the metal the anatomical configuration of the body, and are an especial favourite of the Baltimore Painter; in Campania, a cuirass with three metal disks on the front is more commonly found. Characteristic also is the wide belt around the waist, often decorated with a row of studs. Many actual examples of the various types of armour shown on the vases have been found in tombs at various South Italian sites. In Sicilian, armed warriors appear only in mythological scenes. For travel and hunting purposes, men wear a *petasos*, a large flat hat with a broad brim. A warrior returning in triumph may carry on his spear the trophies of war – a banner or flag-standard, pieces of armour, and may even be followed by his dejected prisoner, with bound hands. The phlyax vases provide many good parodies of scenes from daily life – husband and wife, father and son, the aftermath of a party, the discovery of a foundling (an ever-popular theme of Middle and New Comedy).

The party was clearly an important factor in daily life. Groups of revellers (komasts) are often shown moving rapidly from one place to another, carrying the appropriate food, drink or musical instruments; indoors, those at the symposium would be entertained by cithara, harp or flute players, as well as by mime or sword dancers, dwarfs, jugglers, acrobats, tumblers and the like. Dionysos himself frequently takes part in these revels, and bunches of grapes or vines decorate the scene.

Landscape as such plays a very small part in outdoor settings and is usually rendered conventionally – rows of dots or lines in added white serve to indicate the ground, with flowering plants, saplings and small shrubs to heighten the effect. Trees, often lopped, also help to define the setting; various rocky formations will indicate a spring, a cave or grotto and in some cases the nature of the terrain. The floral settings, which provide the typical background for the heads or figures on the necks of Apulian volute-kraters and sometimes on the body of the vase, consist of elaborately stylised arrangements of various flowers – rock-roses, dianthus, campanula and lilies are the most readily recognisable –

interwoven with spiralling tendrils, palmette and acanthus leaves to form intricate, and often beautiful, patterns which find parallels on the mosaics of the fourth century and may have been inspired by the floral paintings of Pausias.

Of crafts and trade we see but little – the krater in New York showing an encaustic painter putting the finishing touches to a bronze statue of Herakles *[131]* is unique; the fishmonger is the only tradesman who seems to be represented – fish must have been an important element in the South Italian diet and the fish-plates illustrate a wide range of edible Mediterranean fish (bream, wrasse, bass, perch, mullet, squid, etc.) as well as of seafood (scallops, mussels, shrimps, crabs, etc.).

Death and the After-life

As might be expected with vases destined not for use but for the tomb, funerary monuments and the cult of the dead play an important role on the vases from South Italy, as distinct from Sicilian, where the approach is rather different. Three main types of grave monument are commonly found, with a fourth in comparatively infrequent use. They are as follows:

(i) the *naiskos*, which appears extensively in Apulian, occasionally in Lucanian, in Campanian during the Apulianizing phase, but not in Paestan. It seems to come in with the Iliupersis Painter, early in the second quarter of the fourth century and thereafter becomes increasingly popular. The naiskos appears as a shrine-like structure with engaged Ionic columns and shallow side-walls *[156–9, 248–9]*; the ceiling-beams are sometimes shown, and it is usually crowned by a pediment with acroteria; it stands on a plinth, decorated either with ornamental architectural motifs or more rarely with a triglyph/metope or sculptured frieze. Within the interior of the structure are disposed one or more figures, or objects appropriate to the cult of the dead. They are usually painted in added white, like the monument itself, to simulate the marble or stuccoed limestone of the originals, fragments of which have been found in Taranto.

At first only a single figure appears in the monument *[138]*, but it is not long before the number increases to two or three; more than three figures is exceptional, though in at least one instance there are five. Of male figures, the young warrior is very popular – he appears with various pieces of armour (shield, sword, spear, etc.), and others (especially helmets and greaves) may be suspended from the ceiling; sometimes his horse is shown as well. Other male figures include the huntsman, a youth with his pet bird or dog, or holding a phiale, or other form of ritual vessel. He may also appear in the company of an older, bearded man, perhaps his father, or attended by a servant, or in what looks to be a family group. Women, often shown seated, hold fans, caskets, vessels of various kinds, or fillets; the mistress is often accompanied by her maid, and they may wear colourful costumes, usually in shades of orange or yellow, with crimson stripes or borders, like those which appear on Gnathia vases. It is perhaps worth noting that on hydriai only female figures are normally found in the naiskoi, and that the surrounding mourners are often also women; this suggests that such vases were used particularly in the tombs of women. To the naiskos scenes there is nothing comparable in Athenian vase-painting after the disappearance of white-ground lekythoi at the beginning of the fourth century, but good parallels may readily be seen on the later Attic grave-stones, where the figures are represented in ever higher relief until they appear as almost free-standing within the monument. Various objects associated with the cult of the dead (louteria, loutrophoroi, and other vases), or with the activities of the deceased (wool-basket, armour) may replace human figures within the naiskoi; sometimes there are elaborate flowering plants *[178]* which are perhaps intended to convey the message of the triumph of life over death;

(ii) the stele; this generally takes the form of a tall shaft rising from a stepped plinth; it may be surmounted by a pediment, or have a flat top on which offerings or a single large vase, like a cup or a kantharos, are placed. The shaft is usually tied with black and/or white fillets, which may also be looped over the base, on which various offerings (eggs, pomegranates, vases, etc.) may stand. Stelai of this kind regularly appear on the reverses of vases with naiskoi on the front – a practice originated by the Iliupersis Painter – but also as the main design on the obverse. In that form they occur primarily in Apulian, but in both Paestan and Campanian stelai on a much smaller scale appear as subsidiary decoration. A variant of this type is provided by a monument consisting of a tall base, upon which may rest a vase, or a low stele supporting a vase;

(iii) the grave column; this normally rises from a stepped base, and has a fluted shaft, with an Ionic capital. It is in regular use in Campanian *[307]*, less frequently elsewhere, and often serves to represent the tomb of Agamemnon, where Orestes meets Elektra *[346]*;

(iv) a statue of the deceased; this is far less common. It appears once at the tomb of Agamemnon, showing him as a bearded warrior with shield and spear, once at the tomb of Patroclus, and more often as a free-standing figure on a plinth – an athlete, a young warrior, or a woman, in the last instance in a floral setting.

Grouped around the naiskoi and other monuments there are normally figures bearing various offerings, usually with funerary connections (phialai, mirrors, grapes, caskets, paterae, rosette-chains, fillets), but sometimes perhaps associated with the deceased (armour of different kinds). When the mourners number more than two, their arrangement is usually symmetrical and often chiastic if both sexes are involved (i.e. woman/youth; youth/woman). They are always depicted in red-figure, and look to be of much the same age; they include neither the elderly nor children (both of whom may, however, appear in the naiskoi), and cannot therefore be reckoned as members of the deceased's family: probably they are initiates and, since they are neither sorrowful nor lamenting, are present to convey a conventional message of consolation.

In later Sicilian, and especially at Lipari, as we have seen, the approach is rather different; the funerary monuments are no longer present, and the initiates, presumably into some sort of Dionysiac cult, seem to be preparing for some kind of mystical union in the hereafter or to be resting in the Elysian fields.

The Underworld itself is represented on a number of large Apulian vases, on which the standard version shows Persephone with Pluto in his palace [209], round which are grouped a number of figures. These may include the Danaides, Megara with two of the sons of Herakles, Theseus and Peirithoös, Tantalos and Sisyphus; sometimes also with Herakles and Cerberus and the river Acheron, together with Hermes as psychopompos and a Fury or Poina. On [209] three of the judges of the Underworld are also shown, as well as Orpheus, who comes either to bring back his wife Eurydike, or to escort initiates into the Orphic cult to the next world. The Orphic cult played a large part at Taranto and it is therefore not surprising to see Orpheus represented on many vases – playing to the Thracians [32], dismembered by the raging women, as well as in Hades itself; his head, adorned with the typical Phrygian cap, appears on the necks of many volute-kraters, and once it is the subject of an oracular consultation by a man and woman, presumably followers of his cult. Other aspects of the Underworld may be seen on vases showing Amphiaraos standing before Pluto, the Danaides busy about their task of trying to fill the bottomless pithos, once in the presence of a curious-looking daemon, who might be Eurynomos, a blue-skinned monster who fed upon newly-buried corpses. The repetition of the various figures from one vase to another suggests a common source, perhaps a fresco or free painting like the famous one by Polygnotus.

The better understanding of vase-painting in Magna Graecia, made possible by recent studies and by the remarkable finds of the past thirty years, has awakened a greater interest both in its artistic production in general and in the contribution made by the western colonists to Greek civilisation as a whole. With all the new material at our disposal, we can now see the art of Magna Graecia, and especially its vase-painting, as something 'different' from that of Athens, but this should no longer be taken as implying any measure of inferiority, since, if judged on its own merits, the best of South Italian pottery has a great deal to offer us, both artistically and iconographically.

Chronology
Abbreviations
Select Bibliography
List of Illustrations
Acknowledgements
Indexes

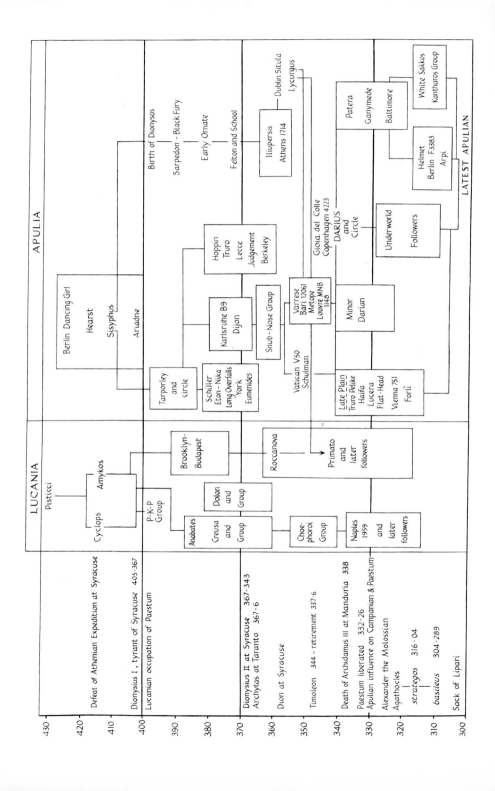

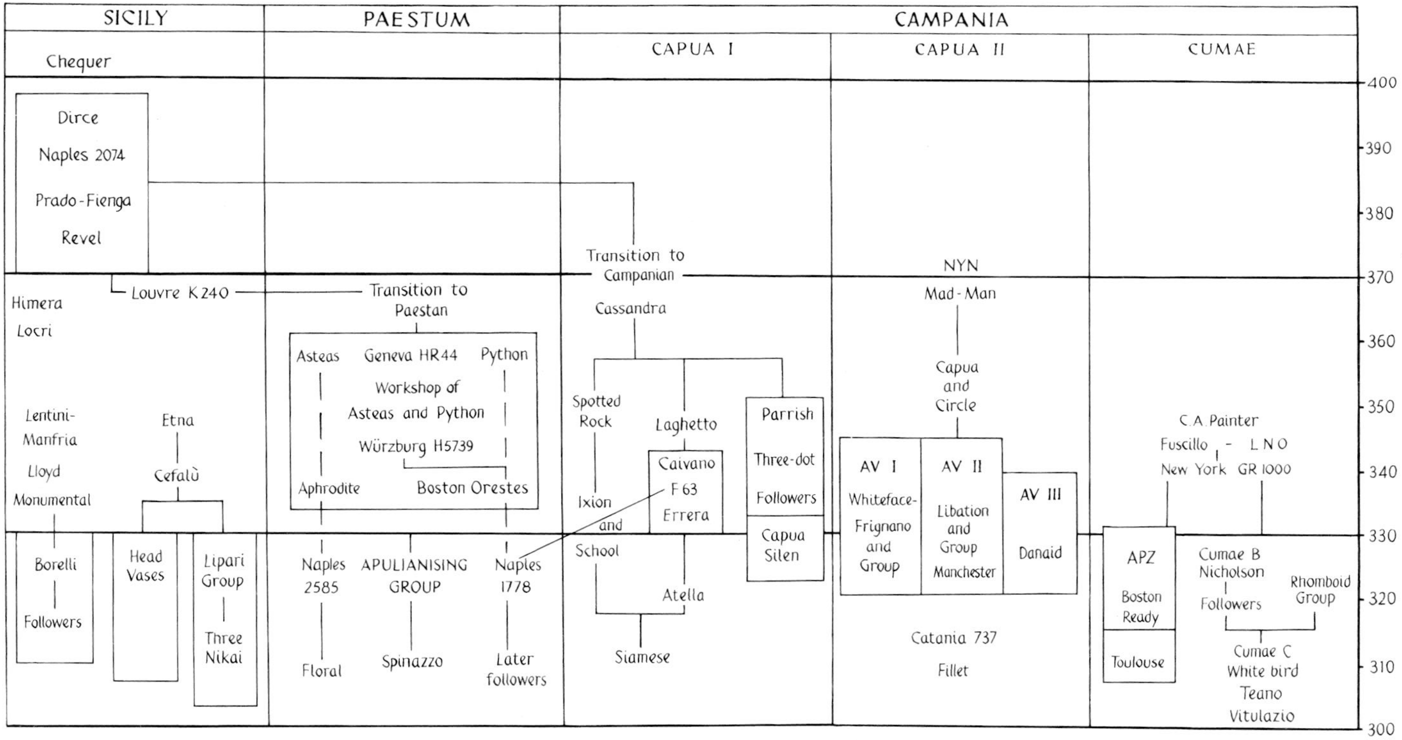

SICILY	PAESTUM	CAMPANIA		
		CAPUA I	CAPUA II	CUMAE

Timeline: 400 — 390 — 380 — 370 — 360 — 350 — 340 — 330 — 320 — 310 — 300

SICILY

Chequer

Dirce
Naples 2074
Prado-Fienga
Revel

Himera
Locri
— Louvre K 240 —

Lentini-
Manfria
Lloyd
Monumental

Etna
Cefalù

Lipari Group
— Three Nikai

Head Vases

Borelli
Followers

PAESTUM

— Transition to Paestun —

Workshop of Asteas and Python

Asteas — Geneva HR44 — Python
Würzburg H5739
Aphrodite — Boston Orestes

Naples 1778
Later followers

APULIANISING GROUP

Naples 2585
Floral — Spinazzo

CAMPANIA — CAPUA I

Transition to Campanian

Cassandra

Spotted Rock — Laghetto — Parrish
Three-dot Followers

Ixion and School
Cuivano F 63 Errera
Capua Silen

Atella
Siamese

CAMPANIA — CAPUA II

NYN

Mad-Man

Capua and Circle

AV I — AV II — AV III
Whiteface-Frignano and Group
Libation and Group Manchester
Danaid

Catania 737
Fillet

CAMPANIA — CUMAE

C A Painter
Fuscillo — L N O
New York GR 1000

APZ
Boston Ready
Toulouse

Cumae B
Nicholson
Followers

Rhomboid Group

Cumae C
White bird
Teano
Vitulazio

ABBREVIATIONS

AA	*Archäologischer Anzeiger*	*Meded Rom*	*Mededelingen van het Nederlands Instituut te Rome*
AJA	*American Journal of Archaeology*		
Ant K	*Antike Kunst*	*MEFRA*	*Mélanges de l'École française de Rome – Antiquité*
Arch Cl	*Archeologia Classica*		
BABesch	*Bulletin Antieke Beschaving*	*Mon Ant*	*Monumenti Antichi (Accademia dei Lincei, Rome)*
CAH	*Cambridge Ancient History*	*ÖJh*	*Jahreshefte des österreichischen archäologischen Instituts in Wien*
BICS	*Bulletin of the Institute of Classical Studies, London*		
BSR	*Papers of the British School at Rome*	*NAC*	*Numismatica e antichità classiche (Quaderni Ticinesi)*
Dial. di Arch.	*Dialoghi di Archeologia*	*NSc*	*Notizie degli Scavi (Accademia dei Lincei, Rome)*
Getty MJ	*Getty Museum Journal*	*Rend Pont Acc*	*Rendiconti della Pontificia Accademia Romana di Archeologia*
JdI	*Jahrbuch des deutschen archäologischen Instituts*	*R.I.*	*German Archaeological Institute, Rome (Photo-Archive)*
JHS	*Journal of Hellenic Studies*	*RM*	*Römische Mitteilungen*

The abbreviations for books to which frequent reference is made
are given in the Select Bibliography

SELECT BIBLIOGRAPHY

The literature on South Italian and Sicilian vase-painting is extensive and the bibliography below is intended only to direct the reader to publications which will provide fuller information on the topics dealt with in the present work.

VASES AND VASE-PAINTERS

The pioneer classifications of Furtwängler (in *Masterpieces of Greek Sculpture*, 1893, 108), Patroni (*La ceramica nell' Italia meridionale*, 1897), Macchioro (*Per la storia della ceramografia italiota*, in *RM* 26, 1911, 187–213; 27, 1912, 21–36 and 163–188; 'I ceramisti di Armento in Lucania', in *Jdl* 27, 1912, 265–316), Tillyard (*The Hope Vases*, 1923, 8–20), Beazley (*Greek Vases in Poland*, 1928, 72–77 and 'Groups of Campanian red-figure', in *JHS* 63, 1943, 66–111), Noël Moon ('Some Early South Italian Vase-painters', in *BSR* 11, 1929, 30–49), and the earlier publications by Trendall (*Paestan Pottery*, 1936; with supplement in *BSR* 20, 1952, 1–52 and *Addenda* in *BSR* 27, 1959, 1–37; *Frühitaliotische Vasen*, 1938, and the updated English version *Early South Italian Vase Painters*, 1974; and, with Alexander Cambitoglou, *Apulian r.f. Vase-painters of the Plain Style*, 1961), have now been incorporated into the three following works, which contain annotated lists of vases attributed to the various painters of Lucanian, Campanian, Sicilian, Apulian and Paestan vases, together with an extensive selection of illustrations, and both general and specific bibliographies.

LCS = A.D. Trendall, *The red-figured Vases of Lucania, Campania and Sicily* (Oxford, 1967), with three Supplements, published as supplementary volumes to the *Bulletin of the Institute of Classical Studies* (I = *Bull. Supp.* 26, 1970; II = *Bull. Supp.* 31, 1973; III = *Bull. Supp.* 41, 1983).
RVAp = A.D. Trendall and Alexander Cambitoglou, *The red-figured Vases of Apulia* (Vol. I, Early and Middle Apulian, Oxford, 1978; Vol. II, Late Apulian, Oxford 1982), with *Supplement* I (= *Bull. Supp.* 42, 1983) and a forthcoming *Supplement* II.
RVP = A.D. Trendall, *The red-figured Vases of Paestum* (British School at Rome, 1987).

Shorter introductory studies to South Italian and Sicilian vase-painting will be found in:–

A.D. Trendall, *South Italian Vase-painting* (British Museum, ed. 2 1976 = *SIVP*), a general guide to the subject based on the collection in the B.M.; see also Dyfri Williams, *Greek Vases* (1985), 56–66.
Margaret Ellen Mayo and Kenneth Hamma (edd.), *The Art of South Italy. Vases From Magna Graecia* (Catalogue of an exhibition held in the Virginia Museum of Fine Arts, Richmond, May–August 1982 = *VMG*), with sections on South Italian vase-painting (by A.D. Trendall), their subject-matter (by Margot Schmidt) and their technique (by J.V. Noble), as well as brief surveys of the individual fabrics.

The following work deals primarily with Apulian, but has useful general observations: Christian Aellen, Alexander Cambitoglou, Jacques Chamay, *Le Peintre de Darius et son milieu* (Catalogue of an exhibition in Geneva, April–August, 1986; *Hellas et Roma* IV = *PdD*).
Short articles on the main fabrics and the more important vase-painters will be found in the *Enciclopedia dell' arte antica* (Vols. I–VII and Supplemento, 1958–1975), under the headings Apuli, Campani, Lucani, Pestani, Sicelioti–Vasi and under the names of individual artists.
Most of the standard works on Greek art or painting contain passing references to South Italian; see, in particular, R.M. Cook, *Greek Painted Pottery* (ed. 2, 1972), 190–201; J. Charbonneaux, R. Martin, F. Villard, *Classical Greek Art* (1972), 292 ff.; Martin Robertson, *A History of Greek Art* (1975), esp. 426 ff. See also: P.E. Arias, M. Hirmer, B.B. Shefton, *History of Greek Vase-painting* (1962), 356–392, with plates 230–240 and colour-plates XLIX–LII.

Recent studies of vases by various South Italian painters include:

Lucanian: Brooklyn-Budapest Painter, K. Schauenburg in *NAC* 14, 1983, 63–83; Sydney Painter, A.D. Trendall in *RVP*, 378–380; Painter of Naples 1959, K. Schauenburg in *Ancient Greek Art and Iconography* (1983), 259–284.

273

Apulian: Darius and Underworld Painters, A.D. Trendall, in *Enthousiasmos* (Festschrift Hemelrijk, 1986), 157–66; Painter of Louvre MNB 1148, id, in *Greek Vases in the J. Paul Getty Museum* 2, 1985, 129–144; Baltimore and White Saccos Painters, P.E. Arias, 'Un nuovo cratere apulo del Pittore di Baltimora' in *Rend Pont Acc* 53–4, 1980–82, 69–90; K. Schauenburg, in *JdI* 99, 1984, 127–160 and *RM* 91, 1984, 359 ff.; L. Todisco in *Arch Cl* 35, 1983, 45–57; id, in *Xenia* 7, 1984, 49–66; Virginia Exhibition Painter, K. Schauenburg in *JdI* 100, 1985, 399–443. See also the article by Ian McPhee in *NAC* 15, 1986, 169–177 which shows the Painter of the Large Egg-Pattern to be Elean rather than Apulian.
Campanian: A.D. Trendall, in *NAC* 12, 1983, 91–106.
Sicilian: N. Stambolidis, 'Some observations on the Sicilian krater 9341', in *Athens Annals of Archaeology* 15, 1982, 143–151; L. Bernabò Brea and M. Cavalier, *La ceramica policroma liparese di età ellenistica* (1986).

ILLUSTRATIONS OF VASES

Several fascicules of the *CVA* (= *Corpus Vasorum Antiquorum*) are also largely devoted to the publication of the South Italian vases in various museum and private collections. Of these the most important are: Great Britain 2 (B.M. 2); Germany 8 (Karlsruhe 2), 19 (Altenburg 3), 23 (Heidelberg 2), 42 (Mainz 2), 50 (Frankfurt 3); Italy 6 (Lecce 2), 11 (Capua 1), 12 (Bologna 3), 32 (Torino 1), 34 (Verona 1), 43 (Trieste 1), 49 (Milano, 'H.A.' coll. 2), 58 (Fiesole, Costantini coll. 2); Japan 1; Poland 7–8 (Warsaw, Nat. Mus. 4–5); Switzerland 5 (Ostschweiz, Ticino); U.S.A. 20 (Toledo 2), 22 (Philadelphia 1). The South Italian vases in the Vatican have been published by A.D. Trendall in *Vasi antichi dipinti del Vaticano: Vasi italioti ed etruschi a figure rosse* (2 vols. 1953, 1955 = *VIE*) and *La Collezione Astarita* III (1976).

Good illustrations of vases, as well as of the sites from which they come and of related objects, will be found in S. Moscati, *Italia Archeologica* (1973) and in volumes 6 and 8 of the Collana Antica Madre (Credito Italiano, 1983 and 1985) entitled *Megale Hellas* and *Sikanie*. The following recently published catalogues of museums and collections in Apulia provide reproductions of vases (often in colour): E.M. De Juliis (ed.), *Archeologia in Puglia* (1983), which gives a rapid survey of all the main museums; id, *Il Museo archeologico di Bari* (1983); id, and D. Loiacono, *Taranto – il Museo archeologico* (1986); Biagio Fedele et al., *Antichità della Collezione Guarini* (1984); Cleto Bucci, *Museo Jatta in obiettivo* (ed. 2, 1986); F. Di Palo, *Museo archeologico Jatta* (1986). Earlier works are referred to in the bibliographies to *RVAp* and *Suppl. I*.

EXCAVATED MATERIAL

As many South Italian vases do not come from scientifically conducted excavations, those which do, have a particular value, since they can be studied in their proper context together with other objects found with them. The publications of the sites listed below, which have been excavated in recent years, are of particular importance for the study and chronology of vase-painting in Magna Graecia. Unless otherwise stated, the references are to the *Notizie degli Scavi* of the year given.

Lucania: Metaponto – *Metaponto* I = Supplement to *NSc* 1975, esp. pp. 355–452; *Excavations in the territory of Metaponto, 1976–1982* (reports by J.C. Carter on excavations conducted by the University of Texas at Austin); Policoro (anc. Herakleia) – *Arch. Forschungen in Lukanien* II. *Herakleiastudien* = *RM* Ergänzungsheft 11, 1967, with a study of the vases by N. Degrassi (pp. 193–231), of which there is an Italian version in *Boll. d'Arte* 1965, 5–37; see also Salvatore Bianco and Marcello Tagliente, *Il Museo Nazionale della Siritide di Policoro* (1985).
Apulia: Gioia del Colle – *Mon Ant* 45, 1960, cols. 145–352; *NSc* 1962, 1–288; Conversano (1964, 100–179); Ugento – *Atti Soc. Magna Grecia* n.s. 11–12, 1972, 99–152. For Tarentine tomb-groups, see *Gli Ori di Taranto* (ed. 2, 1985), 369 ff.; material from Canosa, Ceglie Peuceta and Ginosa is published in the *Studi sull' antico* of the Archaeological Institute of Bari University, vols. 3–4 and 6–7, from Ascoli Satriano and Arpi by F. Tinè Bertocchi in *Le necropoli daunie di Ascoli Satriano e Arpi* (1985), and from Pomarico by Silvia Macchioro in *NAC* 13, 1984, 49–61.
Campania: Many of the tomb-groups in the Neapolitan area excavated before 1940 are published in *Napoli antica* (Exhibition Catalogue, Naples, 1985). *Paestum*: See *RVP*, Bibliography, p. xxvii.
Sicily: Assoro (1966, 232–287), Gela (1960, 67–246; 1962, 341–408), Lentini (1955, 281–376), Manfria (1958, 288–408), Troina (1961, 322–404), Vassallaggi (Suppl. to 1971); Agrigento (*Mon Ant* 46, 1962, cols. 85–198), Butera (*Mon Ant* 44, 1958, cols. 205–672); Himera – Elda Joly, 'Il Pittore di Himera' in *Quaderno Imerese* 1, 1972, 93–105; Lipari – L. Bernabò Brea, *Meligunis-Lipara* II (1965).

The annual *Atti* of the Convegni di Studi sulla Magna Grecia (held at Taranto since 1961) contain much relevant material, as well as accounts of the latest archaeological discoveries in South Italy; these also appear at regular intervals in *Archaeological Reports*.

SHAPES AND TECHNIQUE

Most of the existing studies of vase-shapes deal primarily with Attic, but are still relevant for South

274

Italian. See, in particular, G.M.A. Richter and M.J. Milne, *Shapes and Names of Athenian Vases* (1935); R.S. Folsom, *Handbook of Greek Pottery* (1967), 149–195; W. Schiering, *Die griechischen Tongefässe* (1983); M.G. Kanowski, *Containers of Classical Greece* (1984).

The following deal with particular shapes:– G. Schneider-Herrmann, *Apulian red-figured Paterae* (*BICS* Suppl. 34, 1977), eadem, *Lucanian and Apulian Nestorides* (1980); H. Hoffmann, *Tarentine Rhyta* (1966); K. Schauenburg on alabastra (*JdI* 87, 1978, 258–298), askoi (*RM* 83, 1976, 261–271), dishes or paterae (*AA* 1976, 72–78), oenochoai, shape 8 (*Boreas* 6, 1983, 95–104), situlae (*AA* 1981, 462–483). For fish-plates see Ian McPhee and A.D. Trendall, *Greek Red-figured Fish-plates* (*Antike Kunst*, Beiheft 14, 1987 = *GRFP*), 54–149. For variations between Attic and South Italian vase-shapes see A.D. Trendall, 'On the divergence of South Italian from Attic r.f. vase-painting', in *Proc. 1st Congress Class. Arch. Sydney, 1985* (1988).

The technique is dealt with by J.V. Noble in 'The Techniques of painted South Italian pottery', in *VMG*, 37–47; see also Ingeborg Scheibler, *Griechische Töpferkunst* (1983), and H. Lohmann, 'Zu technischen Besonderheiten Apulischer Vasen', in *JdI* 97, 1982, 191–249.

COMPOSITION

K. Schauenburg, 'Tondokompositionen aus Grossgriechenland', in *JdI* 101, 1986, 159–183.

HISTORICAL BACKGROUND

General: A.G. Woodhead, *The Greeks in the West* (1962); E. Langlotz, *Greek Art, Western* in *Encyclopedia of World Art* vii (1962), 115–173 (esp. 153–161); B. D'Agostino, 'Il mondo periferico della Magna Grecia', in *Popoli e Civiltà della Magna Grecia*, vol. 2 (1974), 179–271; John Boardman, *The Greeks Overseas* (ed. 2, 1980), Chapter 5, with bibliography on p. 276; R. Bosi, *Le città greche d' Occidente* (1980); P.G. Guzzo, *Le Città scomparse della Magna Grecia* (1982); F. D'Andria, *I Greci in Italia* (*Archeo*, Dossier 20, Oct. 1986).

See also *CAH* (ed. 2), vol. vii, part 1 (1984) and the accompanying volume of plates dealing with Sicily and Magna Graecia (pp. 71–80).

For the development of the pottery industry in Magna Graecia see Brian R. Macdonald, 'The emigration of potters from Athens in the late fifth century BC', in *AJA* 85, 1981, 159–168.

Specific: P. Wuilleumier, *Tarente* (1939; repr. 1968); G.C. Brauer, Jr., *Taras* (1986), with bibliography on pp. 215–224; M.W. Frederiksen, *Campania* (B.S.R., 1984); E.T. Salmon, *Samnium and the Samnites* (1967); Angela Greco Pontrandolfo, *I*

Lucani (1982) – M.I. Finley, *Ancient Sicily* (1968); R.J.A. Talbert, *Timoleon and the revival of Greek Sicily, 344–317 BC* (1974); E. Gabba and G. Vallet (edd.), *La Sicilia Antica*, esp. vol. II, part 1 (1980).

SUBJECT MATTER

General

D. von Bothmer, 'Observations on the subject matter of South Italian vases', in *Arts in Virginia* 23, 3 (1983), 28–41.

Mythology

The basic reference works are: W.H. Roscher, *Lexicon der griechischen und römischen Mythologie* (1884–1937), which is now being replaced by the *Lexicon Iconographicum Mythologiae Classicae*, of which three volumes (A-Eros) have been published (1981–86). P. Grimal, *Dictionary of Greek and Roman Mythology* (1986), an English version of his earlier work in French, is of particular value for its references to the ancient sources; also useful are *Room's Classical Dictionary* (1983), John Pinsent, *Greek Mythology* (1969) and Jane Henle, *Greek Myths: a Vase Painter's Notebook* (1973). Excellent illustrations of vases with mythological subjects (mainly Attic) will be found in the 5 volumes of *Helleniki Mythologiá* (Athens, 1987; in Greek).

F. Brommer, *Vasenlisten zur griechischen Heldensage* (1980) lists numerous South Italian vases (under Section D for each entry) with mythological subjects. Konrad Schauenburg has written extensively on mythological subjects on South Italian vases; his publications are listed in *Mythologischer Sach- und Künstlerindex zu den Schriften von K.S. von 1953–1983* (Kiel, 1984), with a subject-index (pp. 12–74), which enables references to a given character to be easily located. *Studien zur Mythologie und Vasenmalerei* (in honour of his 65th birthday in 1986) also contains many relevant articles. Of his own writings published since 1983 the most important for mythology are: 'Herakles und Eulen' and 'Herakles in Neapel' (*RM* 92, 1985, 45–64; 93, 1986, 143–156).

References to works dealing with the mythological subjects represented on specific South Italian vases will be found in the individual entries for each vase in *LCS* and *Supplements* I–III, *RVAp* and *Suppl.* I, and *RVP*.

Recent books or articles on mythological themes, which deal with South Italian vases, include: Eva Zahn, *Europa und der Stier* (Würzburg, 1983); Ruth Lindner, *Der Raub der Persephone* (Würzburg, 1984); F. Brommer, *Herakles II* (1984); K. Schauenburg, 'Zur Telephossage in Unteritalien', in *RM* 90, 1983, 339–358; A.D. Trendall, 'The daughters of Anios', in *Festschrift Schauenburg* (1986), 165–8; id,

'Amphion and Zethos', in *Enthousiasmos* (1986), 157–166; H. Lohmann, 'Der Mythos von Amphiaraos auf apulischen Vasen', in *Boreas* 9, 1986, 65–82; J-M. Moret, *L'Ilioupersis dans la céramique italiote* (1975); A. Cambitoglou, 'Troilos pursued by Achilles', in *Studies in honour of T.B.L. Webster*, vol. II (1988); Emily Vermeule, 'Baby Aigisthos and the Bronze Age', in *Proc. Camb. Phil. Soc.* 213, 1987, 122–152; K. Schefold and F. Jung, *Die Urkönige, Perseus, Bellerophon, Herakles und Theseus in der Klassischen und Hellenistischen Kunst* (Munich, 1988).

Theatre and Drama

L. Séchan, *Etudes sur la tragédie dans ses rapports avec la céramique* (1926) is still basic, though now rather out of date. A.D. Trendall and T.B.L. Webster, *Illustrations of Greek Drama* (Phaidon, 1971) illustrates many South Italian vases with dramatic themes; lists of these will be found in T.B.L. Webster, *Monuments illustrating Tragedy and Satyr-play* (ed. 2, 1967 = *BICS*, Suppl. 20) and *Monuments illustrating Old and Middle Comedy* (ed. 3, 1978, by J.R. Green = *BICS*, Suppl. 39). See also Anneliese Kossatz-Deissmann, *Dramen des Aischylos auf westgriechischen Vasen* (1978). For stage settings see S. Gogos 'Bühnenarchitektur and antike Bühnenmalerei' and 'Das Bühnenrequisit' in *ÖJh* 54, 1983, 59–86 and 55, 1984, 27–53.

Phlyax Vases (ed. 2, 1967 = *BICS*, Suppl. 19) by A.D. Trendall lists vases with scenes or single figures from phlyax plays; for representations of masks see his article 'Masks on Apulian r.f. vases' in *Studies in Honour of T.B.L. Webster*, vol. II (1988). An important new phlyax vase is discussed by F.G. Lo Porto in *Studies Trendall* (1979), 107–110. See also Oliver Taplin, 'Phallology, Phlyakes, Iconography and Aristophanes', in *Proc. Camb. Phil. Soc.* 213, 1987, 93–104. The section by M. Cavalier in L. Bernabò Brea's *Menandro e il teatro greco nelle terrecotte liparesi* (1981), 259–302, illustrates several vases from Lipari with scenes associated with the theatre; see also *Da Eschilo a Menandro*, catalogue of an exhibition in Lipari, 1987, with many pictures of vases and terracottas relevant to the theatre.

A useful section on the theatre in the later 4th century will be found in *CAH*, Pls, to vol. vii, pt. 1, 141–163.

Daily life

For social contacts between the Greek colonists and the native peoples see, in particular, F.G. Lo Porto, 'Civiltà indigena e penetrazione greca nella Lucania orientale', in *Mon Ant* 48, 1973, 105–251 and Angela Greco Pontrandolfo, 'Segni di trasformazioni sociali a Poseidonia', in *Dial. di Arch.* n.s. 1, 2, 1979, 27–50. For native costumes and armour, as depicted on vases, see: F. Weege, 'Bewaffnung und Tracht der Osker', in *JdI* 24, 1909, 141–162; M. Láng, 'Zur oskischen Frauentracht' in *ÖJH* 18, 1915, Beiblatt, 238 ff. and 32, 1940, 35–55; M. Dewailly, 'Les femmes des guerriers indigènes', in *MEFRA* 94, 1982, 581–623; G. Schneider-Herrmann, in *BABesch* 57, 1982, 147–152; illustrations in A.D. Trendall, *Gli Indigeni nella pittura italiota* (Taranto, 1971); Christiane Saulnier, *L'armée et la guerre chez les peuples samnites* (1983).

For hunting, see J.K. Anderson, *Hunting in the ancient world* (Univ. California, 1985) and for symposia, R. Hurschmann, *Symposienszenen auf unteritalischen Vasen* (1985); F.A.G. Beck's *Album of Greek Education* (Sydney, 1975) illustrates a number of South Italian vases representing different aspects of daily life.

For inscribed pillars, especially in the palaestra, see J-M. Moret in *Revue Arch.* 1979, 3–34 and 235–258.

Death and after-life

K. Schauenburg, 'Die Totengötter', in *JdI* 73, 1958, 48–78; id. 'Unterweltsbilder aus Grossgriechenland', in *RM* 91, 1984, 359–387; H.R.W. Smith, *Funerary Symbolism in Apulian Vase-painting* (Univ. of California, 1972); Marina Pensa, *Rappresentazioni dell' oltretomba nella ceramica apula* (1977). For funerary monuments: R. Pagenstecher, *Unteritalische Grabdenkmäler* (1912); M. Schmidt et al., *Eine Gruppe Apulischer Grabvasen in Basel* (1976); K. Schauenburg, 'Tymboi auf unteritalischen Vasen', in *RM* 85, 1978, 83–90; Hans Lohmann, *Grabmäler auf unteritalischen Vasen* (1976). For the actual tombs see John Boardman and Donna Kurtz, *Greek Burial Customs* (1971), 307–315; also Andrew Oliver, *The reconstruction of two Apulian tomb-groups* (*AntK*, Beiheft 5, 1968).

On vases with Orphic representations see Margot Schmidt, 'Orfeo e orfismo nella pittura vascolare italiota', in *Atti XIV° Conv. di Studi sulla Magna Grecia, 1974*), 105–137.

276

LIST OF ILLUSTRATIONS

70–71 Rome, American Academy 1840. *LCS* 92, no. 477, pl. 45, 5–6; *Supp.* III 48, no. C 56.

72 Toledo 81.110. *LCS Supp.* III 66, no. C 22, pl. VII.

73 Vienna 653. *LCS* 94, no. 490, pl. 46,2; *Supp.* III 50, no. C 83.

74 Matera 9579. *LCS Supp.* III 54, no. C 145; *PhV²*, no. 44, pl. 3c.

75–6 Bari 6264. *LCS* 102, no. 535, pls. 53,1 and 51,8; *Supp.* III 57, no. D 9.

77–8 Paris, Louvre CA 2193. *LCS* 100, no. 517; *Supp.* III 56, no. D 4, pl. IX,3.

79 Paris, Cab. Méd. 422. *LCS* 102, no. 532; *Supp.* III 58, no. D 19.

80 Metaponto 29057. *LCS Supp.* III 60, no. D 26.

81 B.M. F 157. *LCS* 102, no. 533, pl. 52,3; *Supp.* III 59, no. D 21.

82 B.M. F 176. *LCS* 103, no. 540; *Supp.* III 61, no. D 30.

83–4 Brooklyn 09.7. *LCS* 109, no. 559, pl. 55,1–2; *Supp.* III 67, no. BB 2.

85 Kiel, private coll. (on loan to Hamburg). *LCS Supp.* III, p. 69, no. BB 30.

86 B.M. F 179. *LCS* 113, no. 582, pl. 58; *Supp.* III 71, no. BB 47.

87 Budapest 50.191. *LCS* 112, no. 581, pl. 57,5; *Supp.* III 71, no. BB 45.

88 Oxford 1952.235. *LCS* 128, no. 655, pl. 63,5.

89–90 Madrid 11091 (L. 232). *LCS* 119, no. 598, pl. 60,1–2.

91 Munich 3266. *LCS* 120, no. 602.

92 Cambridge (Mass.), Fogg Art Museum 1960.367. *LCS* 125, no. 644, pl. 62,4.

93 Reading 160.51 RM. *LCS* 132, no. 670, pl. 64,1.

94 B.M. F 201. *LCS* 140, no. 780, pl. 65,6.

95 Taranto 8153. *LCS* 141, no. 783, pl. 66,5.

96 Munich 3270. *LCS* 148, no. 826, pl. 69,3–6.

97 Naples 1762. *LCS* 165, no. 917, pl. 72,1.

98 Louvre K 526. *LCS* 165, no. 923, pl. 72,4.

99 Vatican W 1 (inv. 17137). *LCS* 167, no. 926.

100 Louvre K 518. *LCS* 167, no. 931, pl. 73,3.

APULIAN

101 B.M. F 126. *RVAp* I 46, no. 3/1.

102–3 New York L.63.21.5 (on loan from Mr Jan Mitchell). *RVAp* I 46, no. 3/2.

104 Sydney 47.05. *RVAp* I 48, no. 3/15.

105 New York 24.97.104 (Fletcher Fund, 1924). *RVAp* I 46, no. 3/7; *VMG* 82–3, no. 13.

106–7 Gotha 72. *RVAp* I 51, no. 3/39.

108 Paris, Cab. Méd. 931. *RVAp* I 66, no. 4/10.

109 Würzburg H 5697. *RVAp* I 65, no. 4/4a; Kossatz-Deissmann in *Tainia (Festschrift Hampe)*, pp. 281–90, pl. 60.

110 Adolphseck 179. *RVAp* I 72, no. 4/51.

111 Kiel, Kunsthalle B 537. *RVAp* I 73, no. 4/61a; Schauenburg in *Meded Rom* 41, 1979, 21–27, pl. 9.

112–3 Bologna 537. *RVAp* I 80, no. 4/100.

114 Ruvo 820. *RVAp* I 85, no. 4/142. Photo *R.I.* 64.1225.

115 S. Agata, former Rainone coll. 1. *RVAp* I 96, no. 4/224; *PhV²*, no 59.

116–7 Once Swiss Market. *RVAp* II 1045, no. 5/15a.

118 Vienna 894. *RVAp* I 117, no. 5/125.

119 B.M. F 168. *RVAp* I 124, no. 5/208, pl. 40,5.

120 Leningrad 299 (St. 1775). *RVAp* I 129, no. 5/260; *PhV²*, no. 31.

121 Bari 6257. *RVAp* I 139, no. 6/31. Photo *R.I.* 62.1165.

122 Karlsruhe B9. *RVAp* I 136, no. 6/8.

123 Pulsano, Guarini coll. 18. *RVAp* II 1047, no. 6/14a; *Antichità della coll. Guarini*, p. 60, no. 2, pl. 68.

124 Taranto 61059. *RVAp* I 147, no. 6/90, pl. 46,1.

125 Bari 3899. *RVAp* I 148, no. 6/96; *PhV²*, no. 18. Photo *R.I.* 62.1161.

126 Ruvo 620. *RVAp* I 154, no. 6/165. Photo *R.I.* 64.1214.

127–8 Vatican T 7 (inv. 17946). *RVAp* I 148, no. 6/95.

129 Cleveland 24.534. *RVAp* I 161, no. 6/216.

130 Taranto 117503. *RVAp* I 262, no. 10/18, pl. 86,1.

131 New York 50.11.4 (Rogers Fund, 1950). *RVAp* I 266, no. 10/47; *VMG* 96–8, no. 27.

132 Christchurch (N.Z.), Univ. of Canterbury 116/71. *RVAp* I 273, no. 10/83, pl. 90,5.

133 Malibu, J. Paul Getty Museum 71 AE 248. *RVAp* I 275, no. 10/103.

134 New York 20.195 (Rogers Fund, 1920). *RVAp* I 266, no. 7/8, pl. 53,4; *VMG* 84, no. 14.

135 Malibu, J. Paul Getty Museum 72 AE 128. *RVAp* I 167, no. 7/12, pl. 54,6.

136 Melbourne 90/5. *RVAp* I 172, no. 7/49.

137 Taranto, Ragusa coll. 74. *RVAp* I 174; *PhV²*, no. 115, pl. 8b.

138–9 B.M. F 283. *RVAp* I 193, no. 8/7, pl. 61,1–2.

140 Milan, 'H.A.' coll. 239. *RVAp* I 193, no. 8/4, pl. 60,3.

141 Boston, M.F.A. 1970.235. *RVAp* I 194, no. 8/11, pl. 61,3.

142 New York L.63.21.6 (on loan from Jan Mitchell). *RVAp* I 212, no. 8/152, pl. 67,1.

143–4 Parma C 97. *RVAp* I 217, no. 8/206, pl. 69,3–4.

145 London, Victoria and Albert Museum 2493–1910. *RVAp* I 396, no. 15/6, pl. 137,5.

146 Ruvo 1372, *RVAp* I 402, no. 15/36. Photo *R.I.* 64.1230.

147 Essen, Folkwang Museum 74.158 A 3. *RVAp* I 404, no. 15/44a; H. Froning, *Griechische und italische Vasen*, pp. 214–9, no. 89.

148 B.M. F 271. *RVAp* I 415, no. 16/5, pl. 147.

149 B.M. 1931.5–11.1. *RVAp* I 416, no. 16/10, pl. 149,1.

150 B.M. F 352. *RVAp* I 418, no. 16/20, pl. 151,3.

151 Karlsruhe B 4. *RVAp* I 431, no. 16/81, pl. 160,1.

152–3 Vatican V 14 (inv. 18047). *RVAp* I, 226, no. 9/5.

154–5 Geneva 2754. *RVAp* I 230, no. 9/38, pl. 72,1–2.

156 Ruvo 603. *RVAp* I 241, no. 9/111. Photo *R.I.* 64.1211.

157 Tampa (Florida), Museum of Art 86.102 (ex Noble coll.). *RVAp* I 249, no. 9/187, pl. 82,1; *VMG* 120–1, no. 42.

158 Bari, Lagioia coll. *RVAp* I 253, no. 9/224, pl. 84,3.

159 Brussels A 1381. *RVAp* I 289, no. 11/16.

160 Once Basel Market, MuM. *RVAp* II, 1057, no. 11/98b.

161 Sydney 49.11. *RVAp* I, 304, no. 11/182, pl. 96,2.

162–3 Lecce 609. *RVAp* I 319, no. 12/16, pl. 99,1.

164 Richmond (Va.) 76.37. *RVAp* I 331, no. 12/126a; *VMG* 118–9, no. 41.

165 Naples 2887. *RVAp* I 323, no. 12/55; Lohmann, *JdI* 97, 1982, 213, fig. 18.

166–7 Sydney 69. *RVAp* I 382, no. 14/169, pl. 130,3–4.

168 Karlsruhe 65/100. *RVAp* I 387, no. 14/215.

169 Taranto 135755. *RVAp* I 392, no. 14/257, pl. 136,3.

170 Taranto 8922. *RVAp* I 337, no. 13/1, pl. 108,1.

171 Once London Market (American private coll.). *RVAp Supp.* I 46, no. 13/34,2, pl. V,2.

172 London Market.

173–4 Vienna 1158. *RVAp* I 348, no. 13/101, pl. 113,3–4.

175–6 B.M. F 297. *RVAp* I 357, no. 13/197, pl. 115,5–6.

177 Philadelphia L 64.26. *RVAp* I 372, no. 14/104, pl. 123,1.

178 Once London Market, Sotheby. *RVAp* I 373, no. 14/113, pl. 124,1.

179 Geneva 24692. *PdD* 71–83, 283–4, colour ill. on p. 17.

180 Bari 12061. *RVAp* I 376, no. 14/126, pl. 126,3.

181 Once London Market (American private coll.). *RVAp Supp.* I 72, no. 18/16e, pl. X,4.

182 Malibu, J. Paul Getty Museum 84 AE 996. *Getty MJ* 13, 1985, p. 171, fig. 26.

183 Malibu, J. Paul Getty Museum 82 AE 16. *RVAp Supp.* I 100, no. 20/278a; *Greek Vases* 2 (Occasional Papers on Antiquities 3) 1985, 129–144.

184 Malibu, J. Paul Getty Museum 86 AE 680. *Getty MJ* 15, 1987, p. 163, no. 17 (ill.).

185 W. Berlin F 3291. *RVAp* I 426, no. 16/60, pl. 156,4.

186 Bari 20054. *RVAp* II 457, no. 17/1, pl. 161,1.

187 Copenhagen 4223. *RVAp* II 463, no. 17/37, pl. 165,1.

188 Geneva, private coll. *PdD* 90–94 (ill.).

189 Geneva HR 69. *PdD* 85–90 (ill.).

190–1 Barletta 659 (912). *RVAp* II 474, no. 18/1, pl. 168.

192–3 W. Berlin 1969.9. *RVAp* II 476, no. 18/6.

194 Basel, Antikenmuseum BS 468. *RVAp* II 480, no. 18/13, pl. 170,3.

195 B.M. F 272. *RVAp* II 481, no. 18/14, pl. 169,1.

196 Basel, Antikenmuseum S21. *RVAp* II 482, no. 18/16, pl. 171,4.

197 Geneva HR 44. *PdD* 97–108 (ill.).

198 Los Angeles Market.

199 Los Angeles Market.

200 Melbourne, Geddes coll. A 5:3, ex Sotheby, *Sale Cat.* 9 Dec. 1985, no. 173 (colour ill.).

201 Naples 3220. *RVAp* II 497–8, no. 18/47.

202 New York 11.210.3 (Rogers Fund, 1911). *RVAp* II 489, no. 18/20, pl. 174,2.

203 Naples 3253. *RVAp* II 495, no. 18/38, pl. 176,1. Photo R.I. 71.454.

204 Naples 3254. *RVAp* II 495, no. 18/39; *FR*, pl. 89.

205 Miami (Florida), private coll. *Festschrift Schauenburg* (1986), pls. 30,1 and 31.

206 Los Angeles Market.

207 Geneva, private coll. *PdD* p. 25 (colour ill.), and pp. 181–4.

208 Richmond (Va.) 80.162. *RVAp Supp.* I 84, no. 18/281c; *VMG* 128–132, no. 50 (ill.).

209 Munich 3297. *RVAp* II 533, no. 18/282, pl. 194; *FR*, pl. 10.

210 Geneva, Sciclounoff coll. *PdD* 190–199 (ill.) and colour-plate.

211 Melbourne, Geddes coll. A 5:4. *Enthousiasmos* (Festschrift J.M. Hemelrijk, 1986), p. 164, fig. 8.

212 Naples, private coll. 23. *RVAp* 543, no. 18/357, pl. 205,5.

213 Pulsano, Guarini coll. 25. *RVAp* II 553, no. 19/56a, pl. 207,3; *Antichità della coll. Guarini*, pl. 105,1.

214–5 B.M. F 325. *RVAp* II 562, no. 20/5, pl. 209,5–6.

216–7 Zurich, Mildenberg coll. *RVAp* II 566, no. 20/41, pl. 212,1–2.

218–9 Vienna 76. *RVAp* II 579, no. 20/176, pl. 219,3–4.

220–1 Lecce 730. *RVAp* II 599, no. 20/365, pl. 231,4.

222 Bloomington, Indiana University Art Museum 77.109. *RVAp* II 607, no. 21/27, pl. 233,3.

223 Bari, Malaguzzi-Valeri coll. 49. *RVAp* II 617, no. 21/96, pl. 235,5–7.

224–5 Malibu, J. Paul Getty Museum 71 AE 301. *RVAp* II 656, no. 22/76, pl. 243,8.

226 Liverpool University. *RVAp* II 654, no. 22/47, pl. 241,4.

227 (1) Once London Market. *RVAp* II 664, no. 22/153, pl. 248,1. (2) Once London Market. *RVAp* II 664, no. 22/158, pl. 248,3. (3) Kiron, Goldfine coll. *RVAp* II 680, no. 22/400, pl. 252,6. (4) Bari 1179. *RVAp* II 697, no. 22/597, pl. 259,2. (5) Milan 66/1957. *RVAp* II 709, no. 22/734, pl. 263,4. (6) Policoro S 271. *RVAp* II 713, no. 22/778, pl. 264,9. (7) Kassel T 603. *RVAp* II 715, no. 22/809, pl. 265,8. (8) Rheinbach, Koch coll. *RVAp* II 719, no. 22/865, pl. 266,5.

228 Once Ascona, Galleria Serodine. *RVAp Supp.* I, 126, no. 22/874a, pl. 23,6.

229–30 Zurich, Roš coll. *RVAp* II 727, no. 23/7, pl. 268,1–2.

231 Ruvo 1613. *RVAp* II 732, no. 23/39, pl. 270,1.

232–3 Once London Market, Sotheby, *Sale Cat.* 9 Dec. 1985, no. 174A (ill.). *RVAp* II, 744, no. 23/145b, pl. 275,5–6.

234–5 B.M. F 294. *RVAp* II 748, no. 23/179, pl. 277, 1–2.

236 New York 17.120.240 (Isaac D. Fletcher Bequest). *RVAp* II 754, no. 23/231, pl. 280,1; *VMG*, p. 40, fig. 2.

237 (1) Column-krater, Bologna 582. *RVAp* II 747, no. 23/171. (2) Column-krater, once Milan Market, ex Arnò coll. *RVAp* II 747, no. 23/176. (3) Dish, Göttingen 583d. *RVAp* II 768, no. 24/23; Schneider–Herrmann, *Paterae*, no. 128A. (4) Situla, Bonn 103. *RVAp* II

772, no. 24/89 (where incorrectly listed as an amphora). (5–6) Oenochoe (shape 8), Kiel B 572. *RVAp Supp.* I 138, no. 25/66b. (7) Plate, Armidale 69/1. *RVAp* II 805, no. 25/75, pl. 300,2. (8) Skyphos, Leiden K 1977/11. 1. *RVAp* II 806, no. 25/92, pl. 300,6. (9) Column-krater, Vatican Z 26. *RVAp* II 811, no. 25/147; *VIE*, pl. 36g.

238–9 Melbourne D 88/1969. *RVAp* II 796, no. 25/3.

240 Swiss private coll. *RVAp* II 795, no. 25/1, pl. 294.

241 Geneva, Sciclounoff coll. (ex London Market), Sotheby, *Sale Cat.* 14 July 1986, no. 175 (ill.).

242 Once Zurich Market. *RVAp Supp.* I 70, no. 18/11a, pl. 19,1, where incorrectly associated with the forerunners of the Darius Painter.

243 Ruvo 779. *RVAp* II 822, no. 26/36, pl. 307,6. Photo *R.I.* 64.1249.

244 Canberra 65.20. *RVAp* II 826, no. 26/89, pl. 311,2; J.R. Green, *Antiquities*, pp. 52–3.

245 Zurich, Rôs coll. 67. *RVAp* II 830, no. 26/129, pl. 315,1.

246 Once Basel Market, MuM. *RVAp Supp.* I 145, no. 26/516a, pl. XXV,9.

247 Hamburg, private coll. *RVAp* II 850, no. 26/488; *Kat. Hamburg*, pp. 365–6, no. 313.

248–9 Toledo 77.45. *RVAp* II 862, no. 27/13, pl. 322; *VMG* 164–7, no. 68 (ill.).

250 Vienna 94. *RVAp* II 861, no. 27/5, pl. 320,1.

251 Geneva, Sciclounoff coll. *PdD* 215–224 (ill.), colour-plate p. 26.

252 Ruvo 424. *RVAp* II 865, no. 27/24, pl. 324,2.

253 Bari, Macinagrossa coll. 26. *RVAp* II 871, no. 27/57, pl. 333,2.

254 (1) Plate by the Stoke-on-Trent Painter, Brooklyn 50.50. *RVAp* II 889, no. 27/242, pl. 341,1. (2) Lebes gamikos by the Stoke-on-Trent Painter, Fiesole 1149. *RVAp* II 890, no. 27/259, pl. 341,4. (3) Kantharos, Taranto 123596, by the T.C. Painter. *RVAp* II, 902, no. 27/487, pl. 343,7. (4) Stand, Bari,

Macinagrossa coll. 52, by the Painter of the Macinagrossa Stand. *RVAp* II 904, no. 27/515, pl. 344.3. (5) Amphora, Vatican V 48, by the Copenhagen Head Painter. *RVAp* II 951, no. 28/322. (6) Volute-krater, once Athens Market, Acheloös 50, White Sakkos Painter/ Kantharos Group. *RVAp* II 962, no. 29/3, pl. 375,4. (7) Kantharos, once Hattatt coll., Kantharos Group. *RVAp* II 997, no. 29/438. (8) Kantharos, Marburg 788 – Kantharos Group, Painter of Marburg 788. *RVAp* II 1011, no. 29/826, pl. 389,10. (9) Amphora, Palermo 2244, by the Painter of B.M. F 339. *RVAp* II 1032, no. 30/102, pl. 399,4.

255 Tampa (Florida), C.W. Sahlman coll. Zewadski *Ancient Gr. Vases in Tampa Bay colls.*, *Suppl.* I, 15–20, ill. on pp. 21–24.

256 Geneva, Sciclounoff coll. *RVAp* II 961, no. 29/2a; Schauenburg, *RM* 90, 1983, pls. 79–81.

257 Once London Market, Heim Gallery. *RVAp Supp.* I 182, no. 29/B, pl. XXXVI.

258 San Simeon 5509. *RVAp* II 974, no. 29/154, pl. 381,7.

259 Boston 76.62 (Gift of T.G. Appleton). *RVAp* II 980, no. 29/228, pl. 384,5.

260 New York 56.171.63 (Isaac D. Fletcher Fund; ex Hearst coll.). *RVAp* II 907, no. 28/1, pl. 345.

261 Vatican AA 5. *RVAp* II 910, no. 28/13; *VIE*, pl. 39b.

262 Berlin F 3383. *RVAp* II 918, no. 28/58, pl. 353.

263 Naples 3236 (82269). *RVAp* II 918, no. 28/60, pl. 354,2–4.

264 Foggia 132723. *RVAp* II 925, no. 28/90, pl. 360,2.

265 Foggia 132726. *RVAp* II 925, no. 28/91, pl. 361.

266 Tampa (Florida), C.W. Sahlman coll. *RVAp* II 926, no. 28/96, pl. 362.

267 B.M. F 237. *RVAp* II 933, no. 28/128, pl. 367,1.

268 New York, private coll. *RVAp Supp.* I 174, no. 28/86b, pl. XXXIII,2; *VMG*, pp. 178–9, no. 73 (ill.).

269 Basel BS 484. *RVAp Supp.* I 174–5, no. 28/86f; Margot

Schmidt, *AntK* 27, 1984, 34–40, pls. 8–10.

270 Mannheim Cg 230. *RVAp* II 1025, no. 30/45, pl. 396,6.

271 B.M. F 156, from the Blacas Tomb. *LCS* 211, no. 1/61; *Supp.* III, 105, no. 103.

272 Lipari 11806. *LCS Supp.* III 108, no. 120, pl. XII,4; *RVP*, no. 1/45, pl. 4c.

273 Capua 7554. *LCS* 225, no. 2/1, pl. 88,1.

274 Erlangen I 264. *LCS Supp.* II 188, no. 2/41a, pl. 34,3–4.

275–6 B.M. 1928.7–19.3. *LCS* 250, no. 2/148; *SIVP*, pl. 11.

277 Naples, private coll., ex Sotheby, *Sale Cat.* 12–13 Dec. 1983, no. 409 (ill.).

278 Naples 870 (82744). *LCS* 276, no. 2/342, pl. 112,6.

279 Philadelphia L 64.219. *LCS* 280, no. 2/376, pl. 114,7.

280 Paestum 5427. *LCS* 298, no. 2/510, pl. 119,6.

281 Naples 147950, from Frignano. *LCS* 307, no. 2/567, pl. 123,1.

282 Naples, private coll. *NAC* 12, 1983, 91–94, figs. 1–4.

283 Once London Market, Christie's, *Sale Cat.* 6 May 1982, no. 211, ill. on p. 28; *LCS Supp.* III 147, no. 2/584b.

284 Cambridge 248. *LCS* 316, no. 2/645, pl. 124.

285 Boston 03.822. *LCS* 323, no. 2/718.

286 Oxford 1894.5 (V528), from Capua. *LCS* 339, no. 2/802, pl. 133,5.

287 Kiel, private coll. *LCS Supp.* III 158, no. 2/792a; Schauenburg, *AA* 1976, 218, figs. 6–8; *Kat. Hamburg* 402, no. 344 (ill.).

288 New York 06.1021.240 (Rogers Fund, 1906). *LCS* 339, no. 2/801, pl. 132,5; *VMG*, pp. 206–7, no. 90 (ill.).

289 Once London Market. *LCS Supp.* III 160, no. 2/822b.

290 Naples, private coll.

291 San Diego, private coll. *LCS Supp.* III 168, no. 2/903a, pl. XIX,5.

292 New York 06.1021.225 (Rogers Fund, 1906). *LCS* 361, no. 3/5,

pl. 138,4–5; *Supp.* III 173, no. 3/7.

293 Naples, private coll. *LCS Supp.* III 177, no. 3/49c, pl. XX,2.

294 Paris, Cab. Méd. 1046. *LCS* 375, no. 3/115; *PhV²*, no. 133, pl. VId.

295 Zurich, Roŝ coll. *LCS* 381, no. 3/139, pl. 147,1.

296 Boston 69.1142. *LCS Supp.* I 69, no. 3/139a, pl. 16,4; *Supp.* III 185; Emily Vermeule in *Studies Hanfmann* (1971) 177–188, pls. 46–9.

297 New York 06.1021.236 (Rogers Fund, 1906). *LCS* 380, no. 3/124, pl. 145,2.

298 B.M. 1957.2–12.24. *LCS* 385, no. 3/177, pl. 148,6.

299 Vatican, Astarita 58. *LCS* 400, no. 3/269, pl. 155,1–2; *VIE* Astarita 3, pl. 10,1–3.

300 New York 01.8.12. *LCS* 402, no. 3/284, pl. 158,1; *VMG* 210–11, no. 92 (ill.); colour-plate p. 15.

301 Louvre K 261. *LCS* 406, no. 3/299, pl. 159,1.

302 Naples, private coll. *LCS Supp.* III 199, no. 3/304f, pl. XXIII,3.

303 Sydney 51.17. *LCS* 406, no. 3/305, pl. 160,4.

304 Melbourne D 14/1973. *LCS Supp.* III 201, no. 3/337a.

305 Sydney 71.01. *LCS Supp.* II 223, no. 3/340a, pl. 38,4; Trendall, *Rev Arch* 1972, 310, fig. 1.

306 Manchester IV E 30. *LCS* 415, no. 3/359.

307 Hamburg, Termer coll. *LCS Supp.* III 208, no. 3/495a; *Kat. Hamburg*, 395 ff., no. 341

308 B.M. F 207. *LCS* 430, no. 3/496, pl. 171,3.

309 B.M. F 194. *LCS* 430, no. 3/495, pl. 171,2.

310 Louvre K 334. *LCS* 439, no. 3/577, pl. 173,1.

311 Sydney, Phillip Adams coll. 70. *LCS Supp.* III 211, no. 3/612a.

312–13 Budapest 51.41. *LCS* 453, no. 4/12, pl. 175,5–6.

314 Newark (N.J.) 50.330. *LCS* 455, no. 4/19, pl. 176,1.

315 Naples RC 144 (85873). *LCS* 460, no. 4/70, pl. 178,1.

316 Mannheim (ex Lugano, Bolla coll.). *LCS Supp.* III 217, no. 4/64a, pl. XXV 3–4; MuM,

Auktion 70, 14 Nov. 1986, no. 224, pl. 59.

317 (1) Bell-krater, Geneva, Hartmann coll. *LCS Supp.* II 234, no. 4/201b, pl. 41,4 (CA Painter). (2) Bail-amphora, Sudbury Hall. *LCS Supp.* III, no. 4/219c, pl. XXVI,3 (CA Painter). (3) Bell-krater, Vatican U 43. *LCS* 491, no. 4/378 (Painter of New York GR 1000). (4) Squat lekythos, once London Market. *LCS Supp.* III 243, no. 4/551b (APZ Painter). (5) Bell-krater, Madrid, Palacio de Liria 28. *LCS* 532, no. 4/745, pl. 210,3 (now attributed to the Nicholson Painter; see *Supp.* III, 250). (6) Plate, Birmingham 1297.85 *LCS* 543, no. 4/812 (Branicki Painter – Rhomboid Group). (7) Bell-krater, once London Market. *LCS Supp.* III 256, no. 4/860a (Painter of B.M. F 229). (8) Kemai, Würzburg 884. *LCS* 569, no. 4/1004 (near Fratte Group). (9) Bell-krater, Naples, private coll. *LCS Supp.* III 261, no. 4/1030a, pl. XXX, 5 (Vitulazio Painter).

318 Paestum 5232, from Paestum. *LCS* 477, no. 4/260, pl. 184,4.

319–20 New York 96.18.25 (GR 1000). *LCS* 485, no. 4/323, pl. 187, 1–2.

321 Naples 856 (82768). *LCS* 497, no. 4/412, pl. 192.

322–3 New York 06.1021.231 (Rogers Fund, 1906). *LCS* 502, no. 4/429, pl. 196.

324 Melbourne, Geddes coll. C 6:0. *LCS Supp.* III 237, no. 4/434b.

325 Naples 127977, from Cumae. *LCS* 508, no. 4/512, pl. 199,3.

326–7 Boston 63.3. *LCS* 516, no. 4/607, pl. 201, 1–2.

328 Once Baden, Roŝ coll. *LCS* 519, no. 4/644, pl. 204,1–2.

329–30 Salerno, Sopr. Ant. from Montesarchio T. 462. *LCS Supp.* III 248, no. 4/667d.

331 Sydney 46.01. *LCS* 523, no. 4/668, pl. 206,1.

332 Vienna 129. *LCS* 540, no. 4/782, pl. 211,6.

333 Stockholm N.M. 20. *LCS* 540, no. 4/777, pl. 212,6.

334 Leningrad 3008. *LCS* 552, no. 4/882, pl. 215,5.

335 Naples 128131, from Cumae. *LCS* 557, no. 4/907, pl. 218,5.

336 Frankfurt H 5. *LCS* 558, no. 4/912, pl. 220,1.

337 Naples 132444, from Teano. *LCS* 559, no. 4/916, pl. 220,5–6.

338 Naples 132442, from Teano. *LCS* 560, no. 4/918, pl. 221,1.

PAESTAN

339 Louvre K 240. *RVP*, no. 1/94, pl. 11c.

340 Lipari 927. *RVP*, no. 1/99, pl. 12f.

341 New York, private coll. *RVP*, no. 1/101, pl. 13b.

342–3 Basel, Antikenmuseum Z 313. *RVP*, no. 2/8, pl. 17 c–d.

344–5 Melbourne D 391/1980. *RVP*, no. 2/24, pl. 21 c–d.

346–7 Geneva HR 29. *RVP*, no. 2/1, pl. 15; *PdD* 264–9 (ill.), colour-plate on p. 28.

348 New York 1985.74 (Gift of D. von Bothmer). *RVP*, no. 2/2, pl. 16a.

349–50 Malibu, J. Paul Getty Museum 81 AE 78. *RVP*, no. 2/129, pls. 49–51.

351 Naples 2873 (81847), from Paestum. *RVP*, no. 2/135, pl. 57.

352–3 W. Berlin F 3044, from S. Agata. *RVP*, no. 2/125, pl. 44.

354 Rome, Villa Giulia 50279, from Buccino. *RVP*, no. 2/130, pl. 54b.

355 Madrid 11094 (L. 369), from Paestum. *RVP*, no. 2/127, pl. 46.

356–7 Paestum 21306, from Paestum. *RVP*, no. 2/137, pl. 59 a–b.

358 Louvre K 570. *RVP*, no. 2/140, pl. 60.

359 Basel, Antikenmuseum. *RVP*, no. 2/141, pl. 61.

360 Paestum 4794, from Paestum. *RVP*, no. 2/142, pl. 62a.

361 Paestum 26631, from Paestum. *RVP*, no. 2/151, pl. 65.

362 Paestum 26633, from Paestum. *RVP*, no. 2/152, pl. 66.

363 Paestum 26635, from Paestum. *RVP*, no. 2/154, pl. 67b.

364 Vatican U 19 (17106). *RVP*, no. 2/176, pl. 73a; *PhV²*, p. 46, no. 65.

365 Madrid 11445 (L. 433). *RVP*, no. 2/186, pl. 76.

366 Japanese private coll. *RVP*, no. 2/223, pl. 83b.
367 B.M. F 149, from S. Agata. *RVP*, no. 2/239, pl. 88.
368–9 Paestum 21370, from Paestum. *RVP*, no. 2/240, pl. 89.
370 Louvre N 3157, from S. Agata. *RVP*, no. 2/241, pl. 90.
371 B.M. 1917.12–10.1. *RVP*, no. 2/244, pl. 91.
372 Vatican AD 1 (17370). *RVP*, no. 2/245, pl. 92.
373 Paestum 21369, from Paestum. *RVP*, no. 2/248, pl. 93d.
374–5 Paestum 82.15. *RVP*, no. 2/271, pl. 100 c–d.
376 W. Berlin 4532. *RVP*, no. 2/272, pl. 100e.
377 Richmond (Va.) 81.72. *RVP*, no. 2/285, pl. 104c; *VMG* 240, no. 113.
378 Hamburg, Termer coll. *RVP*, no. 2/349, pl. 112a.
379 Louvre K 244. *RVP*, no. 2/306, pl. 107e.
380–1 Würzburg H 5739. *RVP*, no. 2/379, pl. 118; *Kat. Hamburg*, p. 379, no. 328; Simon, *Werke der Antike* (1983), p. 148, no. 67.
382 Malibu, J. Paul Getty Museum 80 AE 155,1. *RVP*, no. 2/418, pl. 129a; *VMG* 229–30, no. 105.
383 Okayama, Kurashiki Ninagawa Museum 79. *RVP*, no. 2/424; Simon, *Cat.*, p. 144.
384–5 Paestum 20303, from Paestum. *RVP*, no. 2/963, pl. 145; Greco, *Pittore di Afrodite*, pls. I–V.
386 Paestum 20295, from Paestum. *RVP*, no. 2/964, pl. 146; Greco, *PdA*, pls. IX–XIIIa.
387 Tampa (Florida), Zewadski coll. *RVP*, no. 2/971, pl. 150.
388 Paestum 26605, from Paestum. *RVP*, no. 2/978, pl. 154 a–c.
389–90 Boston 99.540 (H.L. Pierce Fund). *RVP*, no. 2/1004, pl. 158; *VMG*, pp. 237–9, no. 112, colour-plate on p. 22.
391 B.M. F 154. *RVP*, no. 2/1001, pl. 157a.
392–3 Sydney 48.05. *RVP*, no. 2/1007, pl. 160 a–b.
394 Toledo 77.30. *RVP*, no. 2/956; *VMG* 236–7, no. 111; *GRFP* IIIA/34, pl. 37b; *CVA* Toledo 2, pl. 118.
395 Naples 1778 (82127), from

Paestum. *RVP*, no. 3/2, pl. 167a.
396 Paestum 20347, from Paestum. *RVP*, no. 3/14, pl. 170a.
397 Paestum 5134, from Paestum. *RVP*, no. 3/168, pl. 182a.
398 Paestum 5184, from Paestum. *RVP*, no. 3/341, pl. 192a.
399 Madrid 11226. *RVP*, no. 3/342, pl. 192g.
400 Naples 2585 (82084). *RVP*, no. 3/420, pl. 201d.
401 Once Ascona Market, Galleria Serodine. *RVP*, no. 3/393, pl. 198c–d.
402 Paestum 24603, from Paestum. *RVP*, no. 3/448, pl. 204 c–d.
403 Paestum 24602, from Paestum. *RVP*, no. 3/449, pl. 205.
404 Geneva, Sciclounoff coll. *RVP*, no. 3/450, pl. 206; Moret, *AntK* 21, 1978, pl. 21; Sotheby, *Sale Cat.* 13 July 1987, no. 284, ill. on p. 99.
405 (1) Madrid 11249. *RVP*, no. 3/476, pl. 211a. (2) Paestum 5104. *RVP*, no. 3/544, pl. 215d. (3,4) Paestum 5105. *RVP*, no. 3/505, pl. 213c–d.
406 Paestum 5422, from Paestum. *RVP*, no. 3/584, pl. 218a.
407 Paestum 22872, from Paestum. *RVP*, no. 3/597, pl. 220c.
408 Paestum 5656, from Paestum. *RVP*, no. 3/622, pl. 221 b–d.
409–10 Paestum 26796, from Paestum. *RVP*, no. 3/625, pl. 222 c–d.
411 Philadelphia L.29.46. *RVP*, no. 3/628, pl. 224b.
412 Paestum 5188, from Paestum. *RVP*, no. 3/631, pl. 224d.
413 Paestum 27027, from Paestum. *RVP*, no. 3/643, pl. 227 a–b.
414–7 Paestum 26713, from Paestum. *RVP*, no. 3/662, pl. 232.
418 Paestum 48432, from Paestum. *RVP*, no. 3/701, pl. 235b.

SICILIAN

419 Oxford 1884.709 (V480). *LCS* 584, no. 2, pl. 225,3–4.
420 Syracuse 43011, from Scordia. *LCS* 585, no. 6, pl. 226,1.
421 Ferrara 6891, from Spina, Valle Pega. *LCS* 587, no. 16, pl. 226,8.
422 Syracuse 47099, from Lentini. *LCS* 589, no. 27, pl. 228,1.

423 Gela 642, from Manfria. *LCS* 593, no. 45, pl. 230,3.
424 Milan, Scala 749. *LCS* 595, no. 68, pl. 231,1; Mirabella-Roberti, *Museo Teatrale alla Scala*, no. 45, figs. 48–9.
425 B.M. F 473. *LCS* 597, no. 82, pl. 232,3.
426 St. Petersburg (Florida), Lemonopoulos coll., ex Lugano, private coll. *LCS Supp.* III 274, no. 46b; Trendall, *NAC* 9, 1980, pp. 89–113; MuM *Auktion 70*, 14 Nov. 1986, no. 226, pl. 60.
427 Lipari 10647, from Lipari. *LCS Supp.* III 275, no. 46e; Bernabò Brea and Cavalier, *Ceramica policroma* (1986), p. 7, figs. 2–3.
428 Lipari 9341 D, from Lipari. *LCS Supp.* III 275, no 46f.
429 Syracuse 66557, from Syracuse. *LCS Supp.* III 276, no. 98a.
430 Lipari 2297, from Lipari. *LCS Supp.* III 276, no. 46g.
431 Oxford 1937.283. *LCS* 599, no. 89, pl. 234,1.
432 Basel, Antikenmuseum BS 478. *LCS Supp.* III 276, no. 101a (Frontispiece to *LCS*, vol. II; text, p. 695).
433 Reggio Calabria 8998. *LCS* 607, no. 135, pl. 238,3.
434 Sydney 57.02. *LCS* 613, no. 190, pl. 239,8.
435–6 Hillsborough (Calif.), Mrs R.A. Hearst. *LCS* 615, no. 206, pl. 240,1–2; *Supp.* III, 279, with additional bibliography.
437 Lentini 1602, from Lentini. *LCS* 617, no. 216, pl. 241, 2–3.
438 Agrigento AG 3016, from Agrigento. *LCS* 618, no. 219, pl. 241,4.
439 Moscow 505. *LCS* 619, no. 228, pl. 242,3; *Antique Painted Pottery in the Pushkin State Museum* (1985), no. 78, figs. 142–3.
440 Palermo GE 4730, from Falcone. *LCS* 626, no. 278, colour frontispiece to vol. I; Bernabò Brea and Cavalier, *Ceramica policroma* (1986), 86–88, figs. 93–96.
441 Zurich E.T.H. B 24, from Adrano. *LCS* 628, no. 281, pl. 244,1–2; *CVA* Switzerland 5, IV S, pl. 50,1–4.
442 Palermo, Mormino coll. *LCS* 631, no. 299, pl. 245,1–2.
443 Palermo, Fondazione Mormino

222. *LCS* 633, no. 314, pl. 247,5–6.
444–5 Lipari 749 A, from Lipari. *LCS* 635, no. 326, pl. 249,4–6; Bernabò Brea and Cavalier, *Ceramica policroma* 17, figs. 15–17.
446 (1) Bottle, Sydney 47.214. *LCS* 638, no. 337, pl. 251,1 (Sydney Bottle Group). (2) Pyxis, Syracuse 45860, from Paternò. *LCS* 648, no. 422, pl. 252,10 (Paternò Group). (3) Lekanis, Syracuse 29575, from Centuripe. *LCS Supp.* III 293, no. 369l, pl. XXXII,4 (Centuripe Group). (4) Lekanis, Syracuse 31590,

from Centuripe. *LCS Supp.* III 293, no. 393a, pl. XXXII,7 (Macclesfield Painter). (5) Lekanis, Palermo, Mormino coll. *LCS* 647, no. 411, pl. 252,1 (White Ivy Group). (6) Lekanis, once London Market. *LCS* 647, no. 412, pl. 252,2 (White Ivy Group). (7) Lekanis, Munich SL 487. *LCS Supp.* I 110, no. 432a, pl. XXVIII,1 (Portale Painter – White Stripe Group). (8) Lekanis, Trieste 5386. *LCS* 650, no. 441, pl. 252,3 (White Stripe Group).
447 Naples 794 (82889). *LCS* 655, no. 448, pl. 253,2.

448 Lipari 9345 A, from Lipari. Bernabò Brea and Cavalier, *Ceramica policroma*, p. 59, fig. 60; *LCS Supp.* III 301, no. 450a.
449 Lipari 745 A from Lipari. *LCS* 655, no. 450, pl. 254,2; Bernabò Brea and Cavalier, p. 68, fig. 65.
450 Lipari 276 L. from Lipari. *LCS* 655, no. 451, pl. 254,1; Bernabò Brea and Cavalier, p. 50, fig. 46.
451 B.M. F 251. *LCS* 657, no. 464, pl. 254,4.
452 Lipari 9132 B, from Lipari. *LCS Supp.* III 304, no. 504a.

ACKNOWLEDGEMENTS

The author and publishers are deeply grateful to the many museums, galleries, auction-houses and private collectors, referred to above, for their kindness in providing photographs of vases in their possession and for granting permission to publish them. They are also indebted to Professor J.C. Carter for the photograph of Ill. 4, to Professor Erika Simon for that of Ill. 383 and to Dr Robert Guy who, with the permission of the authorities concerned, took the photos of Ills. 396, 402, 405, 407–10, 412–16.

The author would like to express his sincere thanks to the directors of the relevant museums, to Messrs. Sotheby's of London and New York and Messrs. Christie's of London, to Numismatic Fine Arts Inc. of Los Angeles, to numerous private collectors, and, for particular help in various matters, to Dietrich von Bothmer, H.A. Cahn, Jacques Chamay, Charles Ede, Robert Guy, Ian McPhee, Jean-Marc Moret, M.K. Steven and Dyfri Williams. He is also greatly indebted to Professor John Boardman and Pat Mueller for their invaluable assistance in the production of the book and to Valda Lane for the typing of the manuscript.

Ap = Apulian, C = Campanian, L = Lucanian, P = Paestan, S = Sicilian. Illustration numbers are in italics

INDEX II : GENERAL

Index to significant references in the text, with select illustration numbers in italics

Polychrome style, Canosan, 16, 99, 100, 102. —, Centuripe, 16, 240. —, Lipari, 238
Pool, reflecting, 79, 87; *141*
Praxitelean, hair style, 240; pose, 89, 100, 164

Rhyton, 10, 77, 199; *121, 246*
Rock(s), agglomerate (spotted), 13, 77, 161; *280, 283*. —, hollow, 13, 77, 204, 208; *168, 193*. —, lava-flow, 13, 160; *282*. — piles, 63, 84, *174, 216, 218, 244*

Samnites, 157, 160, 165, 168
Satyrs, *see* Dionysos in Index III
Satyr-play, 19, 20, 22, 75, 262; *2, 9, 104*
Sculpture, 23, 27, 86, 91
Shapes, general, 9–11, 196. *See also* individual shapes
Ship, prow of, 88; *197*
Signatures, 14, 196, 200
Situla, *Figs. 2/3; 148, 228, 275*
'Skewer of fruit', 198, 204; *390, 392, 400*
Skyphoid pyxis, 208, 209, 235, 237, 241, 242; *Fig. 2/6; 414, 421, 426, 434–5, 449*

Skyphos, 10; *22, 66, 101, 222, 285*
Sophocles, 88, 236, 262, 263
Stage, phlyax, 12, 75, 165, 200, 236, 262; *Fpce, 120, 125, 304, 340, 352, 424*. —, tragic, 12, 236, 261; *429*
Stamnos, 10, 26; *45*
Statues, 19, 22, 27, 78, 165, 266, 267; *52, 131*
Stele scenes, 164, 165, 168, 267; *139, 191, 230, 239, 261, 302*
Symposium (banquet), 13, 80, 168, 172, 202, 268; *58, 142, 315, 372–3*

Temples, 28, 79; *52, 140, 358*
Theatre, influence of, 9, 12, 20, 22, 28, 75, 77, 78, 87, 88, 161, 165, 169, 198, 200, 202, 236, 255, 262–4
Three-quarter view, faces in, 20, 22, 26, 27, 28, 60, 63, 78, 80, 86, 87, 98, 158, 161, 164, 234, 237, 240
Thunderbolt, of Zeus, 19, 28, 76, 90, 101, 256, 257, 263; *55, 208, 266*
Timoleon, 16, 232
Tumbler (acrobat), 199, 265; *341*

Underworld, 81, 90, 96, 97, 99, 257, 268; *151, 209*

Volute-krater, 9, 14, 17, 21, 23, 27, 28, 56, 79, 81, 85, 86, 97, 196, 201, 265; solid handles, *36, 44, 72;* open-work handles, 79, *140;* mascaroon handles, *141, 186–7, 190, 197–8, 204, 236, 238, 248–9, 268*. —, decoration on necks of, 28, 79, 81, 84, 86, 97. —, metal, 85; *180*

Warriors, 18, 57, 58, 74, 75, 82, 86, 101, 157, 159, 160, 161, 164, 165, 166, 168, 171, 198, 199, 203, 205, 266; *18, 37, 70, 93, 278–9, 289, 331, 377;* in native costume, *136, 157, 175, 232, 300, 307, 312, 314, 319*
Wave-pattern, 172, 197, 206, 235
Windows, 42, 77, 165, 168, 198, 202, 205; heads in —, *47, 309, 340, 384, 387*. —, as decorative adjunct, *125, 127, 142, 326, 402*

'Xylophone', 80, 87, 157, 167, 168, 170, 187, 204; *147, 194, 325, 386*

Youths, draped, 13, 18, 21, 25, 29, 56ff, 63, 75ff, 84, 92, 94, 100, 160ff, 169ff, 197ff, 201ff, 209, 234; *there are numerous illustrations*

INDEX III : MYTHOLOGICAL SUBJECTS

Greek mythology is discussed in general terms on pp. 12–13 and 255–264; not all the subjects there referred to are reproduced in the illustrations, but those which are not can readily be found by consulting the relevant indexes in *LCS* and *Supplements I–III, RVAp* and *Suppl.* I, and *RVP*. References to illustrations are in italics

Acheloös, 236; *428*
Achilles, 63, 88, 97, 240, 256, 258, 259; *34, 198, 202*
Actaeon, 58, 256; *82*
Admetos, 87; *196*
Adonis, 90, 98, 200, 256–7; *251, 349*
Adrastos, 24, 236, 261; *427*
Aegisthus, 101, 161, 259
Agamemnon, 258–9. —, tomb of, 12, 60, 205, 267; *60, 91, 389, 406*
Aigeus, 259, 260; *110*
Aigina, 18, 19, 257; *4*
Aiolos, 263; *210*
Ajax, 200, 258, 260; *273, 354*
Alkestis, 87, 259; *196*
Alkmene, 28, 90, 158, 159, 200, 202, 263; *55, 206, 355, 367*. —, (?), in phlyax scene, 201; *364*
Amazonomachy, 13, 24, 27, 57, 85, 96, 172, 259; *27, 36, 50, 54, 80, 181, 260*
Ampelis, 236, 258; *430*
Amphiaraos, 96, 97, 261, 268
Amphion, 91, 261; *29, 61, 211*
Amphitryon, 28, 90; *55, 206, 367*
Amykos, 21, 260; *17*

Amymone, 257; *378*
Andromache, 91; *258*
Andromeda, 12, 26, 78, 85, 97, 158, 161, 260, 263; *44, 132, 182*
Anios 12, 89, 90, 258; *205*
Antigone, 88, 263; *115, 200*
Antiope, 261, 263
Aphareus, sons of, 90; *208*
Aphrodite, 24, 85, 88, 90, 93, 94, 98, 172, 200, 204, 207, 240, 256; *49, 184, 197, 202, 236, 251, 256, 275, 349, 364, 446, 449. See also* Paris, Judgement of
Apollo, 21, 22, 28, 62, 88, 96, 101, 238, 256, 263; *8, 20, 49, 52, 56–7, 62, 97, 99, 136, 148, 199, 241–2, 265, 360, 371, 386, 444*. —, statue of, 19, 22, 28, 256; *8, 52*
Arcas, 78
Ares, 257
Argonauts, 21, 23, 27(?), 260; *19, 47(?)*
Ariadne, 26, 56, 87, 259; *45, 72, 194*
Artemis, 21, 28, 58, 96, 97, 101, 238, 256; *20, 49, 56, 82, 241–2, 253, 265, 445*. —, Bendis, 76, 256

Assembly of deities, 87, 97, 255; *208, 210, 260*
Astrape, 85, 257; *184*
Athena, 22, 26, 28, 75, 87, 97, 165, 172, 256–7; *25–6, 46, 50, 57, 59, 99, 106, 111, 190, 371*. —, statue of, 200; *43, 304. See also* Paris, Judgement of
Atlas, 91
Auge, 236; *424*
Aura, 55, 93, 257; *66*

Bellerophon, 26, 160, 161, 166, 260; *46, 48*
Boreas, 161, 257; *149, 286*
Busiris, 259

Cadmus, 164, 200, 201, 202, 260; *296, 359, 370*
Callisto, 12, 78, 256; *135*
Cassandra, 88, 200, 237, 258; *187, 354*
Cecrops, daughters of, 78
Centauromachy, 24, 27, 87; *49, 53, 195*
Cepheus, 26, 85, 263; *44, 132, 182*
Chimaera, 26; *46*
Chrysippos, 97, 99, 260, 263

287